THE KINNING OF FOREIGNERS

Transnational Adoption in a Global Perspective

Signe Howell

Berghahn Books
New York • Oxford

First published in 2006 by

Berghahn Books

www.berghahnbooks.com

© 2006 Signe Howell

Library of Congress Cataloging-in-Publication Data

–CIP data to be supplied–

British Library Cataloguing in Publication Data

A catalogue record for this book is available from
the British Library.

Printed in the United States on acid-free paper

ISBN 1-84545-184-8

To Desmond and Tika, with love

CONTENTS

LIST OF FIGURES

LIST OF TABLES

PREFACE

My research on transnational adoption started in 1998 as part of a collaborative project entitled 'The Meaning of Kinship in Contemporary Norway'.[1] We were intrigued by what we regarded as the restricted scope of British and American anthropological research on assisted procreation. While research on new reproductive technology (NRT) had been very exciting and had given kinship studies a new lease of life and a new direction (e.g. Edwards 1993; Franklin and Ragoné 1998; Strathern 1992), we were surprised that the researchers limited their investigation to the technological aspects of new trends in the procreative universe. Perhaps because I had adopted a child myself,[2] I felt that adoption ought to be included in anthropological studies of 'unnatural' reproduction; not least because so many involuntarily childless couples who fail to give birth through NRT turn to adoption. To study transnational adoption in Norway in tandem, as it were, with technologically assisted conception, was a challenging and exciting project.

As I began the research, I realised that the scope was going to be much larger than originally anticipated. The practice of Norwegian transnational adoption, though anthropologically fascinating in itself, has, in this book, become the springboard for a more ambitious project. My aim has been to place it within a broad context of contemporary Western life. The practice has become part of a global movement of persons and concepts, and I became intrigued by the wider social and political implications of moving children from one biological, sociocultural, geographical and national reality to another. Not only is the potential for mutual suspicion between donor and receiving countries high; cultural values regarding the meaning of children, families and relatedness vary greatly among the different parties involved, giving rise to mutual incomprehension. In Europe, racism is spreading; boundaries along racial and ethnic lines are increasingly being erected between those who belong and those who do not. As transnational adoption has grown in volume and in the number of countries involved, the practice has become the concern of national and international agencies who seek to regulate it. As a result, a vast array of experts has become activated. To adopt a child from another country has, to a large extent, been taken out of the hands of the individuals concerned and placed firmly in the hands of the state. To bring into the bosom of the family children whose early start in life has been difficult, who look different from their new parents and countrymen, and who come from poor countries whose sociocultural traditions are unfamiliar, is a courageous enterprise. However, as I hope to show, drawing on substantial empirical material, the transaction is running surprisingly smoothly.

In presenting my findings, I have identified three main themes – kinship, governmentality and globalisation – each of equal analytical significance, but attributed different weighting in different chapters according to the particular topic addressed. Informed by anthropological kinship theory, I examine how notions of the child, childhood, and relatedness vary across time and space, and how diverse persons are made kin through a process of what I call 'kinning'. Further, I study the rise of the significance of expert knowledge in the exercise of national and international policy regarding practices of kinning in general and transnational adoption in particular. Finally, through case studies from four countries from which children are adopted to Europe, I examine how transnational adoption both depends upon and helps to foster the globalisation of Western rationality and morality. As a result, the book covers a wide span of complex issues; but my argument is that it is only by treating the three themes as profoundly interlinked that we may begin fully to grasp the dynamics of the practice.

The project has necessarily been both multi-sited and wide-ranging. Social anthropology provides insights which other disciplines cannot provide, but classic social anthropological methods can be used only to a limited extent in an enterprise such as this. My two previous ethnographic projects were located in small, relatively bounded communities in Malaysia and Indonesia where long-term participant observation was the main method. That was clearly not possible in this case, and the project has therefore been a challenging one. It may perhaps be characterised as 'borderland' anthropology (Ortner 1996). The book may thus be read as an example of how anthropological methods can be combined with a historical approach, supplemented by a wide variety of written sources ranging from laws and legal debates to psychological literature and special interest group publications. (See the Postscript for a discussion of the methods employed.)

The world of transnational adoption is a world of contradictions and paradoxes. It is also a world filled with emotionality and personal happiness. The fact that I am the mother of an adopted daughter has rendered the ethnographic field more personal than my previous ones. I have, at times, become more emotionally involved than I am accustomed to as an anthropologist, and this has made it necessary to exercise a high degree of reflexivity. The empathy that I experienced with the anxieties and happiness of the couples that I studied has, I am convinced, proved a strength rather than a weakness. Whether this has biased my interpretation is for others to judge.

Notes

1. The project was started with my colleague at the University of Oslo, Marit Melhuus, who focused on new reproductive technology (Melhuus 2001, 2003, 2005). Values and practices in the world of transnational adoption are in constant flux. Because adoption is increasing in volume and, as a result of new countries becoming involved as both donors and receivers, many institutional and legal changes have occurred during the writing of this book. I have not been able to systematically check all of these beyond 2004.
2. My husband and I adopted a baby girl from Nepal in 1986 while we were still living in Britain. One reason that I was first alerted to transnational adoption as a topic for research was that when we moved to Norway I was amazed to discover that, in stark contrast to Britain, not only was the practice very common, but that the state had developed a clear infrastructure to deal with it.

ACKNOWLEDGEMENTS

A great number of individuals and institutions from many different countries have assisted me in my project. I want to thank them all for their interest and support. The two largest Norwegian adoption agencies, Verdens Barn and Adopsjonsforum, were positive and co-operative right from the start, and made it possible for me to participate in many different social and professional fora. In particular I want to name Ketil Lehland, Toril Juvet Hermansen, Gro Hoft Solstad, Kristin Holtedal, Astrid Ødegård and Toril Andersen. I also want to thank the many Norwegian adoptive parents, and their children, for their willingness to engage in formal and informal conversation and surveys, and for permission to use photographs. Gro Fivesdal, founder of the Adoptive Parents Association, included me in their activities. Knut Steenberg and Morten Stefansen from the Ministry of Children and Family gave me several opportunities to interview them. Staff at various orphanages in India, Ethiopia and the Holt Organisation in Korea all received me in a positive manner and enabled me to appreciate some of the challenges that they have to face in their daily work.

I want to thank my colleagues in the Department of Social Anthropology at the University of Oslo, in particular those who participated in the project 'Transnational Flow of Concepts and Substances' (funded by the Norwegian Research Council) of which my project was a part. I want to thank my colleagues from England, France, Spain, Hungary, Italy and Lithuania with whom I participated in the European Commission funded project 'Public Understanding of Genetics: A Cross-cultural and Ethnographic Study of the "New Genetics" and Social Identity' under Framework 5 and the Quality of Life and Management of Living Resources Programme; contract number QLG 7–CT–2001–01668. Marit Melhuus, with whom I thought up the project in the first place, and who has worked alongside me in the projects listed above, deserves special thanks.

The first draft was written during six months' sabbatical in 2003 spent as a Visiting Scholar at the Sociology Department at the University of California, Berkeley. Barry Thorne and Shelly Errington both provided numerous insightful comments. The invitation to spend two weeks as Visiting Professor at the Department of Anthropology, University of Gothenburg, in 2004 enabled me to rework the manuscript in congenial surroundings. I am grateful to Wil Burghoorn and the graduate students for their interest and comments. Former graduate student, now colleague, Sidsel Roalkvam not only invited me to join her, Tom and Isak to accompany them to collect their daughter Sarah in Ethiopia, but she also read an earlier version of the whole manuscript and gave me the courage to complete. Nora Hoff provided comfortable and friendly conditions for me to finalise revisions.

Nancy Frank and Frøydis Haugane provided library support and Frank Silye helped with computing problems. In addition, the following individuals have contributed with critical and encouraging comments at different stages of the research and writing: Erdmute Alber, Paul Ketil Botvar, Ånund Brottveit, Monica Dalen, Carol Delaney, Jeanette Edwards, Geir Follevåg, Sarah Franklin, John Gillis, Olivia Harris, Keith Hart, Joan Hollinger, Marianne Lien, Sarah Lund, Susan McKinnon, Diana Marre, Audhild Roel, Anne-Lise Ryvgold, Jim Scott, Peter Selman, Olaf Smedal, Barbro Sætersdal, Aud Talle, Ketil Tronvoll, and Kari-Anne Ulfsnes. Finally, I am grateful to the anonymous readers who provided pertinent and helpful comments. This final version has benefited from their insights.

But most of all, I want to express my gratitude to my husband Desmond McNeill who, as usual, has supported the endeavour and has been my sparring partner throughout. And to Tika, without whom I would never have thought of such a project.

Oslo
August 2005

PART I

Adoption – Biology or Sociality?

Chapter 1

Desire and Rights: Transnational Movement of Substances and Concepts

Blood Is Thicker Than Water is not only axiomatic in studies of kinship, it is a fundamental axiom of European culture. Even if this axiom were true as a biological fact, even if the most extensive scientifically acquired evidence showed it to be true … the point remains that culture, even were it to do no more than recognise biological facts, still adds something to those facts. The problem remains of just what the socio-cultural aspects are, of what meaning is added, of where and how that meaning, as a meaning rather than as a biological fact, articulates with other meanings … But the axiom does not hold water even for the sociobiologists … They only claim to account for *some* aspects of *some* of the relations between very close kin. This leaves a good deal to be accounted for.

D.M. Schneider, *A Critique of the Study of Kinship*

Transnational Adoption: Local and Global Values and Practices

Since the late 1960s, transnational adoption has emerged as a global phenomenon. The last thirty years have witnessed a rapid increase in the movement of infants and young children from the poor South (and more recently from the former Soviet bloc) to eagerly awaiting prospective parents in the rich North. Due to a sharp decline in infants being made available for adoption locally, involuntarily childless couples in Western Europe and North America who wish to create a family have to look to the developing world. As infertility increases amongst couples in Western Europe and North America, at the same time as the value of parenthood takes on new dimensions, to remain childless is becoming an unacceptable condition. Two options are available for involuntarily infertile couples: assisted conception, though the use of new reproductive technology (NRT), or adoption. For reasons that will be elaborated below, in many European countries today (but not in the USA where domestic adoption still out-numbers transnational adoption) adoption is practically synonymous with transnational adoption. An estimated 35,000 children were adopted annually in this manner during the late nineteen-nineties reaching 40,000 in 2003; and despite improvements in new reproductive technology, the number of adoptions continues to increase. More than half (approximately 20,000) of the children that arrive in the West each year become Americans. The rest are spread across Western Europe with a large proportion going to the Scandinavian countries.[1] Today, Norwegians adopt children from more than twenty countries in Asia, Africa, Latin America and the former Soviet bloc and, in terms of per capita, lead the world. My research on this phenomenon in Norway forms a core from which I explore some general theoretical and analytical issues raised by the practice. Bringing into the bosom of the family children from alien countries who, on the whole, will look very different from their parents, is a challenging enterprise that raises issues of personhood, kinship, family, children, identity, race, ethnicity, and nationality. In particular, adoption – whether domestic or transnational – raises questions concerning the significance attributed to biogenetic relations versus social relations within a lived world of kinship, both in Europe and elsewhere. In addition, with an increased state involvement in matters of family life, transnational adoption raises questions of the role of expert knowledge and the relationship between the nation-states of the North and the South. These are the subjects of this book.

Two questions immediately present themselves. Firstly, to what extent, and according to what criteria, is the movement of so many children across kin, social, cultural, racial and national boundaries successful? I shall seek to provide some answer to this and suggest that, by and large, the children settle down very well, but that their movement from one country to another is enmeshed in numerous professional and official anxieties resulting in a number of 'dos and don'ts'. Secondly, what does it take to make this movement possible? This question goes to the heart of my argument. I suggest that transnational adoption is possible because the child given up for adoption becomes a naked child;[2] often literally naked, but, more importantly in this context, socially naked. The child is denuded of all kinship; denuded of meaningful relatedness whether its identity is known or not.[3] As such, the child is the example *par excellence* of the autonomous individual – so central in contemporary Western thinking. But this also, paradoxically, renders him or her a non-person; in a sense, non-human. By being abandoned by relatives (whether biological or not is irrelevant in this context) and left for strangers to look after, the children are at the same time 'de-kinned' by them (see below), removed from kinned sociality. Entering the non-personal world of an institution (usually an orphanage), the abandoned child who is earmarked for adoption overseas enters a liminal world. Here he or she awaits a new set of kin persons.

I suggest that this social nakedness makes adoption across national fron-
tiers possible, makes it a morally acceptable act. The new parents from an
alien country are allowed by the state of the birth country to remove such
non-persons and to 'kin' them to themselves. The nakedness enables the
state to relinquish a citizen, and the new state to accept one, because she
will not be naked in her new country. She enters it fully clothed in new relatives. By this act biology is rendered insignificant, sociality becomes all-
important. While this may seem a little fanciful, I shall nevertheless seek to
make the case, returning to it throughout the book.

Analytical Approach

Three main analytical threads are central to my argument and will be
referred to throughout the book. They are: the anthropology of kinship; the
growth of psychology and the psychological-based professions which
enable the consolidation of governmentality; and the globalisation of
morality and rationality. My intention is to interlink these three compo-
nents in order to cast a fresh and illuminating light on the complexity of
the ideology and practice of transnational adoption.

Several issues arise which I regard as analytically challenging. Not only
does the practice raise interesting questions relevant to the anthropological study of kinship, but it also becomes relevant to questions of globalisation – globalisation of morality, knowledge and rationality rather than of
the market system and neoliberal economics; of power relations on a
national as well as transnational scale; of issues of race, ethnicity, identity
and personhood; and finally, questions of attributed significance of place,
belonging and relatedness. What is particularly interesting to me is that
transnational adoption activates a number of issues that range from the
most intimate sphere of the life of individuals to macro-politics on a global
level. Several levels of relationships are activated in connection with
transnational adoption. Each has its own raison d'étre and each gives rise
to its own set of values and interactions. I shall be exploring each of them.
First, there is the relationship between nation-states, acting as agents –
each has its own legal provisions that have to be accommodated before an
adoption may be completed; second, the relationships that are informed
by international conventions, between international agencies and national
agencies in donor countries; third, the relationship between adoption
agencies in receiving countries and the local institutions that look after
children released for adoption overseas; fourth, the relationship within the
receiving country between prospective adoptive parents and the public
authorities that decide on their application; fifth, the relationship between
the prospective parents and the adoption agency; sixth, the relationship
between the adoptive parents and their adopted child(ren); seventh, the

relationship between transnationally adopted persons themselves; eight, the relationship between adoptees, adoptive families and the adoptees' country of origin; and, finally, the relationship between the adoptees and their biological relatives.

My presentation and interpretation spring out of an anthropological approach whereby I investigate the themes as cultural issues, i.e., cultural constructions of representations, discourses and values anchored in world-views within specific historical and social contexts. I will not debate the rights or wrongs of the various theories about children and the significance of biogenetics; my task is to identify the posited 'truths' in various relevant arenas and to deconstruct them – to show that they are, in fact, cultural issues. My analytical tools will be the anthropology of kinship, an argument about the constituting role of expert knowledge and governmentality, and the globalisation of Western discourses about kinship and childhood and of Western understanding of morality and rationality. This first, introductory chapter sets the scene for subsequent topics, discussions, arguments and interpretations.

While an examination of the Norwegian values and practices concerning adoption in general, and transnational adoption in particular, constitutes a central focus of this book due to the in-depth research that I have done on the practice in Norway (Howell 1999, 2001, 2002, 2003a and 2003b; Howell and Melhuus forthcoming, Melhuus and Howell forthcoming), I use the Norwegian situation as a springboard to address a number of questions of wider applicability. Adoption, in the sense that a child is brought up by persons who are not his or her biological parents, but who treat the child according to local norms of parent–child relationship, has probably been practised in all societies at all times. However, an obvious, but nevertheless important, fact is that adoption as a discursive practice varies enormously – both across societies and over time. Adoption cannot be understood in isolation from a broader examination of cultural attitudes to personhood, family, parenthood and childhood.

A central argument of this book will be that infertile couples in Norway and the other Scandinavian countries[4] regard their condition of infertility as dramatic and unacceptable because without children they cannot become a 'normal family', an ambition that the majority of Norwegian couples give as the reason for the efforts they invest in NRT and adoption. Their childlessness not only prevents them from participating on an equal footing with their contemporaries who do have children, but it also makes their kin status within their family circle ambiguous. Without children a number of significant kin categories, such as those of mother, father, grandmother, grandfather, remain empty categories in a particular family setting. Childlessness thus excludes those affected from engaging in meaningful sociality. Most importantly, they are prevented from experiencing motherhood and fatherhood – lived categories that, in recent decades, have become culturally necessary for the development of a full individual person. In light of this, it is not surprising that Norway, Sweden and Denmark have a very high rate of adoption from overseas in per capita terms. Because of the special personal and emotional nature of adoption in general and transnational adoption in particular, one encounters a number of paradoxes and contradictions in attitudes to the practice, both amongst those directly concerned – as adoptive parents and adoptees – and amongst those employed to instigate and supervise the practice, whether in donor or receiving country.

By and large, the children settle down well. The vast majority become incorporated into their new familial, cultural and national statuses seemingly without serious difficulty. In itself this is rather sensational, not least because most adoptees look very different from their new parents and kin, so that the nature of the relationship cannot be hidden. In North America and Western Europe, for the past couple of hundred years, kinship has been predicated upon the biological bond between parents and children. In such social and cultural settings, the question arises of how it is possible to incorporate children into a family who not only have no biological connection to their new relatives and look very different from them, but who also originate from distant unknown countries. This question goes to the heart of the anthropological study of kinship. And I shall argue that the answers may be found here also – although it requires some fundamental rethinking.

Another central question that will be addressed in this book is how mechanisms are established so that adoption of children across national borders, and even across continents, can be conducted to the satisfaction of all parties concerned.[5] This takes us to questions about the role of the state in organising the private lives of its citizens. Throughout the twentieth century, the state has increasingly involved itself in governing people's home life, manifesting what Foucault (1991) has termed 'governmentality'. Moreover, in the case of transnational adoption, this active involvement of state powers has taken on a global dimension. The interference of the so-called international community in the internal politics of sovereign states has become more marked. Children in adoption are moved from the jurisdiction of one country to that of another; from countries less developed economically and technologically in the South to the much wealthier North where there is a growing demand for them. The diffusion of ideas, however, moves in the opposite direction: from the liberal democracies of the economically developed Western nation-states to those that are less developed in the South and in Eastern Europe – but who provide the children so desired by the North. I shall examine this ironical situation from the point of view of a globalisation of Western knowledge, rationality and morality. This has to be linked to a parallel growth in so-called expert knowledge which has resulted in a number of professions that derive their expertise from psychological discourses. This group of professionals I call psycho-technocrats. I shall suggest that two ideological concepts, anchored in Western understanding, have emerged as pivotal in the discursive practices of transnational adoption: those of the autonomous individual and the best interest of the child. Closely linked to these two are discourses about rights: human rights and children's rights.

To explore through the lens of adoption the global processes and the mechanisms of governmentality, both local and global, that are currently transforming childhood itself is a major aim of this book. It is equally important to investigate the reactions to these processes in those non-Western countries that send children to the West for adoption; that is, to what extent they adopt, adapt, resist and reject Western values.

Exploring the Three Analytical Approaches

Underlying my whole exposition is the argument that in transnational adoption one may observe a two-way, asymmetrical movement of substances and concepts. Substances in the form of children move from the South to the North; and concepts, in the form of moral values and psychological discourses (expressed most clearly in international treaties), move from the North to the South. These processes will be analysed from the point of view of kinship, expert knowledge and governmentality, and globalisation.

Adoption and Kinship

As a social practice, adoption has received surprisingly little attention from anthropologists, and yet it goes to the very heart of what we take to be kinship and, I argue, its study can throw new light on established questions concerning the nature of relatedness. Studying transnational adoption enables me to examine comparatively, and from a novel perspective, cultural values concerning procreation, reproduction, family, kinship, children, and the perceived relationship between biogenetic and social relatedness, as well as issues of race, ethnicity and nationality. On the bases of my findings, I argue for an unexplored phenomenon of kinship studies that I call 'kinning' (Howell 2003b). By kinning I mean the process by which a foetus or newborn child is brought into a significant and permanent relationship with a group of people, and the connection is expressed in a conventional kin idiom. Kinning need not apply only to a baby, but to any previously unconnected person, such as those connected through marriage. What kinning does in adoption is to transform the autonomous, non-social individual to a relational person. Henceforth the person is clearly anchored in necessary and unchanging relations. I wish to suggest that kinning is a universal process, marked in all societies by various rites of passage that ensure kinned subjectivation, but that it has not generally been recognised as such. One may identify three aspects of kinning: to kin by nature, to kin by nurture, to kin by law. Adoption in Europe involves the two last aspects only, although the first constitutes the model. The study of kinship is the study of formalised relationships, and such relationships are not just, or even primarily, the business of the individuals concerned, but of society.

To kin a person, even a new-born baby, is nowhere a trivial or automatic process. At a societal level a new kin relationship must be made manifest for the person to become a member of the kin community. De-kinning may also occur when a previously kinned person is thrown out of the kin community for some reason or another, or when a newborn child is never kinned due to the fact that it is going to be abandoned. According to my argument, de-kinning is what makes adoption of abandoned children possible.[6] In some societies, such as contemporary Europe, adoption is an extreme example of kinning, but not a unique one. Because adoption is a practice that challenges those kinship ideologies that base themselves upon the constituting value of biological connectedness, it throws existing values and practices into sharp relief. Moreover, dilemmas often arise within adoptive families concerning the status of their connectedness and the identity of the adoptee. These may be subjected to current psychological theories concerning the relative weighting attributed to biological or environmental factors.

Adoption, Expert Knowledge and Governmentality

I suggest that contemporary Western ideology of family life, children and childhood is the result of an increasing influence of psychological theories on identity, personhood and child development as these have been developed within academic psychology during the twentieth century. Modern psychology has had a profound effect upon how we think of what it means to be a human being and a gendered person. A constituent premise of Western psychology is the autonomous individual. Ever since Kant 'threw new light on the understanding of human nature by insisting on man being autonomous, i.e. self legislating' (Svendsen 2004), Western philosophical and ideological traditions have maintained the ontological and moral autonomy of the individual person, and this has also underpinned social theory. Many theorists have pointed out that an increasing individualisation is intimately linked with increasing institutionalisation (Vike 2002: 58). This has led to a discourse of human rights where universal rights are anchored in the autonomous individual, but an individual who is dependent upon state institutions to secure the rights. This discourse has found its most graphic and influential expression in the UN Declaration of Human Rights of 1948 and the more thematically focused UN Convention on the Rights of the Child of 1986. However, this ontological centrality of the autonomous individual was not an understanding shared by our ancestors, nor is it shared by a number of non-European cultural traditions. In many non-Western understandings it is the relational, not the individual, which is constitutive of personhood. The full implications of such a premise are not appreciated in the West and, hence, are not taken account of in Western-derived measures directed at the Third World.

Psychologically derived theories have given rise to new professions of child therapists, educators, and social workers in Western Europe and North America. The experts have become increasingly the arbiters of knowledge. They seek to ensure that their knowledge is put to effective use within the increasingly state-controlled institutions that provide education, health and other services pertaining to children, something which has resulted in childhood becoming, arguably, 'the most intensely governed sector of personal existence' (Rose 1999: 123). The overarching aim of these 'psycho-technocrats', (as I term them) is, however, benevolent, intended to safeguard 'the best interest of the child'. This concept, which remains largely unexamined, underpins all recent legislation, national and international, as well as a range of institutionalised concerted actions initiated by public bodies and NGOs (non-governmental organisations) that are aimed at children. The part played by the psycho-technocrats in creating and maintaining discourses about children and childhood and in establishing practices and institutions held to be appropriate, is another theme of the book.

Legislation dealing with children and adoption, and the establishment of those institutions that ensure the application of the laws, may be interpreted as examples of what Foucault has termed governmentality. Foucault argues that the welfare of the population became an increasing concern of the emergent state (1991: 100–101). According to Foucault, in Europe since the Enlightenment, 'good government' became not simply the exercise of authority over people within the state or the ability to discipline them but, more importantly, the desire to foster their prosperity and happiness (ibid). Moreover, governmentality may be understood as an attribute of the modern nation-state whereby people are primarily perceived of as citizens of the state. Power operates less as an external force and more as an internalised understanding by which people cooperate with the agents of the state in aiming, not only for improvement of society and institutions established in order to promote the common good, but also self-improvement in ways which appear to be voluntary. Because the raison d'étre of the state's involvement is to ensure 'the best interest of the citizen', the benevolent state feels morally justified in governing the private lives of its citizens. It is therefore not surprising to find that adoption has become highly regulated in all Western countries and that most countries that adopt children overseas by now have some form of legal provision that regulates the practice – both domestically and transnationally (Chapter 7 examines the adoption laws of the USA and Norway, and Chapter 8 the two international conventions of relevance).

Governmentality implies the cooperation of the citizens. The idea of universal welfare for all is an important part of the modern welfare state. The Nordic countries are often thought of as prime examples of the modern welfare state and Vike argues that in its form it has linked individual rights to public services, and 'thus propagated a unique and very modern brand of individualism, (2002: 61). This makes a focus on transnational adoption in Norway particularly interesting.

At a personal and emotional level, adoption necessarily involves three parties – often referred to as the adoption triad: the biological parents, the adoptive parents and the adopted child. Somehow the interest of all three parties must be taken into account, and one theme of this book is to explore, comparatively and historically, the different weighting given to these three actors in different adoption systems; in other words, whose best interest is at any given time or place held to be paramount. Adoption and transnational adoption today also involves other sets of relationships: that between the state and its citizens, and that between states. In a broader social sense, the practice of adoption and transnational adoption today has been taken out of the hands of the private parties concerned and subjected to an increasing involvement of a series of public and semi-public institutions. These include local and national government departments in both donor and receiving countries, adoption agencies and orphanages, international organisations of various kinds, as well as an increasing number of 'psycho-technocrats' whose expert knowledge has been instrumental in shaping discourses, values and the practice of adoption.

I suggest that contemporary Western ideology of family life, children and childhood is the result of an increasing influence of theories of identity, personhood and child development as these have been developed within academic psychology. My examination of the growth and spread of 'psy' expertise (Rose 1999), which is linked to the growth of state control over its citizens, is further used to investigate the extent to which one may detect a trickle-down effect of these developments in Europe to those countries which send children to Europe. In the case of adoption, this global governmentality derives its legitimacy from contemporary psychological knowledge as this is made into the basis for action by social workers and other professionals.

Adoption and the Globalisation of Rationality and Morality

The rapid increase in the scale of transnational adoption, and the geographical spread of donor countries, have led to the establishment of universal guidelines for its supervision. This is a phenomenon that, I suggest, may be examined as yet another manifestation of globalisation. It is, however, globalisation of a somewhat particular kind, not usually included in scholarly debates; namely a globalisation of rationality and morality which has received very little attention from commentators (e.g. Baumann 1998; Cassels 2000; Featherstone 1990). Just as the globalisation of technology and the market ideology have emanated from Europe and North America, and power remains firmly in the hands of institutions anchored in these nations, so too with the practice of transnational adoption. Western rationality and ethical understandings, loosely understood, today shape and control the practice. Western normative rationality with regard to the meaning of children, childhood, parenthood and families is exported and enforced in the many countries that send children to the West. Transnational adoption is a transaction whose sole purpose involves what is generally thought of as the most precious and intimate part of peoples' personal lives, namely having and bringing up children. This domain, that until about one hundred years ago was left more or less untouched by state authorities, has today become one that is circumscribed by numerous laws and regulations – both nationally and internationally. At the same time the meaning of child, mother and father, and of childhood and parenthood, have changed dramatically. These ideological changes affected adoption discourses nationally and internationally.

The practice of transnational adoption not only involves the two nation-states directly concerned in any one adoption transaction – the donor country and the recipient country – but has also become the concern of the international political and humanitarian communities. The adoption of children from one country to another has been made the subject of intense scrutiny by various international organisations and NGOs, and deliberate attempts have been, and continue to be, made at regulating it according to internationally accepted norms.[7] I argue that transnational adoption may be analysed as a two-way process between donor and recipient countries, which is not necessarily balanced. While children move in adoption from the South (including Eastern Europe) to the North, posited universal ideas and values concerning personhood, childhood, parenthood, family life, children and the treatment of children move from the North to the South. This latter movement is most clearly manifested in the implicit and explicit values expressed in international treaties such as the two mentioned above. But traces of contemporary Western thinking on these matters may also be found in recent local legislation and practices in donor countries. We may thus discern a globalisation of Western concepts and values that emphasise a discourse of rights of various kinds, a normative ambition that seeks to impose a single moral universe.

As it is practised, transnational adoption reveals features of asymmetric exchange. Children move in one direction, values and concepts (and to some extent money) move in the opposite one; but it is not an exchange between equals. The dice are loaded in favour of the northern players – despite the fact that they are the main beneficiaries. They not only get the children they strongly desire, they also – albeit from the best of motives – lay down the procedures as to how to carry out the transaction. Their motive is, in most cases, a genuine desire to improve conditions for children in the Third World in ways which go far beyond mere economic development and, hence, alert the citizens in these countries to (Western) rationality, morality and the discourse of rights. Deriving its impetus from democratic ideals of individualism, equality and rights, this globalisation of values makes itself felt as a moral mobilisation of these values. As such, the effort reveals clear overtones of the 'white man's burden' (Howell 2003b). Such a moral crusade absolves those involved from the need to seek enlightenment about indigenous ontology and values; in their humanitarian quest, local practices are easily rendered irrelevant.

Western views about children and about their (and their parents') needs and 'best interest' do not necessarily meet with an eager response in the countries from which Western countries adopt children. Some local resistances to this 'crusade' have been experienced, and these, in turn, have affected thinking and practices in receiving countries. One may therefore argue that the transnational movement of concepts and values is not as straightforward as might at first be assumed. It is clear that there is a complexity of attitudes that prevail in donor countries regarding the practice of sending children for adoption to well-to-do couples in the rich North. It is a practice that provokes a wide range of emotional and political reactions within each country, and I shall seek to elucidate indigenous notions in donor counties and examine the attitudes that prevail there concerning sending children for adoption to the rich Europe, North America and Australia. In Chapter 9, I examine some of the emotional and political reactions in selected countries from which Europeans and North Americans adopt, namely India, Ethiopia, China and Romania, and try to gauge the extent to which they accept, adapt or reject Western discourses.

There is no single explanation for why children are abandoned. Motives vary from country to country and within each country. Family poverty, the death of the biological mother, the desire for a boy child rather than a girl child, local disasters like wars or epidemics that kill so many people that there is no kin infrastructure remaining that will take care of orphans, social stigma attached to single motherhood – these are amongst the more common reasons for abandoning a child. Whatever the reason, the countries themselves are incapable of looking after the number of abandoned children that fall into their care. Overseas adoption becomes one solution, but due to a number of ideological resistances and complex bureaucracy, only a small minority of theoretically adoptable children are in fact transferred.

To Conclude

Although this book is intended as a contribution to the anthropology of adoption and kinship and as an example of an anthropological approach to the study of globalisation, it is not intended to be confined to an anthropological readership. I have written with a wider audience in mind – not only those who, for personal or professional reasons, are interested in transnational adoption, but also those who take an academic interest in children and childhood and the variations in values and meanings attributed to these categories across time and space. A major aim is to critically evaluate and deconstruct implicit and embedded notions. The historical and cross-cultural comparative study of categories that are so naturalised that even to question them is regarded as unnecessary and provoking, is in itself important work.

My argument will be that everything that has to do with procreation and family life in Western Europe and North America is a manifestation of naturalised knowledge.[8] The variety to be found across space and time in the meaning attributed to concepts and categories – such as family, parenthood, childhood, personhood and, ultimately, human nature – provides an empirical richness that belies attempts to generalise. Studies from non-European countries amply demonstrate the cultural contingency of values about childhood and families. Most anthropologists would argue that it must be an empirical question to what extent it is harmful for a child to be brought up in circumstances other than their natal home (e.g. James and Prout 1997, Stephens 1995, Scheper-Hughes et al. 1998). Yet with the increase in international governmental and non-governmental organisations whose concern is with human rights, and children's rights in particular, there is little doubt that contemporary Western views have assumed a global perspective, and that they carry strong normative ambitions

From a comparative point of view, interesting differences have emerged between Norway, other European countries and the USA concerning attitudes to sensitive issues such as in vitro fertilization, sperm and egg donation, surrogacy, and adoption, as well as in requirements for prospective adoptive parents. These differences are manifested in the laws of each country. Arguably, there are more differences between the USA, on the one hand, and the European countries, on the other, than there are between the European countries. This is my reason for comparing legislation on adoption in Norway and the USA. From this fact alone, it is clear that no 'Western' or 'European' or 'Euro-American' consensus of opinion has emerged. In light of this, serious questions must be asked regarding the appropriateness of terms such as 'the West' or 'Euro-American'. I have, nevertheless, found it necessary in this study to employ them in certain contexts. This is when I talk of Western philosophical traditions and debates which, together with psychological traditions and debates, I argue, have been constituent in the development of moral discourses of personhood, family and childhood, and which have set their stamps on both national and international law. Hence, it is legitimate to talk in terms of a globalisation of Western morality and rationality. This is not to say that this has been a globalisation without resistance. In fact, one of my points is that being confronted with a number of alternative values, the psycho-technocrats and practitioners in the field of transnational adoption have had to adjust their own understandings and demands somewhat. However, to what extent the alternative voices will prevail must remain an open question.

Notes

1. See the statistics in the next chapter for a breakdown in numbers.
2. I use this term because, although many children are not abandoned in the sense of left anonymously in some deserted place, by giving them up for adoption and agreeing to cease all future contact with them, they are in effect abandoned and rendered socially naked.
3. In some countries, e.g. India, it is forbidden to release the identity of an abandoned child's biological origin even when this is known. In some Latin American countries the biological parents may not intend the abandonment to be permanent (Fonseca 2000, 2004), or children may be stolen from their families. Nevertheless, the rhetoric of transnational adoption is that the child is abandoned and hence may be classified as socially naked.
4. I limit myself to the Scandinavian countries as this is the area I know most about. Birth rates vary between countries in Western Europe, and the profile is changing. The past ten years have witnessed a dramatic drop in birth rates in Spain and Italy whereas it is growing in Scandinavia. During the past four years transnational adoption has suddenly taken off in Spain and the per capita rate here rivals that of Norway (Marre and Bestard 2003).
5. Very little, or nothing, is known about the biological parents of most children sent for adoption overseas. Hence we have no way of knowing if they are satisfied or not.
6. Well-known examples of de-kinning in Europe may be found in Victorian novels when an incensed father disinherits his child and exclaims, 'you are no longer a son (daughter) of mine!' By the same token re-kinning may also take place. It is such a process that, I suggest, occurs when a child is abandoned and adopted.
7. Thus sections 21 and 22 of the UN Convention on the Rights of the Child deal directly with matters pertaining to transnational adoption, and the Hague Convention on Inter-country Adoption (1993) further regulates the practice. This is discussed in Chapter 8.
8. That others may have different notions about these matters is to most people incomprehensible. During my fieldwork on transnational adoption this has been brought home to me again and again. 'But, surely, it is only natural that…' is a statement I have met more often in this research than in any other I have been engaged in. Americans are as shocked by Norwegian laws forbidding paid surrogacy as Norwegians are about American laws allowing it.

Chapter 2

A CHANGING WORLD OF FAMILIES: AN OVERVIEW

128 children arrived from China in 2003. Of these, seven were boys – an increase of five from last year. 63 children were under one year of age. 56 children were between one and two years old. 9 children were between 3 and 6 … Five children came from Russia – two girls and three boys … 81 children came from Korea – 32 girls and 49 boys.

2003 *Annual Report of Children of the World*, Norway

Considering the amount of heat generated by debates on international adoption, it is perhaps surprising that so little attention has been paid to the scale of the phenomenon.

P. Selman, *Intercountry Adoption: Developments, Trends and Perspectives*

Transnational adoption began as a North American philanthropic response to the thousands of orphaned children in Europe, mainly from Greece and Germany, who resulted from the Second World War. Following the US Displaced People's Act of 1948 – the first legislative provision made with regard to orphan immigration – and the Refugee Act of 1953, several thousand 'orphaned' children entered the USA to be adopted by American families. This period has been named 'the first era of international adoption' (Altstein and Simon 1991: 3).

The second phase was also sparked off by the news of children being rendered parentless as the result of war; this time the Korean War. The adoption of Korean children represented a dramatic rupture with previous practice insofar as for the first time racially and culturally different children entered Western families to be brought up as if they were their own. Between 1953 and 1962 approximately 15,000 foreign-born children, most of whom were Korean or other Asian (primarily from the Philippines and Thailand), were adopted by American families (ibid.). The vast majority of the early adopters were not involuntary childless couples, but people who felt a moral compulsion to look after the orphans. In particular, many were upset about the treatment that 'mixed race' children received in South Korea, where children resulting from relationships between Korean women and American soldiers were regarded as non-persons by the Korean authorities and public alike. Many of the early adoptions from Korea were precisely these children. Slowly the motivations became less philanthropic, and adoption from the poor nations of the developing world served more and more as a means for involuntarily infertile couples to 'become normal families'. The demand for children from overseas corresponded to a decline in potential adoptees being available domestically. The annual number of transnational adoptees into the USA increased from about 8,000 in 1989 to 11,340 in 1996 and 15,774 in 1998 (Gailey 1999: 54) and is estimated to have passed 21,000 in 2003 (Selman 2005: 4). Since adoption from overseas began, changes have occurred in attitudes to the practice, and in the popularity of particular donor countries. While South Korea remains popular, as do several countries in Latin America, by the late 1990s about half the children adopted into the USA from abroad came from China and Russia (Selman 2000). Although the increase in adoption from overseas in the USA has been substantial, 21,000 is still only a small percentage of the total number of 140,000–160,000 adoptions in the USA per year. Between 1971 and 2001, US citizens have adopted more than a quarter of a million children from other countries (www.adoptioninstitute.org).

Figure 2.1 A new son in the family.

The situation in Europe has been somewhat different. Here, the pattern of childbirth and adoption in Norway is fairly representative. Whereas 425 Norwegian-born children were adopted in Norway in 1965, less than fifty of these were foreign-born. By 1980, transnational adoption had become established, but 68 per cent of all adoptions were still Norwegian-born children. By 1984, this figure had dropped to 43 per cent, and by 1991 it was less than 35 per cent. By this time most of the domestic adoption was adoption by step-parents (Ministry of Children and Family). For couples wanting children, but unable to achieve this biologically, transnational adoption had became the usual method. The year 1998 represented a watershed, when almost 800 children were adopted from overseas (Central Statistical Bureau). In terms of per capita, Sweden used to top the list of transnationally adopted children, but has now been surpassed by Norway. Here adoption from overseas accounts for 1.46 per cent of the annual birth rate; by contrast, the rate in USA is 0.58 per cent (Selman 2000: 2).

Unlike the situation in the USA and, to some extent the United Kingdom, there are virtually no Norwegian-born infants available for adoption. Similar conditions prevail in other European countries. This is attributed to several circumstances. The conditions in Norway are fairly typical: free contraception is available to young people from the age of sixteen to twenty-one; abortion may be obtained on demand (following the Abortion Act of 1979); there is no longer a social stigma attributed to single mother-

Figure 2.2 A family at the seaside.

hood; and generous public financial support is provided to single mothers. All these factors have resulted in a situation where hardly any unwanted babies are born to Norwegian women. Abandoned children are virtually unknown in Europe today. These factors, coupled to a public welfare policy that favours fostering over adoption whenever parents are unable to look after their children, means that those who want to have children, but fail to conceive or give birth, have to look abroad in order to satisfy their desire.

Involuntary infertility has become a social fact in Europe and North America. An estimated 10–15 per cent of all Norwegian couples experience difficulties in conceiving, and attempts at assisted conception have more than doubled over the past ten years in the Oslo region (*Aftenposten*, 6 November 2003). Involuntary infertility may be attributed to several causes. Women in Western Europe are choosing to have babies later; the average age of first-time Norwegian mothers in 1987 was 25.2. Today, in the Oslo region (which accounts for the majority of adoptions), the average age is 29 (*Samfunnsspeilet* 3: 2003).[1] This means that many women are well into their thirties when they decide that the time has come to start a family. In 2001, 48 per cent of all births were to women over 30, whereas in 1991, the figure was 34 per cent (Lappegård 2002). The biological fertility of women is at its peak during their early twenties, and conception becomes increasingly difficult with age. At the same time, the quality of male sperm in Europe and North America is declining, possibly due to environmental pollution of various kinds, resulting in male infertility also becoming more prevalent. According to a recent research report from the Danish Council on the Environment (*Miljøstyrelsen*), every second Danish male has poor sperm quality, which 'may mean that they will have problems in having children' (*Aftenposten*, 9 June 2003). If these trends continue, it seems likely that the demand for adoption will become even higher. Not only are many people experiencing difficulties in conceiving,[2] but more people than before are unwilling to live without children, and therefore the demand for some kind of 'unnatural' procreation increases.[3] There are two options open to those who experience involuntary childlessness and who want children: assisted conception through the use of one or more forms of new reproductive technology, or transnational adoption. Today, many who adopt have already had one or more attempts with NRT.

It is important to note that, contrary to popular understanding, there are more people in the West wishing to adopt than there are children officially made available for adoption from abroad.[4] At the same time, uncared for, or insufficiently cared for, orphaned and abandoned children in poor countries far exceed the number that receive new homes in the rich world. Due to reactions in donor countries, transnational adoption is a political matter between states, not a humanitarian one (see Chapters 8 and 9 for an exploration of why this is so). Adoption of children from the poor South and Eastern Europe should not be understood as an aid project. Transnational adoption is engaged in because Western people want children for their own sense of fulfilment. They are not, in most cases, performing an act of charity – although some may argue that there is mutual benefit. Thus, those adult adoptees who argue against the continuation of the practice, and suggest that Western adults ought to support children in their home lands instead of removing them and 'replanting' them in a new national and familial environment, miss the point entirely.

In order to give a picture of the fluctuations, growth and changes of transnational adoption globally, I present some pertinent figures in Table 2.1:

Table 2.1 Numbers of adoptees by major receiving countries in 1988, 1998, 2003

	1988	1998	2003
USA	9,120	15,774	21,616
France	2,441	3,777	3,995
Italy	2,078	2,263	2,772
Canada	232	2,222	2,181
Spain	93	1,497	3,951
Germany	874	922	674
Sweden	1,074	928	1,046
Netherlands	577	825	1,154
Switzerland	492	686	366
Norway	566	643	714
Denmark	523	624	522

Source: Selman 2000, 2005.

By contrast, figures for 1970 show that the USA adopted 2,409 children from overseas, Sweden 1,150, Netherlands 192 and Norway 115.

As we can see from the figures in the table, most countries, with the exception of Germany, Denmark and Switzerland, witnessed a growth in the total number of children adopted from abroad. Other countries, such as New Zealand, UK, Greece, Israel, Ireland, Luxembourg, Cyprus and Iceland did not start adopting transnationally until the mid-1990s. An increase in numbers is occurring here as well. Selman estimated that by the end of the twentieth century more than 32,000 children were adopted transnationally each year (2000: 19), and shows that 40,791 were adopted in 2003 (2005: 3). An interesting new development is occurring in Spain. Until the 1990s people from other countries came to Spain to adopt children; now Spanish couples go overseas to find children (Marre and Bestard 2003: 5). The practice is growing rapidly; figures from 2001 show that transnationally adopted children represented 1.047 per cent of the Spanish birth-rate. In the region of Catalonia, the figure is 1.61 per cent (ibid.: 19), thereby surpassing Norway.

Table 2.2 Number of adoptees from major donor countries: 1980–88, 1995, 1998 (to ten receiving countries).

1980–8		1995		1998	
Korea	6,123	China	2,559	Russia	5,064
India	1,532	Korea	2,145	China	4,855
Colombia	1,484	Russia	2,014	Vietnam	2,375
Brazil	753	Vietnam	1,249	Korea	2,294
Sri Lanka	682	Colombia	1,249	Colombia	1,162
Chile	524	India	970	Guatemala	1,143
Philippines	517	Brazil	627	India	1,048

Source: Selman 2002.

Table 2.3 Number of adoptees from major donor country to USA and Europe[5] in 2003.

	USA	Europe
China	6,859	3,156
Russia	5,209	2,294
Guatemala	2,328	–
S. Korea	1,790	–
Kazakhstan	825	–
Ukraine	702	1,227
India	472	515
Vietnam	382	459
Columbia	272	1,401
Bulgaria	–	741
Haiti	250	652
Ethiopia	–	593

Source: Selman 2005.

Tables 2.2 and 2.3 clearly show a decline in adoptions from Latin America (with the exception of Guatemala to USA and Colombia to Europe) and from Korea and India; the virtual disappearance of Sri Lanka as a donor country; and the dramatic emergence and growth in adoptees from Russia and China. Today, the USA receives approximately half of all its adoptees from these two countries. While China is a popular donor for Scandinavian couples, Russia is much less so.[6] New donor countries, such as Ethiopia, Haiti, Kazakhstan and Ukraine have appeared. What these figures do not show is the sudden appearance and disappearance of Romania on the scene. I shall discuss the background to some of these figures in Chapter 9.

We can note a dramatic increase in the number of transnational adoptions taking place in which children move from the (by and large) poor developing world[7] to the rich North. But the actual number is small if viewed in relation to the total number of children in institutions in these countries. However, the practice has received, and continues to receive, a large amount of media attention in both receiving and donor countries. Much of what is reported is of a sensational nature, often qualifying as urban myths.[8] Both substantiated and unsubstantiated reports of kidnapping abound – of buying and selling of children, and of children undergoing sham adoption in order to obtain their organs for transplants. Such stories reinforce many people's prejudices in both donor and recipient countries. The persistence of negative reports concerning transnational adoption has contributed to the increased involvement of the state and the international community. Demands for 'good governance' have made themselves particularly felt in this field, to ensure that vulnerable children receive the best possible assistance.

Alternative Methods of 'Unnatural' Procreation

Despite recent improvements in various methods of new reproductive technology, the demand for transnational adoption increases steadily. At the same time, we find a wide variance in national attitudes towards the technology: what is allowed and not allowed; which legal rights and restrictions are applied to the various methods; and what are the rights of the people concerned, such as sperm and egg donors and surrogate mothers. As regards legislation of assisted conception, it becomes increasingly difficult to talk in terms of a 'Western understanding', or 'Western practices and values'. From detailed study of laws dealing with the use of biotechnology in general (and new reproductive technology in particular), as well as the associated adoption laws, we find a great variation in what is taken to be 'normal', acceptable, and desirable in different European and North American countries ('Public Understanding of Genetics' project, unpubl. manuscripts). For example, Norwegian laws about various forms of assisted conception are comparatively restrictive. According to Norwegian law, neither egg donation nor surrogate motherhood is allowed; only sperm donation is permitted. This is in contrast to most European laws that allow some kind of egg donation and in stark contrast to the American situation where advertisements of the following type are regularly found in daily newspapers:

> ARE YOU A GOOD EGG? (Wonderful Egg Donor needed) $12.000. Loving, Ivy-league educated couple searching for egg donor. Jewish great, but not essential ... very attractive; excellent GPA/SATs, brown hair, fair complexion, slender, 5'4' and above, creative, healthy. (*The Daily Californian*, 25 February 2003)

> EGG DONOR for Japanese couple: Asian woman, 21-30, high quality education. Prefer 5'3'or taller. 1500+ SAT or 150+ IQ. **$20.000 for selected candidate.** (Original emphasis)[9]

Not only would such advertisements be illegal in Norway (and most European countries), but they would also be regarded with repugnance by most people. Firstly, to involve money in such a transaction is, ipso facto, to make children (strictly, potential children in this case, but nevertheless) into commodities that may be sold and bought.[10] This goes against common moral understanding of parenthood, an understanding which is clearly expressed in the legal codes. Secondly, the private and unregulated nature of the proffered relationship runs counter to an increasingly accepted view that matters pertaining to procreation, children and family life should be the responsibility of the state, and be handled by properly qualified personnel. To make such arrangements on a private individual basis is illegal, not only with regard to egg donation, but also in the case of adoption. The following advertisement in the same issue of the newspaper would be unacceptable in Norway for the same reasons, namely financial gain and private unsupervised transaction:

> ADOPTION ALTERNATIVE. Are you pregnant and don't know what to do? Loving, openhearted, financially stable woman would like to consider adopting a baby. Free counselling, living expenses and medical expenses. (*The Daily Californian*, 15 February 2003: 7)

To specify the desired qualities of one's future child is not acceptable in Norway. An ideology of chance dominates the discourse of procreation; all kinds of manipulations with nature that are not solely directed at saving life, are highly suspect. Although Norwegian infertility clinics try to match the general appearance of a sperm donor with those of the receiving couple, matters of intelligence, abilities, personality etc. are out of bounds. The same applies to adoption.[11] Thus, once a couple decides to adopt, they may not specify the kind of child they prefer. The ethos is that any child is a gift. To express preferences regarding race, colour, sex, intelligence and looks would be to denigrate the value of the gift, and to question the working of fate. It would also imply that one has the right to interfere with what nature intends. In this sense, biological and adoptive parents are placed in the same category, something which is further borne out in the vocabulary employed by those engaged in transnational adoption (see below). Prospective adoptive parents may specify only the country from which they wish to adopt and give some indication of the desired age range and the extent to which they are willing to accept a child with some form of handicap. My researches have shown that this deliberate emphasis on chance, on the side of the authorities, is not detrimental to adoptive parents' attitudes. Rather, when parents are offered a particular child, even if he or she is not quite what they ideally would have wanted, they hardly ever refuse, and an immediate bonding occurs by the prospective parents with the unseen offered child. Fate becomes an important element in their own familial discourse.[12] These examples are important insofar as they demonstrate major differences in cultural understandings and values between Norway and the USA. A main purpose of this book is to examine cultural differences in attitude regarding involuntary childlessness in both donor and recipient countries, and ascertain in what ways these affect the adoption procedures in, and between, countries. In order to establish a baseline, I turn next to a consideration of transnational adoption, Norwegian style.

Transnational Adoption in Norway

The adoption of an unknown child from an unknown country is a lengthy, complex process that is carried out in accordance with an increasing number of procedures, regulations and laws – both national and international. Although details vary from country to country, the process in Norway is broadly similar to that of other European countries. Adoption is less regulated in the USA and here there also is diversity between states (see Chapter 7).

Although sporadic adoption of children from overseas, mainly from South Korea, had occurred in Norway during the late 1950s and early 1960s, transnational adoption began in an organised manner in the late 1960s. The first children came from Vietnam and South Korea (Dalen and Sætersdal 1992). Later, other Asian countries (e.g. Thailand, the Philippines, Indonesia, Bangladesh, India and Sri Lanka) allowed Norwegian couples to adopt, as did several Latin American countries. Korea and Columbia were for a long time the main suppliers, and although many children continue to be adopted from these countries, today adoptees come from other Asian countries, especially China, from Ethiopia and from the former Communist bloc.

Today (2004) there are more than 17,000 transnationally adopted individuals living in Norway, and about seven hundred arrive each year. The demand to adopt children from overseas continues to increase here as elsewhere. Norway is a wealthy, well-developed country with a population of approximately four and half million people. It is a welfare state where the ideals of social democracy have to a large extent been realised. It may be characterised as a prime example of the liberal democracy: secular and rationalistic, agnostic, and optimistic with regard to the future. It is a country whose population trusts the state and believes that the state actively seeks to provide optimal conditions for its citizens. It is a country where the women's movement of the 1970s and 1980s has borne fruit in socioeconomic terms. Women have entered the labour force on an equal footing with men, and the housewife is a role of the past. It is also a country where the family is high on the agenda – both individually and politically- and where the nuclear family receives an increasing amount of government support in terms of provisions of infrastructure and direct financial transfers. With a birth rate of 1.8 and the fact that an estimated 92–94 per cent of all women have given birth by the time they reach the age of forty – a percentage which in a European context is high (Sundby and Schei 1996) – it is fair to conclude that children are important in contemporary Norwegian understanding of sociality. Family life is culturally elaborated and politically endorsed. Present-day provisions for birth leave are the most generous in the world (Ellingsæter and Hedlund 1998); provided that the father takes a minimum of one month's leave to look after his new child, a couple receives a maximum of twelve months leave at 80 per cent of the salary of whoever takes the leave. Moreover, since the year 2000, mothers have been encouraged to care for their children after the birth leave has expired; they receive financial incentives from the state to do so, and it is legally prohibited for this to be detrimental to their career. These provisions are intimately connected to values at large. Cultural expectations hold that women, and increasingly men, cannot be fulfilled unless they experience motherhood and fatherhood. Implicitly these roles are understood to be grounded in the nuclear family, not in individuals. Although the divorce rate is high, serial monogamy is common, and many couples cement their relationship with a child. All these factors put enormous pressure upon those couples that find themselves unable to have their own children.

Despite liberal legislation about contraception, abortion, cohabitation and homosexual partnership, Norway is surprisingly conservative and restrictive when it comes to procreation. As mentioned, surrogacy is not allowed, egg donation is not allowed and the practice of new reproductive technology is strictly controlled. Sperm donation, on the other hand, is permitted. While couples are entitled to these subsidised attempts at assisted conception, only married couples have this right (Melhuus 2005).[13] The same restrictions apply to adoption. Although single women may under special circumstances be permitted to adopt, the general rule is that only married heterosexual couples may do so. Changing gender patterns have also resulted in a public visibility of homosexual couples who, may enter into legally binding partnerships. Pressure groups representing them are demanding the right to adopt and the right to receive assisted conception. Following the general election in October 2005, a new Social Democratic government was elected. While in opposition they had argued for relaxing the criteria and it remains to be seen if they change the laws. According to the law, there is a lower age limit of twenty-five to adopt. No upper limit is specified in the law, but the Ministry issues directives from time to time. At the moment no applicant over forty-five years of age will, under normal circumstances, be accepted. Criteria for being acceptable adoptive parents are specified by the largest adoption agency, The Children of the World, in the following manner, '[a]n adoptive family ought to be as little as possible different from other families. The adopted child ought to be the youngest in a family. There ought to be at least two years' gap in the age of an adopted child and the applicants other child(ren)'.

Despite pressure from organisations of the involuntary infertile, the government is resisting demands to classify infertility as a disease.[14]

The Process of Becoming Adoptive Parents

In order to appreciate what is involved in the process of adopting a child from another country, I will present an overview of the Norwegian procedure. In formal terms, this does not diverge markedly from those of other Scandinavian countries or Holland, but the procedures are in many ways different from those of the UK and the southern European countries, as well as North America. One main difference is whether so-called private adoptions are permitted. Another is whether the finalising of an adoption is an administrative matter or whether each case has to be heard before a judge.

Once a Norwegian couple decides to adopt a child from overseas, they embark upon a time-consuming and complex process. From start to finish it rarely takes less than three years; often it takes longer. To some extent, the time it takes is dependent upon the country from which a couple wishes to adopt. But as these may change their practice, due to levels of demand and national policy, little can be taken for granted. There are three different authorities that have to be approached and who must give their approval before an application is sent to the country from which the couple desire to adopt a child. These are the Social Services department of their local authority, the special section dealing with adoption within the Ministry of Children and Family, and an adoption agency. It is only the last institution that actually procures a child, but it may not do so until the couple is cleared for adoption by the two public institutions, making the process a prime example of governmentality in action. There is no clear overall consensus about the purpose of transnational adoption, not least because there is, at times, a tension between the personal desires and priorities of prospective adoptive parents and the legal requirements encoded to ensure the proper conduct of all the various parties involved, i.e., professionals, public administrators and adoption agency personnel.

On the one hand, adoption is presented as a social event – the bringing together of adults and children who are total strangers, and with radically different sociocultural backgrounds, in a framework of kinship. On the other hand, as the vocabulary employed indicates (see next chapter), the whole purpose of the exercise is to create a lasting relationship of as-if biological parents and as-if biological children, and forge them into a family. Throughout, the parents (and the professionals involved) oscillate between a biogenetic model of relatedness and an environmental one.

In Norway, three government-certified, non-government organisations (NGOs), handle the actual adoption. They are in close contact with the adoption section of the Ministry of Children and Family. It is the agencies who maintain regular relationships with the various relevant public individuals and institutions in donor countries, as well as with specific institutions that look after children to be released for adoption. The latter are mainly orphanages. Once a couple has decided to adopt, they want the event to happen fast, and they feel very frustrated by what they regard as unnecessarily long-drawn-out procedures preceding the acceptance to go ahead. There are two stages that have to be gone through: scrutiny by various publicly appointed persons and institutions at both local and national level who may or may not grant permission to adopt, and the handling of their case by the adoption agencies who procure the children once permission is forthcoming. The former puts them in direct touch with representatives of the expert professions in the shape of social workers employed by the local government where they live. It is their job to evaluate the couple's suitability not only as parents, but as adoptive parents of a child who will not only look different from themselves, but who will come from a country whose social and cultural reality will, in most cases, be unfamiliar. They write a so-called 'home study report'.[15] Most applicants find this examination of themselves extremely uncomfortable and irksome.[16] Not only do they have to provide legal documents of birth and marriage, and documents concerning job, income, debts, and good behaviour, they are also subjected to investigation of their personal history as individuals and as a couple, which they feel is close to unnecessary prying. Their home will be visited (often several times) and examined; their friends and relatives will be interviewed. All this puts a big strain on them.[17]

Once the social worker has completed his or her report, it is submitted to the local government for approval. If that is granted it is sent to a special section in the Ministry of Children and Family where another scrutiny is made before final approval – or rejection – is issued. (It is a requirement of the Hague Convention on Intercountry Adoption to establish a centralised authority that handles all adoption cases, and as a signatory to the convention, Norway has established such an authority under the auspices of the Ministry of Children and Family.) All this takes time. The duration of the process at the local level varies from local authority to local authority, but six to nine months seems to be the average. At the national level applicants do not have to go for an interview, but there is a huge backlog and it takes about the same time again for an application to be dealt with here. The civil servants in the Ministry decide the kind of child a particular couple should be given, taking into account their stated preferences with regard to country and age; if they should they be allowed to adopt siblings; and which, if any, disabilities a child may have.[18] In parallel with this process, couples register with one of the adoption agencies and choose a country from which they wish to adopt. However, until they have been finally approved, the agency may not approach an orphanage with their application.

Although the criteria for being accepted as parents for a child adopted from overseas are restrictive and normative, only between 4 and 6 per cent of those who apply are rejected (Stefansen, personal communication), a figure which is much lower than is commonly assumed. It may be that rumours of the (assumed) strict criteria prevent all but the conventionally acceptable couples from applying. But it is not correct to think, (as many believe), that adoptive parents come from the wealthier sections of Norwegian society. While there is a slight majority of couples who are highly educated and earn a relatively high income, my studies show that this is much less the case than is assumed in society at large (Howell and Ulfsnes 2002). Even during the early days of transnational adoption, couples from every socioeconomic class became adoptive parents. Nevertheless, there are indications that while good education and high income are not necessary attributes of adoptive parents, what one might call personal resources seem to be so. The process is emotionally demanding and puts a lot of pressure on the couple. For obvious reasons I did not meet those who gave up or divorced along the way; I only met those who persevered and succeeded. They were unanimous in saying that the process was tough, but that they felt that they learnt a lot about themselves and each other. Although it is not statistically documented, a common view amongst adoption workers is that couples with children adopted from overseas divorce less often than do couples with biological children. This may, I suggest, be attributed to the factors just mentioned.

Once a couple has been approved, the adoption agency can approach an orphanage in the relevant country. The three approved adoption agencies collaborate with different donor institutions. Each agency has established a good network of contacts which they are at great pains to maintain and develop. Not only do they cultivate the relationship with staff of actual orphanages, they also seek to maintain good relations with the authorities that are involved in completing the transfer of a child from its country of birth. Although it is forbidden, according to the Hague Convention, to make any payment for children, it is permitted to contribute financial assistance towards the running and the improvement of the orphanage. This is a rather delicate matter (see Chapters 8 and 9), but most Norwegian agencies try to solve the dilemma through donations towards actual projects, such as the improvement of sanitary facilities, or building a new kitchen.

The three agencies that are licensed by the state to undertake adoption from abroad are kept under close surveillance by the relevant section of the Ministry of Children and Family. Whenever an arrangement is made with a new country to receive children for adoption, senior representatives from that country's civil service visit Norway and they sign a bilateral agreement at the highest level. The staff of the Ministry are obliged to keep a close eye on the conditions in all donor countries, and ensure that transactions are carried out in line with Norwegian law and the Hague Convention on Intercountry Adoption; and from time to time representatives from the Ministry accompany adoption agency staff to the various countries in order to check out the situation for themselves.

Unlike biological pregnancy, no one knows how long the transnational adoptive process will last. The couple is now at the mercy of the donor institution and the centralised authorities in the donor country. Their documents have to be translated and certified, and the couple sends a background report on themselves including photos of themselves, their close kin and their home. This is a time when they prepare themselves mentally and emotionally to become the parents of a child born by unknown others – in a distant and unknown land – who, in most cases, will look very different from themselves. After some time, usually from six to twelve months, the waiting couple will be allocated a child. But they still have to wait many months while various bureaucratic and legal procedures are undertaken before they can collect him or her.

Following the 1999 amendment to the Norwegian 1986 Adoption Act, adopted children are given Norwegian citizenship once all formalities in the country of origin are completed, and are issued with a Norwegian passport at the local Embassy. At this point, the child's legal status undergoes an irrevocable transformation. It is now up to the adoptive parents to

Figure 2.3 The Norwegianisation of an adopted child.

make sure that the child will be kinned, and that his or her sense of self and identity will develop in the direction of becoming a Norwegian boy or girl. As I shall show in Chapter 4, this is a task that most embark upon with enthusiasm, sincerity and thoroughness.

Once they opt for transnational adoption, the prospective adoptive parents create a virtual parent–child relationship. The meaning they give the relationship is affirmed through models of kinship that oscillate between the biological and the cultural. What might arguably be described as a quintessentially social form of kinship ends up being alternatively naturalised and denaturalised (Howell 2001, 2003b). Despite many protestations to the effect that proper account must be taken of the transnationally adopted children's 'original culture', and parental attempts at incorporating selected features from countries of origin into their children's childhood, the majority of adoptive parents are, I argue, primarily concerned with a process of kinning their children, and making them to all intents and purposes Norwegian.

The Changing Role of Adoption Agencies

Since they first started, the adoption agencies have expanded their roles, and they are now no longer merely providers of children. From being collections of people whose main qualification in most cases was that they themselves had adopted children from overseas, they have become highly professional organisations whose staff have joined the ranks of the other experts that shape the practice. They no longer exist simply in order to facilitate contact between prospective parents and adoptable children in orphanages in countries where they have contacts; they have become self-appointed educators of prospective parents and the public at large. Through the numerous local branches established throughout the country they provide an infrastructure for adoptive families, and constitute important fora for communication for adoptive parents both before and after their children have arrived. These local branches organise social events, they arrange seminars with invited speakers, and they offer preparatory courses in parenthood for prospective adoptive parents.[19] These courses are usually run by adoptive parents whose children are older and who have taken an active interest in the literature on adoption. A syllabus is prepared by staff at headquarters, consisting of literature deemed to be of relevance. This includes books written by adoptive parents about their experience, books written by adult adoptees, psychological studies undertaken of transnationally adopted children and young adults, articles that debate language learning, difficulties at school, racism etc. The course usually includes invited speakers with relevant expertise, such as psychologists, medical doctors or social workers.

The courses are intended to prepare the couples for this rather special kind of parenthood. Having participated in several such courses, I am left with a strong impression that the prospective parents are interested only in positive information. Although they are given literature that debates possible difficulties encountered by adoptees in settling down in their new circumstances, they seem reluctant to seriously examine such possibilities. The courses are characterised by expectancy and emotionality. By the time the couples have reached this stage, they have been through emotional turmoil and they wish only to look forward to a happy end to their agonies. This is a forum where they can meet others in the same situation, and deep personal bonds are often wrought with others.

In addition, the agencies publish regular journals, which are becoming increasingly glossy and sophisticated in both lay-out and content, covering topics such as education, language acquisition, health, puberty, problems of identity, racism, information on the various donor countries, reports of return journeys etc. In recent years, they have jointly published pamphlets for intending parents, and for adoptees, with titles such as *The Adoptive Family: Information and Guidance for Adoptive Parents* (Carli and Dalen 1997), *Adoption of Foreign Children* (1994), *Who am I? A Brochure Written By and For Those Adopted from Different Countries* (1997). These and similar others are written by people with research or practical experience of the subject (mainly from a psychological standpoint). The agencies further encourage the establishment of associations of young adult adoptees; they arrange lectures and seminars for parents and families; and they arrange the increasingly popular 'motherland' tours for adoptive families, also known as roots... or return journeys.

Figure 2.4 Getting acquainted with the Norwegian way of life.

Figure 2.5 First Christmas in a new country with a new family.

Costs

Adopting a child from overseas is not easy and it is not cheap. It is time-consuming and involves much anxiety on the part of the applicants. In Norway, although the agencies are non-profit-making, they incur costs that the applicants have to cover. Between them, the three agencies receive an annual government grant of one million Norwegian crowns (NOK) (approximately $150,000), but this covers only a small portion of the costs. There is a continuing debate in the media about the level of state subsidy that ought to be allocated to the practice. But since successive governments have refused to define involuntary childlessness as a disease, the national health system is not bound to cover all costs in connection with obtaining a child – either through IVF or adoption. In Norway, the agencies levy a flat fee for all, regardless of the actual cost involved. At the time of writing, the fee ranges from 65,000 to 70,000 NOK ($US9,000–10,000). In addition there will be the cost of collecting the child in his or her country of origin – if the parents wish to do this, or if the country in question insists on it. The Norwegian state reimburses the couple 20,000 NOK.[20] approximately $US 3000) once the child has arrived in Norway.

In America, no public funding is available for covering the cost of transnational adoption, but part of the costs may in some states be tax-deductible. Most agencies charge each applicant according to actual expenses incurred in each case, plus a fee due to the agency. It is estimated that an average adoption will cost between $US 10,000 and 15,000 plus travel expenses. While the costs in both Norway and the USA are clearly substantial, they are not, contrary to widespread belief, prohibitive for most couples. To put it in perspective: in Norway, to adopt a child from overseas costs about half the price of a new car. In America (where cars are cheaper) the cost is more or less equivalent to a new car.

To Conclude

Transnational adoption is about making kinship; it is about creating significant kinned sociality when biology fails to do the job. From an ad hoc and sporadic practice, often based on personal relationships and often undertaken in a spirit of charity, it has turned into a highly organised and regulated practice whose purpose, in most cases, is to provide involuntarily infertile couples with the possibility to become a family. Ultimately, transnational adoption raises profound questions about inclusion and exclusion, and about belonging. In the following chapters, the implications of these issues will be explored. In the next chapter I explore some variations over time and space in the significance attributed to biological relatedness – to being of the same flesh and blood – in understanding kinship.

Notes

1. On a national basis it is 27.
2. It is difficult to put absolute numbers on this. However, whereas spinsters and bachelors in the past did not expect to have children, today the marital status of individuals does not represent such a barrier. In Norway, at any rate, whether married or single, there is a strong tendency today to feel a sense of incompleteness if one goes through life childless.
3. At 1.8, the Norwegian birth rate is one of the highest in Europe. According to recent studies, there is an increase in three-child families and people express a desire to have many children. This in itself demonstrates the high value placed on family life and intensifies the pressure upon those who are infertile.
4. Based on the example from China, it is widely assumed that the great majority of adoptees are girls. This is not the case. In Norway, for example, during the period 1997–2002, approximately only 5 per cent more girls than boys were adopted (Central Statistical Bureau).
5. Since the USA and the (sixteen) European receiving countries do not always adopt from the same countries, a blank is left where no figures are available.
6. Adoption agencies expected a rush of applications in the early 1990s for children from former Soviet countries because they look more like Norwegians. However, after an ini-

tial interest, the demand declined. Several reasons have been suggested. Children from Romania and Russia were reputed to be suffering from various handicaps due to neglect. Also many adoptive parents wish to make the relationship explicit and hence prefer children who cannot be mistaken for their biological children.

7. The picture is more complex. In Latin America huge discrepancies in wealth mean that sections of the population are very poor and it is their children that are given up for adoption. South Korea does not count as a developing nation. Here the social stigma attached to illegitimacy explains the continued abandonment of infants.

8. Despite persistent stories in Brazil of children being abducted for organ transplant, investigations have not found any evidence of this (Fonseca, personal communication).

9. In the same newspaper (all under the general heading of 'Help Wanted' and amidst the ads for staff for summer camps, sales representatives, and house cleaners) was the following advertisement: 'Sperm donors wanted $50 per acceptable sample. If you're healthy, aged 18–40 and can make weekly visits for a year, call us'. The contrast with the ads for eggs is startling. Not only does sperm come considerably cheaper, the requirements made of the donors are much less stringent than those of egg donors. The gender implications are interesting, but beyond the scope of this book.

10. I return to a discussion about the immorality of money in Chapter 8.

11. Again, this differs from the USA. Prospective American adoptive parents are also very demanding in the qualities they look for in an adopted child.

12. Norwegian prospective adoptive parents can, however, also be quite demanding. My examination of application forms submitted to two agencies during the period 1969–2000, indicates that most couples prefer a young child and most would prefer one without special needs (Howell and Ulfsnes 2002). According to the director of an adoption agency, Norwegian couples are perceived by many donor countries to be very inquisitive about the health of their children. By contrast, Italian couples have a reputation amongst donor countries to be willing to adopt not only older children, but also handicapped ones (personal information by orphanage director in India, confirmed by the director of an Italian adoption agency).

13. Changing gender patterns have resulted in a public visibility of homosexual couples who may enter into legally binding partnerships. Pressure groups representing them are demanding the right to adopt and the right to receive assisted conception. Following the general election in October 2005, a new Social Democratic government was elected. While in opposition they had argued for relaxing the criteria and it remains to be seen if they change the laws.

14. Were they to do so, this would put a heavy financial burden upon the public health system.

15. At the time of writing, Norway has not, as opposed to Sweden, Denmark and Holland, devised a standard procedure and questionnaire to be used by all personnel throughout the country. Only one local authority, Bergen City Council, has appointed a person whose job it is to handle all applications. There is, therefore, a certain amount of arbitrariness, and applicants are aware of this – a fact which deepens their insecurity.

16. Many argue that there are no checks at all on people who wish to become biological parents, and that the desire for children that they themselves feel ought to be enough. 'We have so much to offer a child', they say, 'why can we not be allowed to just give it?'

17. In most European countries such studies are undertaken by some kind of public agency, but in the USA this is often done by a private organisation, and this may constitute one of the heavy costs involved in adopting from overseas (Bartholet 1992).

18. Prospective parents may not state a preference for sex or colour. There is little freedom of choice regarding their prospective child's qualities.

19. Unlike some countries, e.g. Sweden, Denmark and Holland, such courses are not obligatory in Norway, but discussions are being held with the Ministry of Children and Family with the aim to make them so.

20. The actual amount of this subsidy varies from year to year.

Chapter 3

KINSHIP WITH STRANGERS: VALUES AND PRACTICES OF ADOPTION

In medieval society the idea of childhood did not exist.
P. Ariés, *Centuries of Childhood*

Adoption customs [in 'traditional societies'] rest on a mental attitude difficult to conceive for those nurtured in Western traditions.
R. Lowie, *The Encyclopaedia of Social Sciences*

There is a strong attitude of shame related to biological parenthood [in Benin] and an attempt to deny it.
E. Alber, 'Denying Biological Parenthood'

Conception, Birth and Fictive Kinship

Franklin and Ragoné argue that 'an important genealogy of modern anthropology can readily be traced through its relationship to a core set of ideas related to reproduction, or "the facts of life"' (1998: 2). Indeed, the early founders of the discipline (Morgan, Maine, McLennan, Engels, Frazer, Rivers, Malinowski, Radcliffe-Brown) made a comparative study of ideas of procreation and kinship their starting point for analysing social organisation (ibid.). Kinship, it was argued, is about what a society does with the phenomena that develop from the biological facts of sexual intercourse, pregnancy and parturition; facts that Morgan thought to be universally crucial for understanding kinship. The fact of birth (begotten, conceived and born by whom to whom) has been, and continues, to be the pivotal analytic reference point.

Although these theoreticians were at pains to declare that kinship should be studied as a classification system of significant others, they nevertheless maintained a biological model of procreation and kinship as their point of reference. Social practices that seemed to emphasise different criteria for relatedness (cf. Bouquet 1993)[1] emerged as highly problematic or were dismissed as 'fictive kinship'. Despite the heavy criticism levelled at this approach (e.g. Needham 1971, Schneider 1984[2]), the centrality of a biological frame of reference for kinship studies has been hard to relinquish. By introducing terms that distinguish pater from genitor, and mater from genetrix, attempts have been made to resist the conceptual fusion of biological and social relations (Barnes 1973). But a predilection to analytically emphasise the biological connection remains. The issue of adoption is well suited for testing such basic assumptions. Adoption is practised in some form or other in all known societies, and as a social practice it goes to the heart of what we take to be kinship. And yet it has received surprisingly little attention from anthropologists.

Adoption both challenges and confirms unreflected notions about relatedness. As a social practice, adoption is meaningless without a biological model for kinship as a reference. But it is a two-way semantic process. Adoption provides meaning to the biological, the 'made' relationship and, at the same time, limits the meaning of the 'natural' relationship. Kinship studies have taught us to study relations, not individuals. Adoption allows us truly to focus upon the quality of 'relationness', to elicit meanings of kinned relations and of processes of kinning.

My research on transnational adoption in Norway has demonstrated two related facts: firstly, that biology remains the model by which most Norwegians approach kinned relatedness, and secondly, that adoptive parents do not regard their relationship with their adopted children as in any sense fictive; rather it results in a kinship that is highly self-conscious. I have argued elsewhere (Howell 1999, 2001, 2003b) that we can observe amongst Norwegian adoptive parents, as well as adoptees, a tendency to fluctuate according to context between foregrounding and backgrounding biology and sociality as explanatory models for kinship. However, it is the biological understanding that remains the model for their understanding of the parent–child relationship. This may be explained by the supremacy of what Schneider has called the Euro-American 'Doctrine of Genealogical Unity of Mankind' (1984: 174).

The concept of classificatory kin has not freed anthropologists from the dominant influence of biology. Continuation of, and recruitment to, the kin group and the various systems of descent that ensure this, became the analytical focus of most Anglo-Saxon anthropology during the first half of the twentieth century.[3] Whenever a biological frame of reference is deviated from, such practices have been labelled as 'fictive kinship' or 'pseudo kinship' (e.g. Barnard and Good 1984: 150–52). In one of only two references to adoption in his introductory book, *Kinship and Marriage: an Anthropological Approach*, Fox states,

Genetic kinship is the model for fictive kinship relations. The most obvious case is adoption. In many societies, large-scale adoption or 'fosterage' is practiced, and most people do not in fact rear their actual children, but there is nothing to stop the system working 'as if' they did. No society treats this in an arbitrary fashion ... Once we accept that 'consanguinity' is a socially defined quality, the definition of kinship holds. What we must avoid doing is foisting our own particular view of consanguinity onto the rest of mankind, however 'true' we may think it is. (Fox 1967: 32)

While Fox's caveat about failing to view consanguinity as a socially defined quality is well taken, more problematic is his unquestioned acceptance of the validity of the terms 'fictive kinship' and 'actual children'. These and similar terms have, however, been incorporated into anthropological kinship discourse without meeting much opposition. Goody confirms this general trend when he says, 'The institution of adoption, whether considered comparatively or not, should be looked at in the context of other quasi-kinship relationships such as fostering, god-parenthood, etc.' (J. Goody 1969: 56). At the meeting of the American Anthropological Association in 1998 a session listed as 'Fictive kinship' attracted a large audience, demonstrating that the concept is alive and well in the minds of many anthropologists. Against this and others who persist in such usages I want to argue that fictive or pseudo kinship can never be an analytical category. This does not mean that the notion of 'fictive kinship' may not be relevant in particular social settings, but as an empirical, not an analytic category.[4]

There are some notable exceptions to the assumption that kin are created solely by the act of conception. Based on her fieldwork among the Hue in New Guinea Highlands, Meigs notes that, 'while many people hold a biological view of kinship, others, especially those who live in Highland New Guinea, have a different concept of kinship' (Meigs 1986: 117). The Hua, she says, are not interested in distinguishing between real and not-real kin, nor do they pay any attention to genealogy. Moreover, according to Hua thinking, children are 'built', originally from menstrual blood and semen, and later from nurture. She states that two people not related by birth can create kinship by feeding each other, or through unilateral feeding (particularly of a woman's milk, of food, and of water) (ibid.: 201). In Hua thinking, food of all kinds, including semen that builds the foetus, includes *nu*, a vital essence invested into food by the person who produces it. 'Thus, when you eat a food you are ... eating some of the nu vital essence of another person. Eating, by this logic, relates people, making them kin because it mixes their *nu*' (ibid.). From this social fact she concludes that earlier anthropologists' characterisation of these Highland kinship systems as incorporating an extensive use of 'fictive kin', is misplaced. The incorporation of kin is not fictive, or some kind of pretence, she argues, but must be regarded as a *different understanding* of kinship (ibid.: 200). In my view this is a perfectly legitimate conclusion. It is congruent with the argument that I put forward about adoptive practices in Europe. However, as witnessed by the quotations cited above, the term 'fictive kinship' continues to be used in contemporary anthropological texts, thus revealing an inherent bio-focus of anthropologists. In order to enlarge our understanding of kinship, we should break with such substantive categories as fictive or quasi-kinship relationships and look instead at the values surrounding the quality of the relationships in each case. In this endeavour, we are helped by examining attitudes and practices towards adoption in social settings where a biogenetic understanding of meaningful relatedness is not paramount.

Due to the increasing rigidity of the questions that were posed, kinship lost its central position in anthropology during the 1980s and 1990s. In his critique of kinship studies, Needham concludes that the dearth of theoretical advances within kinship studies is not due to a lack of data, but the poverty of the conceptual frameworks of analysis (1971: 2). However, following a number of breakthroughs in bio-medical research, new reproductive technology and the transplantation of body organs, it became no longer possible to maintain a clear divide between nature and culture, a divide that had been a mainstay of traditional kinship studies. By abandoning some concepts and introducing new ones, kinship studies revived. Examining implications of the new biomedical research, M. Strathern (1992) delivered a final analytic death blow to 'nature'. This new-found anthropological interest in biotechnology is not only bringing kinship back into focus, but is also raising pertinent questions about personhood and the basis for significant relatedness. However, while anthropologists argue that biology in social worlds is best understood as a social construct, influential members of other disciplines and professions do not share this understanding. Familial relations continue to be thought of as founded upon biological connections between autonomous individuals. This is clearly expressed in family law and this view is being globalised through international conventions (see Chapters 7, 8, 9).

Some Early Scholarly Interest in Adoption

Adoption cannot be understood in isolation from a broader examination of cultural attitudes to personhood, family, parenthood and childhood. In what follows I shall consider some examples of values and practices regarding the kinning of non-biological children in societies whose ontological understandings vary from that of Western Europe. In order to demonstrate the fragility of seemingly fixed categories I also provide a brief historical overview of changing attitudes in Europe and North America. Transnational adoption is a recent phenomenon; adoption is ancient. In order to understand the former it is useful to relate it to the latter.

I define adoption to mean the practice whereby children, for a variety of reasons, are brought up by adults other than their biological parents, and are treated as full members of the family amongst whom they live. The adults in these cases are acknowledged to assume what one would recognise as the parental responsibility of overseeing the children's care, nurture, training, education, and of fixing them on a path of subjectivation and relatedness with significant others. In other words, they kin them. I regard it as useful to distinguish adoption from fostering. The latter has an element of temporality about it, and the jural status of the child is not affected (cf. E. Goody1982: 336). Strict legal aspects of adoption are more relevant in societies subsumed under a codified legal system, but jurally informed practices pertaining to the organisation of relationships within and without a kin idiom are relevant in most places. Although there are numerous brief references to adoption and/or fostering practices in ethnographic monographs from all over the world, very little sustained interpretative interest has been directed at this social phenomenon. It is surprising that anthropologists whose preoccupations were with segmentary lineage systems in Africa and elsewhere have ignored adoption in their studies.

We know that in many places, and at different times, adoption of children has received public attention, and that measures to regulate it were perceived to be necessary. For example, the Babylonian code of Mammurabi, the oldest comprehensive set of written laws in existence, gives a prominent position to 'Adoption and wet-nursing' (Goody 1969: 55). Similarly, the laws of ancient China, India, Greece and Rome included reference to adoption and the practice occupied a large portion of Maine's Ancient Law (1931 [1861]). Maine, and also Fustel de Coulange, linked adoption to the perpetuation of agnates over time. Unlike those who came after him, Maine regarded adoption as an important factor in kinship studies. He characterises it as a 'legal fiction' (Goody prefers the intriguing term 'social fiction'), as one of the means whereby society 'took its first steps towards civilization' because it opened for incorporation of strangers as kin, and thus progressed from an emphasis on the bonds of kinship to the ties of contiguity as a basis for common political action. The practice was important because it 'permitted family relations to be created artificially' (Maine 1931: 21–22, 107 in Goody 1969: 67).

Goody provides a very useful survey of adoption as practised in Rome, Greece, India and China and gives a summary of both Maine's and Mayne's (see below) deliberations on the topic. Despite his insight that adoption could prove an important contribution to kinship studies, Goody cannot rid himself of biological thinking – characterizing the practice as a quasi-kinship relationship. He is unequivocal on this point when he states that '[t]he act of adoption ... involves the transfer of an individual from one filial relationship to another, from a "natural" relationship to a "fictional" one' (ibid.: 58).

Goody divides the function of adoption into three main types:

1. To provide homes for orphans, bastards, foundlings and the children of impaired families.
2. To provide childless couples with social progeny.
3. To provide an individual or couple with an heir to their property.

While the first function looks to the needs of the children, the last two centre upon the adopter. Goody argues that the third aspect of adoption is that which manifests the greatest variety on a cross-cultural basis. Indeed, a question of inheritance for the childless couple was a consideration that prompted the first Norwegian Adoption Act of 1917. Only recently has the first function become central anywhere.

Adoption in ancient Rome was primarily a means for continuing the agnatic line. However, it is important to note that in Roman practice, economic concerns were not divorced from religious ones. Adoption thus provided an individual man with a son and heir, one who 'could inherit the property, continue his line and perpetuate his worship. ... the inheritance of property and the worship of the dead were intimately connected in Roman society' (Goody 1969: 60, Hollinger 1992). Thus, Roman adoption was the concern of the wealthy and powerful. It was a choice taken by individual men and women for the reasons just stated. People preferred to adopt grown men and women, and often a relative or the child of another powerful family was adopted, thus enhancing alliance between them. Several Roman emperors chose to adopt their successors rather than let chance favour a son.[5] Similar preoccupations with succession and inheritance underpinned adoption in Athens. Here a man adopted his daughter's husband or one of her sons, thus keeping the practice within the family network. Property and worship were the main concern in Athens, but some complicated legal provisions existed which enabled an adopted man to revert to his status if his own natal kin left him significant wealth. Both in Rome and Athens only a citizen might be adopted. A slave or a foreigner could not enter into an equal relationship with other citizens, nor might they perform the worship of the ancestors.

Mayne's monumental study, Treatise on Hindu Law and Usage (1878), included 117 pages devoted to the legal provisions for adoption in Hindu India. Again, the overriding concern seems to be to provide male continuation for the agnatic lineage. Both in India and in China, the most eligible person for adoption was the son of a brother, and this continues to be the ideal today. Being of the same agnatic line, he may perform the funerary rites for his adoptive father. However, where no nephew was available, Hindu law allowed the son of a brotherless daughter to be transferred in adoption. (I return in Chapter 9 to a discussion of adoption practices in contemporary India and China.) Goody does not consider the possibility that male infertility might be the source of childlessness. He identifies two main alternative courses of action open to the heirless man, apart from adoption: breeding through the appointed daughter or replacing the barren wife with another (ibid. 71). Of course, in non-scientific understandings of procreation and reproduction, the respective roles of men and women in conception and gestation must be taken into account when considering non-biological options within marriage. In many parts of the world the source of infertility is attributed to women.[6]

Goody's survey demonstrates the complexity of adoption. We learn from his perusal of the written records of European and Far Eastern antiquity that adoption was a relatively common phenomenon, and that its prime functions were to provide a man with an heir to his worldly goods, and to honour him in his posthumous role as an ancestor. In some cases, adoption involved a complete rupture with the biological family, whereas in other cases the adoptee maintained some kind of relationship with it. In none of the examples discussed by Goody and Maine is the motivation for adoption the welfare of destitute or unwanted children; the practice is engaged in exclusively in order to satisfy the needs of adults. As we shall see, this attitude began to change during the first half of the twentieth century.

Changing Meanings of Children, Childhood and Family in Europe and the USA

Contemporary Euro-American notions of childhood, as a particular stage in life qualitatively different from adulthood, is a relatively recent development. As Cunningham rightly suggests, the meaning attributed to childhood at any given time cannot be studied in isolation from society as a whole. Examining trends in economic, political, intellectual and social life in nineteenth-century Europe, the thrust of his argument is that '[i]t has been the economic development of the western world which has allowed for both the shift in the experience of childhood from work to school, and for the emergence of the idea that childhood should be a time of dependence' (1995: 3). These ideas were first developed by Philippe Ariés whose seminal work *Centuries of Childhood* (1962), was to set the agenda for future studies on the history of childhood among social historians and anthropologists alike.[7] Tracing sociocultural ideas from the Middle Ages to the present, Ariés developed a hypothesis which has become the standard debating point for subsequent studies by social historians and anthropologists, namely that the *idea* of childhood[8] is of recent origin. What is often forgotten by critics and commentators is that Ariés was primarily seeking to understand the particularity of the present by comparing and contrasting it with the past, and that what struck him as characteristic of the present was the way in which social life and the emotions were centred in the family (1962: 7) He argued that there was a connection between the idea of childhood and the idea of the family, and that just as the idea of the family was absent from European thinking until the seventeenth century, so also the idea of childhood. Life before that time, he argues, 'was lived in public' (ibid.: 392). Social relations were developed and maintained outside the family, the family being 'simply an institution for the transmission of a name and an estate'. This changed when the family gradually assumed 'a moral and spiritual function', until today, when 'our world is obsessed by the physical, moral and sexual problems of childhood' (ibid.: 295, 296). He found that the main reason for this change could be traced to the development of the educational system whereby the state began to take on a responsibility for the education of children, a development that I analyse as a manifestation of governmentality. Material from many non-European societies bears out his argument that ideas of childhood and family as we know them today are contingent and not universal – as is argued in international conventions. But his suggestion that, as the family advanced as a focus for social life, sociality more generally retreated, is not borne out by my study of Norwegian adoptive families (I return to these points).

In a recent study on the social history of the Northern European and white Protestant North American family, Gillis makes a useful distinction between what he calls 'the family we live *with* and the family we live *by*' (1996: xv, my emphasis). By the family we live with, he means the actual family we live in; and by the family we live by, he means the changing ideas of the meaning of the family, as an imagined social unit 'expressed through myths and ritual that are so embedded in our everyday lives that they remain virtually invisible, or, when detected, are put in the category of folklore, primordial and timeless' (ibid.: xvii). In other words, his is a study of implicit values that inform practice. It is, I suggest, the 'family we live by' of contemporary Northern Europe and North America that largely has given rise to the prescriptions of the UNCRC (UN Convention on the Rights of the Child) and the Hague Convention. Gillis's focus is not on children, but on the growth of the family as a social and cultural value in this region. His work is important for my study of transnational adoption for two reasons. Firstly, the 'family we live by' model is useful for interpreting past and current practices in Norway as well as in the countries that Norway adopts from. Secondly, it enables me to contextualise the moral and normative values about childhood and family life that have influenced present-day psycho-technocrats and been instrumental in the formulation of various laws and international treaties.

From the late Middle Ages through the late eighteenth-century Europeans had clear images of what constituted the good family life, finding support for them in Christianity. From the nineteenth century onwards we may note a shift among the middle classes of Protestant northern Europe and the USA in that they began to create 'a distinctive set of family times and homeplaces', i.e., secular life anchored in time and space became important in the construction of identities. Before that time, he suggests, people paid little interest to questions of origin. Places that represented genealogical roots were not of much concern (ibid.: 14). Furthermore, the connection between giving birth and giving nurture, the equating of bio- logical maternity with motherhood, was not generally made in Europe until the mid-nineteenth century. Women's fertility rate was high, as was their mortality rate, and it was often impossible for a woman to nurture all who were born to her. It was common for children to be brought up by oth- ers, and this was not regarded in negative terms. While the convergence of maternity and womanhood proceeded fastest amongst the middle classes, informal adoption of children by relatives was still common amongst them well into the nineteenth century – a practice that went on much longer among the working class (Gillis 1996: Ch. 8). Children would eat and sleep in the house of nearby kin, or, when older, be sent away to live with more distant relatives. 'It was not until the inter-war period of the twentieth century that parents could expect most, if not all, of their children to be their responsibility until they saw them married' (ibid.: 155). Previously, he argues, anyone who nurtured a child was called 'mother', and the sym- bolic value attached to the biological mother was not common.

With minimal moral and emotional emphasis being placed on the nuclear family, the house was an open place where few distinctions of belonging were apparent, a place where people came and went, but that was not invested with emotional potency. In towns, people spent more time in pubs and clubs than in the house where they slept. It was not until the nineteenth century 'that people began to think of home as something families could make for themselves', and this was a time when '... the modern quest for a homeplace began in earnest' (ibid.: 110).[9] Houses became homes. This involved a radical shift in the attributed meaning of motherhood, fatherhood and childhood. 'Never before has every father, mother, and child been expected to be a role model' (ibid.: xix). Those role models trickled-down, as it were, from the middle classes to become incor- porated into all of society, and Gillis argues that the 'significance of the Jewish Mother is indistinguishable from the Italian Mama or the English Mum', and that people everywhere have become attached in novel ways to their homeplaces.[10]

Although they differ regarding the precise timing of the changes, and argue that allowances must be made for different cultural values in differ- ent countries, most social historians today seem to agree on a general sce- nario regarding changes in European attitudes towards childhood. Not least due to the influential writings of John Locke (1690) in England and J.J. Rousseau in France (1762), the eighteenth century did represent some kind of watershed in attitudes because, as Cunningham puts it, 'Some people began to see childhood not as a preparation for something else, whether adulthood or heaven, but as a stage of life to be valued in its own right' (1995: 61). In other words, the 'idea of childhood' emerged and became a meaningful social category and, as I shall show in Chapter 6, a psychological category. Cunningham discerns three major stages of change. In the latter part of the eighteenth century, children began to be classed together with slaves and animals as 'recipients of the sentimentalism and humanitarianism that characterised [this period]'. A kind of backlash occurred during the first half of the nineteenth contrary when the parent–child relationship became more distant and formal. This changed again during the second half of the nineteenth century when the dominant view became one that not only made childhood a separate stage in life, 'but the best of those stages' (ibid.). Under the impact of Romanticism, what came to be understood as 'the childlike quality' of the child became entrenched, leading to a celebration of innocence. This attitude was in sharp contrast to the Puritan one of some centuries earlier according to which children were viewed as inherently sinful; and hence in urgent need of strict control and shaping.

In Europe and North America, the celebration of childhood as a period of innocence and happiness led to the felt need to make arrangements to preserve and guide these qualities because children embodied hope for the future. The responsibility for proving a suitable upbringing was placed firmly on adults biologically related to the child, or, failing that, on society at large. According to the modern Western view of a proper childhood, a child should have a carefree, safe, secure and happy existence and be raised by caring and responsible adults inside a family home (Panther-Brick 2000: 4). This may be characterised as 'a shift in the balance of power between adult and child' (Cunningham 1995: 184).

These studies are highly illuminating and helpful to my own project. Taken together, they challenge the opinions voiced by present-day psycho-technocrats and others with an interest in governing childhood and parenthood, that contemporary values and practices are not only good and right, but also somehow 'natural'. Such a view finds its more clear expression in the pre-eminent and normative role allocated to the family and the home in the UN Convention on the Rights of the Child (UNCRC), in whose preamble it is stated, inter alia, 'the family, as the fundamental group of society and the natural environment for the growth and well-being of all its members and particularly children'. In this connection it is of interest to look at a practice which challenges conventional conceptions about the European family, namely the abandonment of children.

Abandoned Children

In Europe, the practice of abandoning infants was at certain periods not only common, but socially acceptable (Boswell 1988, Fuchs 1984, Panther-Brick and Smith 2000). Panther- Brick goes so far as to state '[it is] salutary to recognise that child abandonment was central to European culture during a period fundamental to Western civilization (even in Florence, 'the city that was the very centre of European Renaissance' (2000: 14). In the Catholic countries of Southern Europe, foundling homes were established by the Church during the Middle Ages. By the seventeenth and eighteenth centuries they had spread to most major towns in south and central Europe (Fuchs 1984). A feature of many foundling homes was the so-called wheel, a cradle placed outside a convent or hospital that rang a bell whenever a baby was placed inside it'.[11] Anonymity of the mother was thus ensured, at the same time as she knew that the child would be cared for. Not infrequently, however, the child was furnished with an identity tag, thus enabling the mother, or parents, to reclaim it at a later stage should they so wish. The practice might then be intended less as a case of abandonment, but more as a method for poor people to leave non-productive children to the care of others (Sá 2000: 30–31).

Rather than decreasing, the practice of abandonment increased until it reached a peak by the mid-nineteenth century when it is estimated that over 100,000 babies were abandoned in Europe every year (Kertzer 2000: 72–73). In Paris, as many as one-fourth of all newborn babies and half of all illegitimate babies were left each year at the state-run foundling home (Fuchs 1984: xi). In the second half of the nineteenth century, foundling homes were established also in Protestant Northern Europe, but accompanied by moralising debates about the practice of abandoning children (Sá 2000: 28). Moreover, the separation of mother and child – viewed with horror today – could be observed in other domains also. Wet-nursing was common in many parts of Europe where it might be interpreted as a form of circulation of children (Sá 2000: 27). It was also practised by upper-class women in Victorian England (and elsewhere in Europe) who did not want the encumbrance of the practice and who were frightened of losing their figure. Later, wet-nursing became associated with high mortality levels and with poverty, as well as with an increase in illegitimacy (Cunningham 1995: 92–93) and lost its status as being morally acceptable. Fuchs, in her study of abandoned children in France, states that during the nineteenth century the authorities increasingly came to regard families as the proper unit for raising children, and attitudes towards abandonment began to change.

One might expect that adoption would be regarded as the ideal solution for the care of the thousands of abandoned children in France and elsewhere during this period. But familial adoption was very rare. Legal adoption was unknown. The main reason for this, according to Fuchs, was the emerging view that the state 'legally, morally and financially [should be] responsible for its indigent and neglected citizens, a responsibility that legal adoption would have nullified' (1984: 30). In light of changing attitudes throughout the nineteenth and twentieth centuries, whereby the value of the home increasingly was emphasised in influential circles (cf. Gillis 1996), the abandonment of children came to be viewed with moral disapproval. It has been argued that a crucial aspect of childhood in modern Western eyes is domesticity and that '[t]he place for childhood to take place is inside – inside society, inside a family, inside a private dwelling' (Ennew 1995: 202). It follows from this that life for a child outside a family and a home – whether it be on the streets, in an institution, in a live-in sweat shop or, worst of all – in a brothel, is abhorred. Contemporary ideas in Northern Europe and North America hold that children must be saved from such destinies wherever possible. It is in this light that we may understand Ennew's claim that children without homes – street children - have become a major moral concern of contemporary aid projects. Furthermore, it is in this light that we may understand the preoccupation with the nuclear biologically constituted family and the inherent value attributed to home life that underpins the UNCRC.

As the nineteenth century progressed, it became increasingly regarded as morally reprehensible to leave one's child to be cared for by strangers. This coincided with the biological tie between parents and children being made the subject for a moral responsibility. Biogenetic connectedness became the unquestioned superior basis for a kinned relationship, and remains so until the present. Many Victorian novels describe the abandoned or lost child being reunited with his or her biological relatives. From the mid-nineteenth century onwards, children who were abandoned anonymously became by this act denuded of kinship, de-kinned; and abandonment took on a new and derogatory meaning. The children became hostages to fortune. The reported rough, indeed cruel, treatment of children in orphanages may, I suggest, be attributed to their carers regarding them as being outside society, due to their being outside biologically based kinned relatedness. Abandoned children in Europe were socially naked. This made them not only anomalous, but placed them beyond the scope of individual moral responsibility.[12]

A similar fate befalls abandoned children today in the Third World. The situation here, however, is complex. Brazil, for example, sends children for adoption to Europe and the USA on the understanding that they have been abandoned. Fonseca has shown that many poor Brazilian mothers would leave a child at an orphanage and consider the arrangement temporary. They expected to bring him or her home 'as soon as things got better' (2000: 8). Although they signed a form that released the child for adoption, many did not understand the implications of this and were dumbfounded when they came to pick up the child at some later stage to be told that he or she had been adopted abroad. Whether the staff at the institution knew what might happen is not clear, but my point is that they regarded the concept of abandonment as legitimate grounds for adoption. The abandoned child is ipso facto denuded of kinned relations and as such may be transferred to new kin. Today, with the growth of the various rights discourses all of which are predicated upon the value of the autonomous individual, the de-kinned child is an object of pity and compassion and has become the responsibility of the 'world community'.

Anthropological Studies of Adoption

If little anthropological research has so far been directed at adoption, virtually none has been done on transnational adoption. By contrast, there is a large body of psychological, or psychologically derived, studies of adoption, and a few psychological studies from Sweden, Norway and Holland on the fate of those adopted transnationally. These will be considered in Chapter 6. In what follows, I present some anthropological studies that examine practices of adoption in Africa, Melanesia, Polynesia, and the Andes – societies where adoption is central to the indigenous kinship system as well as to notions of personhood and sociality. My focus is on the value attributed to biogenetic connectedness between parents and children, and in what ways other factors are constitutive for creating meaningful parent-child relationships. The examples provide some theoretical challenges to received wisdom in contemporary Europe and North America. I conclude the chapter with a look at a few studies on adoption in contemporary USA and Australia.

Whenever anthropologists have turned their gaze on adoption, the results are fascinating. Articles by Meigs and Anderson from Melanesia, by Weismantel from the Peruvian Andes, and by Alber from Benin, as well as Modell's studies from the USA are all thought-provoking in the extreme, fully validating my claim that adoption practices go to the very heart of the anthropological understanding of what kinship is all about. However, no clear pattern of adoption practices emerges. In some societies, children continue to have regular and meaningful contacts with their biological parents; indeed the transaction strengthens ties between kin groups. In other societies, the fact of adoption is kept secret. In summing up an early article on adoption for the 1930 edition of the *Encyclopaedia of Social Sciences*, Lowie says, 'adoption customs [in 'traditional societies'] rest on a mental attitude difficult to conceive for those nurtured in Western traditions' (Lowie 1930: 460). Whatever else these studies demonstrate, they certainly show that to kin a child successfully is not dependent upon biogenetic connectedness.

Africa

Adoption and fostering are common in many African societies. Goody's posited three main functions of the practice are not, however, very helpful in understanding the dynamics of adoption in Africa. Property and the inheritance of property is rarely the motive. While adoption may provide childless couples with children, the practice of polygamy ensures children in an extended patrilineal household. Adoption certainly provides homes for orphans and, until recently,[13] some family member would take over the responsibility for an orphaned kin as a matter of course. None of these factors, however, explain adoption and fostering as a systematic social practice. Esther Goody's work on 'social parenthood' and fostering in Africa (e.g. 1982), argued that it was rational for a society to share tasks between biological and social parents. She elicited five functions of parenthood that can be shared between biological and social parents: begetting and bearing, status entitlement and rearing reciprocities, nurture, training and sponsorship, (Goody 1982: 7). Bledsoe similarly pursues a functionalist line of argument. According to her, the practice of adoption and fostering minimizes the risk of famine and helps to provide care for the sick and elderly (Bledsoe and Isongo-Abanike 1989). Several commentators stress the fact that the system of adoption provides an enduring link between the families concerned (ibid., Alber 2003). Among the Kikuyu of Kenya, rights on both parental sides are not completely transferred and the adopted child will continue to have contact with his or her biological kin, In Botswana 'Tswana customary adoption might involve a direct request for a child and rights of inheritance depends on whether the adoption is recognised by the elders in the community' (O'Collins 1984: 291). Adoption as a permanent rupture from the biological parents is rare in Africa (J. Goody 1969: 75). But fostering or a form of mutual exchange of children is not uncommon.

Recently, Alber's work from the Baatombu in Northern Benin pursues a different line of argument from those mentioned above. Rather than reduce adoption to a functionalist explanation of social usefulness or continuation of the lineage, she demonstrates the presence of a fundamentally different ontology as regards the meaning of family, children and childhood from that of contemporary Europe and North America. Alber argues that the Baatombu to some extent deny biological parenthood. 'There is an attitude of shame for an individual to claim ownership over his or her biological children'. This is linked to a desire to 'demonstrate publicly that one has nothing to do with one's biological children' (Alber 2003: 496). The reasons for engaging in such a widespread practice are complex.[14] Baatombu are patrilineal and practise virilocality. Divorce is frequent and women often initiate this. Without biological children, women may engage in new relationships without hindrance. However, if they have social children (i.e. permanently fostered), this is not regarded as an impediment.

Fosterage used to be the norm. Until about sixty years ago, more than 90 per cent of all children were in fosterage and Alber estimates that about 30 per cent of young adults today have been. Another reason for adopting away one's children is that it may be regarded as better for the children not to be brought up by their natural mothers (ibid.).

A traditional kinship system that resulted in virtually all children being adopted once they had been weaned from their biological mother, is in the process of being transformed. Nevertheless, her study shows that the Baatombu understanding of society is intimately connected to the practice of adopting children out. It is regarded as an offence for a pregnant woman to refuse a child to any kin who expresses a desire for her child. Women thus know that the child they bear will be handed over to others, and they deliberately distance themselves emotionally from their child. An interesting feature of the practice is that fosterage follows gender lines. Thus a woman will adopt girls, and men adopt boys. Moreover, in taking children into fosterage, women take them from their own patri-clan or from their mother's family, and men from theirs. No one Alber questioned stated that the moment of being handed over from biological mother to foster mother, or father, was experienced in any way as difficult, although the child, just like a bride, is expected to cry. It is perhaps significant that, according to Baatombu notions of personhood, a child does not become 'knowing' until he or she has reached seven years of age and most children are handed over between the ages of three and six. Adoptive parents take on full responsibility for caring for the child, including bearing the costs of his or her marriage, and they kin the child to their own person and kin network. The practice engenders numerous relationships, which may follow genealogical lines as well as create cross-cutting ties. Although there are taboos and rules of avoidance between biological parents and their biological children, most children do know the identity of their biological parents (unlike the Wogeo who, at least in the past, were unaware of their identity; see below).

Children fall into a broader system of exchanges that are carried out among adult Baatombu, representing the most valuable gift. 'The great value of children makes the gift of a child particularly precious. And it is this great value ... that qualifies them as ideal objects of exchange' (ibid.: 498). Biological parents may derive status from having given a child to a person of high social standing. (ibid. 499). Alber's work demonstrates that, in order to understand practices of adoption, it is necessary to contextualise them within a frame of indigenous world-view, of personhood, kinship, rationality, morality and emotionality. Her analysis challenges an assumed universal psychological and emotional tie between biological mothers and their children; a tie that when broken will cause trauma. The Baatombu case may help us in rethinking some of our ideas. According to Alber, both mothers and fathers regard social parenting as satisfactory and non-traumatic. In this they resemble Norwegian adoptive parents.

Melanesia and Polynesia

Since the work by M. Strathern we have been alerted to the proposition that Melanesian understandings of procreation are concerned less with biological connectedness and more with processes of nurture. Melanesian persons, she argues (1988), must be examined as products of those relations that created them, and a child as an objectivation of relations between a man and a woman.[15] I have already mentioned the Hua in Highland New Guinea who are not interested in distinguishing between real and not-real kin, and to whom that kinship is primarily a question of nurture and of feeding. While Meigs does not make any specific mention of adoptive practices among the Hua, we know from others that this is common in parts of Melanesia. Anderson, for example, has shown that adoption is very common among people living on Wogeo, an island off the north coast of New Guinea. Here up to 40 per cent of the population is adopted (Anderson 2001: 175).

Although the practice may in part be accounted for by a high degree of infertility and a high proportion of children being born outside wedlock – and hence without (social) fathers – adoption cannot be explained by these facts alone. Adoption is 'a means to create historical continuity, and adoption can secure and create alliances and improve situations of conflict' (ibid.). As one would expect from contemporary ethnography from Melanesia, the sociocultural situation is highly complex. Anderson's subtle analysis demonstrates that adoption is an integral part of economic as well as symbolic life. Moreover, deposition of children can also be a way of hiding identity and serve as a means towards manipulating kinship in order to improve one's power and influence. This is because in a society like Wogeo, where patrilineal links are emphasised in relation to succession and inheritance, there exists also a more secret and hidden system of matriliny. Matrilines are the owners of secret magical knowledge and some are regarded as dangerous because of this. By adopting out children from 'dangerous' matrilines, the fact of belonging may be hidden, and the person freed from the stigma and possible conflict (ibid.: 185).

As is the case in Benin, adoption practices are not about copying or supplanting 'natural' or 'authentic' relations, but 'are in themselves essential for the constitution of the social landscape on the island' (ibid.: 176), and, with reference to Strathern's analysis, Anderson makes the interesting suggestion that when a child is adopted on Wogeo, the act objectifies the relationship between biological and adoptive parents. The Wogeo distinguish between fostering and adoption. While the former concerns temporary caring for a person, the latter establishes the child's belonging, name and rights. The vocabulary reflects this distinction. Adoption (*oala*) is glossed as 'to take something out of something that is bundled together and place it in another bundle'. The word which means 'to look after' is used for foster relations (ibid.: 180). Adoptees may or may not be aware of their status and they may or may not maintain relationships with both sets of parents. Adoption of adults also takes place, often as a means to resolve conflicts about land rights between families. However, despite the common assertions that 'we love all children equally', adoption on Wogeo is not without its emotional complexities (ibid.: 182). What the example of Wogeo shows us is that it possible to have a multifaceted understanding of the practice of adoption. Unlike Norwegian couples who want to create a family, and stress the individual emotional aspect of this, the practice on Wogeo is so common and well established that it provides people with a range of motivations for engaging in it. I therefore agree with Anderson's conclusion when she states: 'Adoption must occupy a central position in the analysis of Wogeo social organisation and not only as a theme on its own, or as an addendum to a focus on kinship and descent' (ibid.: 187).

Many anthropologists have commented upon the widespread practice of adoption and fostering in Micronesia and Polynesia, but few have made it the focus for special study. We know that the raison d'étre for adoption varies enormously from society to society in the region. Useful overviews of adoption in the Pacific are made by Brady (1976) and O'Collins (1984: 294–98), from whom I borrow the examples that follow.[16] Amongst the people of the Namoluk Atoll, 'a conspiracy of silence surrounds the adoption and it is considered to be very bad taste to tell a child that he is adopted' (Marshall 1976: 35). On Tonga, on the other hand, where nearly all adult people have some experience of the practice, '[t]he adoptee's continuing relationship with his natural parents may range from infrequent to almost daily contact' (Morton 1976: 78). However, the more frequent the interaction, the more likely is conflict to arise between the two sets of parents – an interesting point in light of the campaigns for open adoption in the USA (see below). On New Hebrides, young children are informed about the adoptive relationship and told the identity of their biological parents but never forced to live with either (Tonkinson 1976: 233); and on the Manihi Atoll to the east of Tahiti both sets of parents have an obligation towards the child but the adopted child's first obligation is to the adopted parents (Brooks 1976: 53).

Finally, that traditional practices are no more static in 'traditional' societies than in European ones is exemplified through reports published over time from the Gunantuna of the Gazelle Peninsula in Papua New Guinea. Meir, who worked amongst them from 1899 to 1914, described adoption as being conducted in secrecy and enacted through a payment of 'traditional' money (Meir 1929: 34). Salisbury, conducting his fieldwork in the same place more than fifty years later, shows that adoption then was a very public event, engaged in by big men in order to enhance their standing through replenishing the number of dependents (Salisbury 1970: 326).

The Andes

In a study of adoption practices among an indigenous community in the highlands of Ecuador, the Zumbagua, Weismantel critiques the persistent dichotomy between nature and culture in kinship studies (1995). The Zumbagua make no such distinction in their understanding of parent–child relationships. Rather, while 'The physical act of intercourse, pregnancy, and birth can establish a strong bond between two adults…other adults, by taking a child into their family and nurturing its physical needs through the same substances as those eaten by the rest of the social group, can make of that child a son or daughter *who is physically as well as jurally their own*' (695, my emphasis). Through eating the same food together and over an extended period of time, the child may become the full member of a non-biological family. Weismantel shows how it transpired that '[e]very adult seemed to have several kinds of parents and several kinds of children. They remembered a man who fathered them, but another who 'husbanded' their growth; they remembered a woman who gave birth to them, but others who fed them and taught them to speak and to know' (ibid.: 689). The social fabric of Zumbagua is made up of small households based on life-long heterosexual marriages, not unlike that of conservative USA, she says, but their notion of relatedness could hardly be more different. In fact every adult seems to have several kinds of parents and several kinds of children. Most adoptions take place within the family and are seen to benefit all concerned. As is the case among the Baatombu, birth mothers are free to give up their children if they do not wish to bring them up (but are not expected to, as is the case amongst the Baatombu). Having relinquished a child during one's youth does not preclude one from adopting one later in life (ibid.: 691).

These studies from societies where adoption represents no challenge to indigenous ontology and epistemology (see also Bowie 2004), clearly defy attempts to universalise a biogenetically based understanding of procreation and kinship. They provide a useful corrective to studies of societies where the dominant discourse is one that privileges biological connectedness. Weismantel's argument is a powerful one, showing that through eating the same food over time, a child may be made one's own physically, and not just jurally; and she contrasts this with the Euro-American insistence 'upon a strictly genetic notion to physical relatedness' (Weismantel: 697). But just because the social practice of adoption of Zumbaguans, Hua, Wogeo, and Baatombu transcend a Western preoccupation with, and asserted primacy of, biogenetic relatedness, this does not mean that adoption in these societies is unproblematic. In all these societies people are fully cognizant of a special relationship between a biological mother (and perhaps father); and not every birth mother may be happy to relinquish her child. However, these examples demonstrate that biological facts of reproduction need not constitute the making of kinship, nor provide a moral reference point for the practice and emotionality of significant relatedness. All the anthropologists cited have, through their careful exposition of ethnographic realities, demonstrated the prevailing sociocentricity of anthropological approaches to the meaning of kinship, relatedness and sociality.

From these studies one may conclude, then, that adoption is what adoption does. In societies where there is an institutionalised practice of bringing up the children of others as if they are one's own, children become kinned to those given responsibility for their care, and the relationship is expressed in conventional kinship terms. Not only do such practices challenge western-centric notions of what kinship is all about – namely relatedness constituted through flesh and blood – but they highlight notions I have encountered in many Norwegian adoptive parents. Weismantel's list of kin-constituting factors (ingesting food, sharing emotional states, being in close physical proximity to people and objects) (1995: 694), are all factors which echo Norwegian adoptive parents' understanding of the relationship between themselves and their children. To the list I would add one more, namely a shared creation of the family's destiny. But this understanding is not the dominant one in Norway among Norwegians at large. Here biogenetics occupies the constitutive explanatory position; and adoptive parents' task is thus much more challenging and complex than it is in the Andes, West Africa or Melanesia.

Contemporary Adoption in Western Countries

In Western Europe and North America, adoption invokes and challenges two profound taboos shrouded in cultural silence: parents, and in particular mothers, should not give up their children, and infertility is a great sorrow and a source of shame. Perhaps for these reasons, the anthropological work that has been undertaken on adoption in the West has tended to focus on the stressful coping with personal realities of the different parties in the triangular adoption relationship (biological parents, adoptive parents and adoptees).

Interestingly, most anthropologists – myself included – who study adoption have a personal interest in the subject due to the fact they have adopted one or more children themselves.[17] No doubt as more anthropologists become alerted to the rich theoretical potential of adoption, we will see a rapid increase in publications on the topic.[18] Although the theoretical and analytical approaches by those already published vary, there are nevertheless certain commonalities in the general approach to, and understanding of, the practice. We all focus upon the relationship between biogenetic and social kinship and highlight the challenges that those involved have to deal with – both on the personal and familial levels and in society at large.

Due to the sensitive and, until recently, secret nature, of domestic adoption in Western Europe and North America, access to informants has been difficult. Much of the available information has been obtained through those – whether parents or adoptees – who have experienced the fact of adoption as in some way difficult, and who have sought help, either from public services or by joining mutual support groups. Some of these have been willing to talk about their experiences to anthropologists. There are, however, methodological dangers in relying upon such a special group of informants insofar as they may represent a minority rather than the majority. Those who have a grievance of some kind tend to be more vocal than those who do not. This represents a real challenge to the anthropologist because there are so many preconceived ideas and prejudices in Western societies about adoption that the few, and often articulate, voices who confirm widespread expectations do so at the expense of those whose experiences are mainly positive.

More than 150,000 domestic adoptions take place each year in the USA, which makes for a very different situation than that in Europe. Judith Modell has been studying domestic adoption in the USA for more than twenty years and as such has contributed to the anthropology of adoption in general (Modell 1988, 1994, 1999, 2002). She has interviewed a selection of biological parents, adoptive parents and adoptees for whom adoption has been experienced as problematic in some way or other. In that sense she does not challenge the tradition that regards adoption as inherently problematic. At the same time she makes the point that those she interviewed were 'critical of the significance of "fictive" in being related' and says that the 'dichotomy of real and fictive (or "not real") pervades the everyday experiences of members of the triad' (1994: x). Despite this, Modell maintains the distinction between fictive and real kinship, a distinction that is addressed directly in her most recent book in which she investigates the novel practice of 'open adoption'. This is a practice whereby biological and adoptive parents not only know about each other but, in many cases, maintain some kind of relationship, enabling the child to relate to both – allowing the parties concerned to 'redesign the fiction of their kinship' (1994: 238). This challenges concepts of motherhood and fatherhood and of family – and thus of kinship altogether (ibid.: 236). While open adoption emphasises the significance of biological connectedness, it at the same time, removes genealogy from the core of the American kinship system, allowing the concepts of mother and father to become plural. I return to a consideration of open adoption in Chapter 7.

American adoption used to be secret. Archives were closed to those concerned. However, largely as a result of increased demand for access to information by birth parents and adoptees, many American states have changed their regulations concerning adoptees' access to their own files and original birth certificates, and more are following suit. Media are full of stories of 'reunions' between birth-parents who had relinquished their children for adoption and the children. At the same time many birthparents are resisting the loss of their anonymity (Modell 2002: 2).

With the recent development in American adoption practices that encourage open adoption, the scene is changing dramatically. 'Adoption is no longer simply a way of making a family or caring for a child ... adoption is a challenge to ideas, symbols and ideologies Americans have long held to be self evident' (Modell 2002: 22). Modell bases her conclusion on an investigation of the different parties' (biological parents, adoptive parents and the adoptees) attitudes and experiences of open adoption. Surprisingly, Modell's conclusion is that open adoption does not create kinship, and this, she says 'has its roots in the inequalities that shape American adoption practices' (2002: 70). She has in mind the fact that 'the delegation of parenthood is based on a judgment of "fitness"' and that in this case 'differences between birth and adoptive parents [to] prevail' (ibid.). Initially meaningful relationships between birth mothers and adoptive parents tend to diminish as time passes. The fact that birth parents have to relinquish their child produces a relationship of moral imbalance where the adoptive parents have the advantage. If this is the case, and Modell makes a strong argument for it, then one may discern a real difference in the relationship between the adoptive and birth parents in the case of domestic adoption in the USA, and in transnational adoption in Norway (and elsewhere). Perhaps because the Norwegian authorities have no dealings with the birth parents overseas, perhaps because the cultural climate vis-à-vis the so-called 'third world' makes direct comparisons impossible and hence does not permit moral sanctions to be invoked, the reigning discourse regarding transnational adoption is that birth parents give up their child for economic or social reasons, not because they in some sense have failed as human beings.

American couples appear to be much more concerned with the quality of the child they receive than do Norwegian adoptive couples. He or she should be healthy, intelligent, and good-looking.[19] This parallels the detailed and specified criteria built into the market for egg and sperm donors in the advertisements discussed in Chapter 2. In her work on transracial and transnational adoption in the USA, Gailey focuses on issues of race, class and gender.[20] Several patterns emerge from her study which show important divergences from my Norwegian material and which confirm serious differences in values between the two countries. For example, adoptive parents she interviewed expressed sympathy with the case of a couple whose adopted son required so much medical treatment that the parents decided to return him to the orphanage in Ukraine from which he came. Secondly, American parents do not concern themselves with the lives of their children before they were adopted. According to Gailey, there is a 'convenient myth in circulation that all adoptees are orphans', which

prevents parents from making detailed enquiries. Thirdly, a large proportion of the well-to-do couples in her sample had carried out the adoption
privately in order to reduce 'the hassle and the wait' involved in going
through a public or regular adoption agency (1999: 68). Finally, one reason
given by many for adopting from overseas rather than domestically, or
using a surrogate mother, was the finality of such a procedure. This contrasts with Modell's findings about the trend towards open adoption. Gailey's interviewees were worried about later getting involved in a battle
with the biological mother over custody. The parents were in no doubt that
they offered a much better life for the adopted children than they would
have had had they remained in their country of birth. Gailey argues that
several of the parents seemed to harbour 'notions of love that were per-
formance-based, subject to evaluation and possible rejection' (ibid.: 73).
She links this to a more general trait observable in contemporary USA,
whereby performance criteria are applied not only to children – whether
adopted or biological – but also to spouses and friends (ibid.: 73, 2000:
308). The case of the 'faulty' child that was returned to the Ukraine mentioned above would appear to exemplify the point.

The couples interviewed by Gailey may be representative of a particular section of American society, the ambitious and upwardly mobile who
want a perfect life for themselves. However, not all American couples have
a similarly demanding attitude. According to employees in donor orphanages with whom I have spoken, confirmed by several Scandinavian adoption workers, many American couples are willing to accept older children
as well as handicapped ones. These American couples, many of whom
come from religious communities, are thus less restrictive in their
demands than those studied by Gailey. Nonetheless, the couples in her
sample do not find their counterpart in Norway.

There is little anthropological work on adoption that draws directly on
psychology.[21] One exception is Telfer whose studies of domestic and
transnational adoption in Australia explore the degree of agency exercised
in the shaping of personal destinies. His thesis is that all parties involved
in adoption experience a sense of incompleteness. He examines how this
sense is manifested, and how those concerned seek to alter it (Telfer 1999:
250). His fieldwork was conducted primarily amongst adoptees who, for
whatever reason, felt a desire to explore their origins in order to establish
a 'settled sense of their own identity'. He developed two 'hierarch[ies] of
biogeneticism' (ibid.: 254) in which he lists adoptees' preferences for meeting biological relatives, and adoptive parents' preferred types of procreation. Adoptees show an overwhelming preference for encounters with
biological mothers.[22] This, he argues, may be interpreted as 'pronounced
penchants for biogenetism' in which the mother scores most highly. In
other words, adoptees seem to think that they share most biogenetic material with the mother. Whereas this last point corresponds with my Norwe-

gian findings, the same is not true of his assertion that all adoptees experience a sense of incompleteness. (see Chapter 6)

Telfer's second hierarchy of biogeneticism concerns the adoptive parents' preferences regarding procreation. The order ranges from unassisted or minimally assisted conception; assisted, but with own biogenetic substances; assisted procreation with sperm donation; assisted procreation with egg donation; to adoption and, finally, fostering. Furthermore, he observed a hierarchy of preferences regarding types of adoption. First choice was a very young local baby with no special needs, followed by the same, but the baby coming from overseas. Next, a toddler from overseas was preferred to a local. At the bottom of the list of preferences came intercountry adoption of older children (ibid.: 258). To my knowledge, no similar study has been undertaken in Europe.

To Conclude

Although cultural values and practices concerning family, parenthood and children vary considerably both across space and time, there are also some continuities. For adults to perform the role of parents to a child with whom they have no biogenetic connection is, and has been, practised in most societies. However, from this, very little, if anything follows. What differs widely is how such a practice is perceived and evaluated in each case and how it links to the local world-view in general and notions of family and belonging in particular.

Open adoption is regarded as radical in the USA, but is by many promoted as the norm for the future. Its popularity may, I think, be directly linked to an ambivalence regarding nature and nurture within discourses about personhood and identity, and to discourses about individual and group rights. The argument that it is a human right to know one's biological origins has been accepted by most American states and is gaining ground amongst politicians in Norway. Such an attitude meets little response with Norwegian adoptive families who have few doubts about the reality of their relationship. It is only when kinning fails that the question of belonging and identity becomes serious. So far, open adoption is not an issue in Norway.[23] I suggest that open adoption is pursued as much for the interest of adults involved (primarily the biological mothers) as for the interest of the children – although the two are linked – and that it is founded upon a profound biocentric understanding of kinship.

In American open adoption, ideologically speaking, the child should be kinned equally to both sets of parents. However, experience shows that this is difficult to achieve. Modell suggests that this may be accounted for by the economic and cultural inequality of the two sets of parents. While this may be part of the explanation, I regard it as likely that emotional factors also are involved. The adopted child and his or her two sets of parents may all experience the relationship as difficult to handle emotionally. But to look for guidance in how to deal with such relationships from seemingly similar practices in non-Western societies, or from pre-nineteenth-century practices in Europe and North America, is not likely to be fruitful. Basic understandings of sociality are sufficiently different in each case to preclude meaningful comparison. To attempt to do so reveals a failure to appreciate the constituting significance of culture. A major obstacle to meaningful comparison is the (relatively recent) Euro-American idea of childhood. Contemporary Western understandings are based on a different ontology from those of other times and other places. The development of these understandings, I argue, is linked to the growth and consolidation of individualism, and the rise of discourses about individual rights. During the twentieth century, the value accorded to having children, and the reasons for wanting them, changed dramatically. According to Scheper-Hughes and Sargent, '[T]he instrumental value of children has been largely replaced by their expressive value. Children have become relatively worthless (economically) to their parents, but priceless in terms of the psychological worth' (1998: 12). It is, I argue, precisely this emotional worth of children which makes them so necessary for the personal fulfilment of couples in present-day Europe and North America, and which becomes a major reason for the increased demand for adoption. This may also account for an increase in the demand by American prospective adoptive parents to seek children from overseas; they do not wish to meet the birth parents; they do not want to risk later conflicts, and, I suspect, they are unwilling to regard themselves as only part-parents. For most, the whole purpose of the exercise is precisely to 'have a child of one's own'. In the next chapter I explore the efforts made by Norwegian adoptive parents in order to kin their biologically unconnected child.

Notes

1. Bouquet characterises relatedness as 'a concept which allows for different nuances' and 'does not presuppose that genealogical relations are necessarily the most important' (1993: 157).
2. In his devastating critique of the anthropological study of kinship, Schneider (1984) argues that American (and European) anthropologists have been misled by the biocentrism of their own cultures and the significance attached to genealogical connectedness. This has led them to asking wrong, irrelevant and leading questions in alien societies.
3. Thus the mother–father–child triad was, until recently, regarded by most anthropologists as the core set of relations. According to Radcliffe-Brown, the 'unit of structure from which a kinship system is built up is the group which I call "the elementary family" consisting of a man and his wife and their child or children, whether they are living together or not' (Radcliffe-Brown 1952: 51). Indeed, Lévi-Strauss directed the thrust of his critique of Anglo-Saxon kinship studies precisely at this premise and argued that the mother's

brother should be treated as an integral partner in the 'atom of kinship' (Lévi-Strauss 1969), thus extending our understanding of kinned relatedness from a myopic focus on descent to include affinal relations. However, biology remained the model for kinship.

4. Barnard and Good makes the point even more strongly when they state that, 'The distinction between "true" and "pseudo-kin" is, of course, not one that can be drawn by you yourself, the fieldworker, because all kinship is socially rather than biologically based' (1984: 154, original emphasis).

5. The beneficial effect of this practice is borne out by the case of the five 'good emperors of Rome'. Nerva (AD96–98) adopted Trajan as his successor. Trajan (98–117) adopted Hadrian (AD 117–138) who in turn adopted Marcus Aurelius (138–157) in order to ensure his succession. Marcus Aurelius reigned for nineteen years but broke the chain of adoption by picking his biological son, Commudus, to be his heir. The historical verdict on Commudus is that his reign was disastrous (Altstein and Simon 1991: 2).

6. On the other hand, according to Malinowski, the matrilineal Trobrianders did not consider that men contributed to conception, an ethnographic report which has provoked heated debates (cf. Franklin 1997).

7. Anthropologists have applied his ideas to argue that in many non-European parts of the world the idea (or category) of childhood does not exist.

8. Ideas of childhood are difficult to ascertain from the early period. Ariés based many of his suggestions on contemporary paintings of adults and children in which children appear as miniature adults, rather than as manifestations of a radically different category of person.

9. From the mid-nineteenth century onwards when the English middle classes began to move to the suburbs, 'the home became the sanctuary for the working man while his wife became the housewife that we have known until recently. Moreover, home and homeland began to be paired in the spatial imagination in such a way that one was inconceivable without the other' (Gillis 1996: 113).

10. While the women's movement of the 1970s dislodged the housewife from her exalted position, the significance of the home as a centre for performing family life continues in Northern Europe.

11. This practice goes on today in several developing countries such as India. See the photograph in Chapter 9 of the basket outside an orphanage in Delhi.

12. This is a highly complex matter. Of course, many individuals felt compassion for de-kinned children and looked after them. But, sufficient evidence exists to argue that a pattern of devaluing abandoned children began to take place during the nineteenth century which continued during the first half of the twentieth century. Indeed, in Norway today a number of children who were brought up in state orphanages after the Second World War are suing the state for the abominable treatment they received.

13. Due to the spread of AIDS in many African countries, families have become disrupted to such an extent that kin are often unable to look after AIDS orphans (Ethiopian adoption bureaucrat, personal communication).

14. Due to the fact that not all social ties are cut with biological parents, Alber calls the Baatombu practice 'fosterage' rather than adoption or fostering (Alber 2003: 489).

15. See Gell (1999) for a reanalysis of Strathern which brings out these points very clearly.

16. Most references to authors are taken from O'Collins (1984), who also refers to Brady.

17. When I started my research project on transnational adoption it appeared, to my amazement, that no other anthropologist had worked on the topic. This turned out not to be quite accurate, since a few started around the same time as myself. To my knowledge, the following are engaged in research on transnational adoption. Christine Gailey (1999, 2000) has studied both domestic and transnational adoption in the USA, Barbara Yngvesson (e.g. 2002, 2004) has studied transnational adoption in Sweden, Jon Telfer (1999) has studied adoption in Australia, both domestic and transnational, Claudia Fonseca has studied domestic adoption in Brazil and adoption of children from Brazil (e.g. 2000,

2004) and Chantal Coullard has studied adoption from Haiti to Canada (e.g. 2003). The most detailed investigation of domestic adoption is Modell's study from USA (1994, 2002). In addition, Agnes Fines (1998) has edited a volume in French on (mainly) European adoption in a historical perspective

18. Towards the end of writing this manuscript my attention was brought to two edited special issues of American journals that deal exclusively with transnational adoption (Sterett 2002; Volkman and Katz 2003) For non-anthropological surveys of transnational adoption in several other countries, see Simon and Altstein (1991) and Selman (2000).

19. She characterizes this as a demand for 'blue-ribbon babies' (ibid.: 68).

20. These findings are based on Gailey's interviews with nineteen parents of children adopted from overseas, all of whom were above average income-earners and had achieved above-average education (Gailey 1999: 54).

21. My own work deals to some extent with these questions (eg. 2002, 2004).Yngvesson has studied transnational adoption in Sweden mainly from the point of view of the adoptees. I will return to her work in Chapter 8.

22. This is followed by father and siblings, then maternal grandparents, maternal aunts, paternal grandparents and, finally, cousins and other distant relatives.

23. To my knowledge, it is not an option seriously considered in any of the countries that send children to Norway for adoption although a new bio-centrism is increasingly observable in some of the donor countries as well. The issue of open adoption was raised briefly during my fieldwork in India, but was rejected out of hand (Chapter 9). Fonseca reports that noone had heard of the practice in Brazil (2000: 27).

Chapter 4

KINNING AND TRANSUBSTANTIATION: NORWEGIANISATION OF ADOPTEES

Almost everything in our lives centred on a wish that was never granted. We did not experience the deep depression that many in the same situation go through, but the longing (*savnet*) was there the whole time. The number of children increased amongst friends and family.

H. Queset 'Det Tomme Barneværelset' (the empty children's room)

In the beginning I almost burst with pride every time I went into a shop to buy baby-food. Everyone could see that I was one of them; someone to be reckoned with. I had become part of the community (*felleskskap et*).

Norwegian adoptive mother with child adopted from China in conversation

To Kin the Unrelated Child

The above statements, by an adoptive father and mother respectively, set the scene for this chapter. The vast majority of Norwegian couples who adopt are unable to have their own biological children. As infertility increases, the value of parenthood has at the same time taken on new dimensions; to remain childless is becoming an unacceptable condition. Studying cultural values concerning procreation, reproduction, family, kinship, children, and the perceived relationship between biogenetic and social relatedness, I discovered a practice hitherto unexplored in kinship studies which I call kinning. The concept of kinning, to which I have already referred several times, plays a central role in my analysis. I use this term to refer to the process by which a foetus or newborn child (or a previously unconnected person) is brought into a significant and permanent relationship with a group of people that is expressed in a kin idiom. People everywhere engage in a process of kinning their new children, i.e. they incorporate them into sets of kinned relationships. The employment of conventional symbols during pregnancy, birth and early years all bear witness to the fact that kinning is not automatic. While those involved in biological birth may think of it as an automatic process, my argument is that it is always a deliberate one, and it is one that is engaged in intersubjectively between existing kin and new kin (whether they are biological babies, affines subsequent to a marriage, adoptees, or other adoptive families). Kinning is thus a universal phenomenon and may be operative in domains of both descent or alliance. The process may, however, not be obvious to those involved and be performed implicitly. In the case of adoption it is clearly marked. This is especially so in transnational adoption due to the open and public nature of this transaction and to the fact that the adopted children usually look very different from their parents. In this chapter I shall explore some ramifications of the process of kinning of transnationally adopted children in Norway. Although my exposition will deal with the Norwegian situation exclusively, much of what goes on there is not greatly different from that in other European countries. Because of several structural and ideological differences in the political systems of the USA and Northern Europe, the legal and administrative situation in the USA is in many respects different, but the emotional and personal aspects of transnational adoption are – with the possible exception of the group of professional middle-class people studied by Gailey (1999) – not very different.

Because transnational adoption in Norway today is such a public practice, taking place in a cultural climate that predicates kinship on biogenetic connectedness, and because adoptive parents engage so deliberately in transcending the fact that they are not biologically connected to their children, my attention was led towards this previously 'hidden' aspect of kinship. Through a process of kinning, which I argue, involves a transubstantiation of the children's essence – their non-physiological being – adoptive parents enrol their adopted children into a kinned trajectory that overlaps their own. Issues pertaining to time, place and body become central in this process; and it is a process which, in most cases, is fraught with tensions, ambiguities, ambivalences, and contradictions, not least because the parents are faced with the dilemma of incorporating the child into their own kin group at the same time as they must acknowledge the existence of unknown biological relatives in a foreign land.

I am concerned primarily with the efforts engaged in by adoptive parents to make their adopted child into *their* child, and a relative to their own relatives. Through a process of kinning and transubstantiation, adoptive parents thus not only incorporate their children into their own kin, they also transform themselves into parents. By so doing, they negate the dichotomy between the social and the biological that is encountered elsewhere in society. It is clear that kinning affects all parties involved. The adoptees certainly undergo very radical changes to their former selves, but the parents also emerge affected. In fact, I wish to suggest that adoptive parents and their children recreate each other intersubjectively both as individuals and as parents and children. In being kinned, the adoptees adjust their personhood through their relations to others (primarily their adoptive parents), just as the adoptive parents, in kinning, adjust their personhood through their relations to others (primarily their adopted children).They all become fixed as kinned persons by virtue of their particular relationships (cf. Faubion 2001: 11–12).

Changing Meanings of Family in Norway

We may notice a shift in Norwegian social life during the postwar period that places a stronger, or at least a somewhat different, emphasis upon the family and the raising of children. From historical and ethnographic material, it is apparent that the past three decades have shown a steady rise in fertility rates and an emotional investment in the nuclear family that is somewhat different from earlier times. A major explanation for this may be found in the radical changes that have taken place in the cultural, social and economic position of women – and the subsequent changes in gender relations within the nuclear family. Despite a high divorce rate and a large number of single parents, the ideal of what constitutes the good life on a personal level remains stable. Family life made up by mother, father, two to three children, surrounded by grandparents, uncles and aunts seems to be what most young adults envisage. Such lived relatedness constitutes normality. To my open-ended question, 'Why did you want to have children?', almost every adoptive parent answered that they wished to become a 'normal family'. With the cultural emphasis on children and family life, it is not surprising that for most adults between the ages of twenty-five and forty-five, social life is centred round having and bringing up children. For those couples that fail to give birth, the social and emotional pressures become great indeed. Again and again, I have been told by adoptive parents how much they longed to be engaged in the wider social world around them, but that without children, without being a 'normal family', they were unable to do so, and remained, according to themselves, excluded.[1] From this I suggest that the dominant motivation for infertile couples to adopt is not to be found in some universal psycho-biological desire to give birth and /or reproduce themselves, nor in the need to establish an heir as was the case in earlier times. Rather, adoption represents a desire for significant sociality within a conventional model of 'the normal family'. In contemporary society this means having children. Children have become part of the means towards personal and relational fulfilment. There is therefore a noticeable shift over time in emphasis: from the individual within networks of other individuals, to parents and children within networks of other parents and children – an interesting finding in the light of increasing individ-ualism in the West.[2] Norwegian media are full of investigative reports about contemporary family life. Articles appear regularly in daily newspa-pers deliberating topics such as the rising age of women giving birth for the first time, the tendency towards increased size of families, the increasing participation of the father in bringing up children, and the facilities that the state ought to provide for families with small children. One may conclude that during the past twenty to thirty years, children and families have taken on a new meaning – a meaning that leads to an increased expectation for emotionally rewarding interaction between kinned adults and children. Having children is ultimately about personal relations which then may be extended into the wider social world.

Biologising and De-biologising the Kinship Discourse

Norwegians' perceptions about their own personal belonging in the con-temporary social world are contrived through personal trajectories worked out in an idiom of kinship. Moreover, the idiom of kinship is predicated upon a biological connectedness of shared substance – in common parlance that of flesh and blood. However, the understanding of substance in these contexts, I suggest, is not only material but includes the insubstantial ele-ments carried, as it were, in the substantive ones. What is important is not so much what substance is, but what it does (cf. Carsten 2001). Blood, for example is a substance, but the significance of its meaning in contexts of kinship is the relational quality of blood as shared between defined cate-gories of kin. To share the same blood (and flesh) means to share not only certain physical resemblances, but also insubstantial qualities, such as per-sonality, interests and abilities inherent in, for example, 'being an Ander-sen'. This may be said to provide the social dimension of kinship, which creates continuity over time, and gives people a sense of 'belonging to a life', to something bigger than the individual (Roalkvam 2001). For the development of their personhood, children need to be fixed in relation to significant others and, through their relatedness to them, to society at large. Plotting their identities, the adoptees have to negotiate two sets of signifi-cant interlocutors in their kinning drama: biological and adoptive parents. Whereas the adoptive parents are active partners in this drama, the biolog-ical parents are, in most cases, silent and insubstantial interlocutors. But in Norwegian discourses on kinship, where a constituting emphasis is placed on the blood-tie metaphor, they are no less important for that. Although flesh and blood as constituent defining criteria for kinship are far from uni-versal, the metaphors are central in most contemporary European and North American understandings, and 'make kinship or genealogical rela-tions unlike any other social bonds' (Schneider 1984: 174).

Where biogenetic connectedness ipso facto signifies kinned relatedness, to create kinship relations where no shared blood can be traced is far from easy. Adoptive families have to come up with some other mechanisms for establishing and legitimising their relationship. Weismantel's argument that the Zumbagua in Peru make no meaningful distinction between biology and sociality in their understanding of the parent–child relationship is instructive in this context. Through eating the same food over time, a child may be made one's own physically, and not just jurally, she says (1995: 695). Moreover, 'they [unlike Western societies] acknowledge the impact of history on the physical self, the regimes of diet and exercise … through which societies produce specific human bodies at specific times' (ibid.: 697). I have encountered similar notions amongst many Norwegian adoptive parents. However, to kin a foreign adoptee in Norway requires more than just feeding, nurturing and placing the adoptee and adoptive parents in close proximity – although these factors are all highly relevant. It requires a conscious effort on the part of the parents, which enables them, their children and kin to participate in the creation of the family's destiny and transcend cultural 'truths' that blood is thicker than water. Their efforts thus go against the general understanding in which biogenetics occupies a constituting explanatory role for kinship, and adoptive parents have to take this into account when they kin their children. Their task is thus much more challenging and complex than is that of the Andeans. Adoptive families do not operate a model of either/or as regards the constitutive and defining role of biology and sociality, but in different contexts foreground one at the expense of the other. They thus employ a dynamic model of kinship (Howell 2001, 2003b); a model, moreover, that allows conceptual, semantic and moral space for both genitor and pater, and genetrix and mater.

If we regard kinship as a classification system that effectuates enduring relationships, achieved through a process of kinning and subjectivation, then it must also be regarded as something that is necessarily achieved in relation with others. Categories are given the same meaning by all parties concerned. Because a doxic European/North American premise of biological connectedness is challenged by adoption, that very assumption is thrown into self-conscious relief. Adoptive parents soon become sensitised to this. Moreover, there is a noticeable change in couples' attitudes during the early stages of becoming adoptive parents. They shift from seeking to produce children from their own bodies to seeking children produced by other, and unknown, bodies. Most become unequivocal in praising adoption as a desirable procreative method. 'To adopt is the natural way for us to have children', a father told me. At the same time, it cannot be disputed that other bodies produced their children. Not only other bodies, but also, usually, bodies that look different from the Norwegian norm and that have therefore borne children who do not look like their new parents. In addition, these children were born in distant lands whose traditions and culture are alien. Not surprisingly, these facts give rise to ambivalent attitudes in the adoptive parents. There is no way they can hide from them, and they are obliged somehow to deal with them in their relationship with their children and with the world at large. They handle this through operating multiple discursive practices. They engage in a process of biologising or de-biologising the defining quality of the relationship according to particular contexts and according to the stages of the child–parent relationship. Thus, in certain contexts they will foreground the biological nature of the relationship while backgrounding the social (and emotional), and, in other contexts, the reverse. Parents create cognitive boundaries between the different contexts, and handle with apparent ease what appear to the anthropologist as contradictory positions (Howell 2001).[3] What my material shows is that the path of adoptive kinning is a bumpy one, but that where it is successful, it ends with privileging the social – the social quality of kinship – at the expense of the biogenetic.

Transubstantiation of Selves: From Foreign to Norwegian

Relatedness that is predicated on blood carries an automatic expectation of meaningful sociality in Norway. Upon learning that they are related (*i slekt*) – however distantly – previous strangers immediately alter the nature of their interaction. Once the blood connection is established, passage of time, distance in place, and lack of interaction, are in themselves no barriers to a genuine feeling of being related. This may be linked to my suggestion that meaningful belonging in the present is contingent in Norwegian thinking upon a demonstrable belonging to the past. Of course, the future becomes predicated upon such continuity, and the reproduction of continuity is anchored in kinned relationships and kinned places. This is the opposite of the adoptive situation. Temporal, spatial and emotional closeness do not in themselves compensate for the absence of shared flesh, blood and history. Adoptive parents somehow have to compensate for this absence in order to achieve kinning of their children. I want to suggest that much of the work adoptive parents engage in before and after the arrival of their adopted child, may be interpreted in terms of a transubstantiation of the child. The social and temporal practices of kinship – and of kinning – as commonly practised in Norwegian adoptive families are aimed at transmitting belonging to the adopted children, to include them in their own kin networks. This may be analysed as a process of transubstantiation. Transubstantiation of the adopted child is a prerequisite for kinning. In order to achieve this, parents must take account of the children's different biological and geographical/cultural origins and former relationships, at the same time as they fix them permanently into their new circumstances. But for the children to become integral partners in the familial present, they must also somehow be integrated into its past. Only then may the adopted children become active partners in the shaping of the familial future. Adoption is a process of inclusion and exclusion that results in self-conscious kinship (Howell 2001). According to *The Shorter Oxford English Dictionary*, transubstantiation means,

> (1) the changing of one substance into another, and (2) in the case of the Eucharist, the transubstantiation of bread and wine into the body and blood of Christ, as a result of which *'only the appearances (and other "accidents")* of bread and wine remain'. (my emphasis)

I find this suggestive in trying to understand the processes that the adoptive parents engage in. Unlike transformation, which changes the form as well as possible content, transubstantiation effects a fundamental change at the same time as the appearance remains. In the case of the transnationally adopted children, their incorporation into their parents' kin transcends the constraints of the blood tie while the outward appearance remains. The substance (biological body) remains; the social essence (being, self) is changed. I argue that this transubstantiation is effected over time, and that it is useful to divide the temporal process during which it occurs into four main stages: pre-pregnancy, pregnancy, birth, and daily life after the child's arrival in its new family. The terms 'pregnancy' and 'birth' are used by the adoption agencies and the adoptive parents – albeit placed within implicit inverted commas. This fact by itself demonstrates the hybridity of the adoption discourse.

Temporal Practices of Kinning

The process that leads to a decision to adopt can be a long and painful one. 'Almost everything in our lives became focused on the desire to have children', I was told by an adoptive father. Once failure to conceive is faced, once assisted conception does not succeed, adoption becomes a joint venture of the involuntary infertile couple. Indeed, many couples will, in retrospect, argue that this very shared involvement in achieving adoption meant that they both contributed equally to the birth, and the subsequent kinning of their child. This is regarded as a positive aspect of adoption. Once they have decided to adopt, most couples put the grief of infertility behind them and concentrate on the promise of becoming a family. Having been approved by the authorities, people know that it is only a matter of time before they will be given a child. Although the incorporation of an adopted child into standard kin structures may, at first glance, seem relatively straightforward, adoptive parents work extremely hard at making themselves and their adopted children conform to a normal family.

Through the various stages that they are submitted to, by creating symbolic pregnancy and birth events for themselves, they normalise their own experiences and forge ties with their child which are analogous to blood ties elsewhere in society.

Pre-pregnancy

What I call the pre-pregnancy stage begins when a couple decides that the time has come for them to have a child. The persistent failure to conceive leads to a round of medical check-ups which may, or may not, include the use of some form of assisted reproduction.[4] People experience a sense of grief at not being able to conceive, and the pressure upon the relationship can become great indeed. 'To want, but not to have children is a crisis … how can you grieve over something that never existed?' asks the Swedish author of a book describing her own infertility who subsequently adopted a child from Vietnam (Weigl 1997: 32). Once a couple has decided to put behind them the fact that their own bodies are not going to produce a child and to adopt instead, their attitude changes remarkably. For many, this is a time characterised by some self-examination. Starting from an unreflected focus upon biology as the model for family, they end up with a rather assertive culturalist approach favouring adoption. Biological criteria for relatedness are backgrounded in favour of social and emotional ones. From a focus on biology they end up with a fairly assertive culturalist approach toward procreation. Adoptive parents are adamant in denying that the love they feel towards their children is in any way different from that of biological parents.

Registering with an adoption agency through which children are allocated, choosing a country, and contacting the relevant section of the local authority in order to be evaluated as suitable adoptive parent material are the first steps that a couple deciding to adopt must take. This is a time when they are adjusting their expectation from that of having their own 'homemade' child, as the jargon runs in adoptive circles, to adopting a stranger. This is the time when they create a mental and emotional space for a non-biological child, born by unknown biological parents in a foreign country, who will be looking quite different from themselves. The as yet unidentified child is being incorporated into its prospective parents' sense of their own identity as expecting parents and the private kinning process has already started. It is a period of hybrid discourses and rapid shifts between biology and sociality as constituting reference points. It is a period during which the unknown child, to all intents and purposes abandoned in his or her country of origin – thereby rendering him or her de-kinned and denuded of meaningful relations – is being kinned into the family of his or her waiting parents and their kin. It is also a time when couples read avidly whatever they can find on the topic of transnational adoption and when they begin to seek out others who have already completed the process.

Pregnancy

Once the couple has received the stamp of approval from the local and national authorities, the pregnancy may be said to have started. Unlike a biological pregnancy, however, pregnant adoptive parents do not know how long it will last and they are completely at the mercy of a number of institutions and individuals in the donor country with whom they have an impersonal relationship. All communication is effected through the adoption agency. Prospective parents have to send the orphanage a dossier with photos of themselves, their home, their close relatives, their pets – if any – and whatever else they regard as significant about themselves. This provides them with a sense of actively relating with the institution even though they have no direct communication with it themselves. They must wait until a child is made available to them in the country concerned, and then for the permission to collect him or her. This takes from one to three years. During the waiting period, the prospective parents continue to make emotional space for the child to come. Many take part in a preparatory adoptive parents' course organised by the local branch of their adoption agency. The courses are run by people who have already adopted one or more children and who can bring their own experience to bear on the topics under discussion. Here the couples meet others in the same situation and they have the opportunity to exchange experiences, feelings, hopes and frustrations. The courses usually last from eight to ten weeks, with weekly meetings, or they may be organised over two weekends with a break in between to allow the couples to digest the information they received the first time round.

Having participated as an observer in several such courses in different parts of the country, I am struck by the general high level of intensity and emotionality at these meetings. The tears are never far away. The prospective parents have a strong desire to talk and to share their thoughts and feelings with other like-minded people. It is common to hear that although their family and friends are very sympathetic to their plight, only those who have gone through the same loops of disappointments and stresses can truly understand the degree of pressure that they have been under and the excitement with which they look forward to the adoption. They listen avidly to stories told by speakers who already have an adopted child. They never seem to get enough details about the visit made to collect the child, about the early period back home with the child, about the child's own tensions and how they adapt to their new environment, about eating, sleeping, crying, growth etc. They appear to have an insatiable thirst for listening and talking. At the same time, they read books about adoption written by various professional experts and about their future child's country of origin. The courses are intended to make the couples accept their infertility and to face the implications of adoption – especially adoption from a foreign country. Many of the values that will come into operation at later stages are transmitted during these courses. At this particular stage, the couples are extremely open to listening to opinions and values. The agencies and their employees are powerful transmitters of notions that shape the prospective adoptive parents' understanding of their future role and responsibilities. Everyone who gives a talk is regarded as an expert, and those members of the caring professions with work experience of transnational adoption are treated with great respect and deference. It is noticeable how individuals who in their daily lives are self-confident and competent become in these arenas insecure, emotional and rather humble.

Birth and Daily Life

The birth of the adoptive child begins when a particular child is allocated a particular couple. The birthing of an adopted child from overseas is a long, drawn-out process. It extends through the time following allocation, the arrival and the early period after arrival. But labour starts the moment that a child is identified as theirs. Upon allocation, expecting parents are sent a photograph of the child and are given whatever personal details about the child are available – or that the orphanage wants to make available. From this time onwards the public kinning of the distant and unseen child is actively pursued. The photograph is duplicated and widely distributed amongst relatives and friends and the child's room is made ready.

When a child is made available, a couple is sent pictures and a brief description, and they are given a couple of days to decide whether they want to accept him or her. I have not yet met a single couple who refused. One look at the picture and the report is usually enough to find some quality that resonates within them. Profound bonds are immediately formed, reminiscent of those experienced by birth parents upon the birth of a child. The following account by an adoptive mother of her child's birth, i.e. when she received the news that a child had been allocated her, is typical. She received a telephone call from the adoption agency at seven o'clock on Tuesday, 8 September 1981, and says: 'I cannot remember if I was standing or sitting, but I do remember the incredible joy that filled me when Kari Berntsen from *Adopsjonsforum* told me that I had become the mother of a tiny little boy. And Lars a pappa.' She continues, 'The name of our boy was Shavran, and he lived in an orphanage in Bombay called Shraddhanad Mahilashan.' Her next statement is very similar to ones I have heard from many adoptive parents, '[f]rom that telephone conversation I realised that it was precisely that boy, Shavran, who was our boy. We had not seen him, not even in a photo, not held him, but I felt so strongly that it was exactly him' (Beheim Karlsen 2002: 15).

This reaction is very common. Again and again, adoptive parents have told me how they experienced an immediate sense of fate upon being told about a specific boy or girl who has been allocated them. They are overcome by a profound sense of destiny that has connected them and the unknown child. Many parents I have talked to believe that the orphanage directors put a great deal of effort into choosing a child[5] that will be most compatible with themselves–if not in looks, then in personality traits or interests. They believe that the report they submitted about themselves is scrutinised by the orphanage personnel in order to match them with the child. Parents rarely feel that it is a matter of chance which child comes to them. Somehow they are 'meant for each other'. Once, at a gathering of parents who had travelled together to collect their infants from China, there were two mothers whose children were born within weeks of each other. One of the mothers said, half-jokingly, to the other, 'I wonder how would it have been if I had been given your child and you mine?' The other mother immediately retorted, 'But that would have been impossible. My daughter is just right for us, but she would not have suited you.' In a similar vein, the new Norwegian father of a six-month-old Ethiopian boy, commenting upon the sturdy physique of his child, told me that, of course, this was his son because they were built alike and, just like him, the son was made for the outdoor life of farming, fishing and hunting.

It will still take several months after allocation before the parents may collect their child. The emotional investment that expecting parents put into their identified, but as yet not encountered, child was well illustrated in a report about a couple whose allocated child died before they had collected it. The parents organised a memorial service in the local church in which they publicly mourned their child in the company of family and friends (*Adopsjonsforum*, April 1999: 21).

From a formal point of view, the child arriving in Norway is treated as a *tabula rasa*. The main actors in its rebirth are the parents, the bureaucracy and the judiciary, all of whom are concerned with the transubstantiation of the child. The child is given a new birth certificate, a new name, new citizenship, new kin and home, new social and cultural expectations, and new relationships beyond the family. The adopted child may be said to be kinned by law and by nurture. This is a time characterised by an extreme effort to de-biologise origins and to transubstantiate the child's essence. Through a number of different measures, the parents engage in an active kinning process of the child, i.e. they incorporate it into their own descent groups. The ultimate aim is to kin the adopted child into its parents' network of relations. One way to achieve this is to create an origin narrative that involves a discourse of fate.

However, the symbolical umbilical cord is not finally cut until the adoptive parents have fulfilled their obligations to the donor country. These vary from country to country and consist primarily of submitting progress reports on the child. Whereas Ethiopia insists on receiving annual reports on the child's progress until he or she reaches the age of eighteen, other countries are satisfied with reports for the first three or four years. These follow a fairly standard procedure, providing details of the child's health and how he or she is adapting to his or her new life. Often photographs are included. Having examined a number of reports that parents send to donor institutions in countries of origin, it is clear to me that attempts are made to distance the children from their origins and to emphasise their incorporation into their new social environment. In the reports, the parents stress how well- received the children have been by their grandparents, uncles and aunts, how happily they play with their cousins and local children and how easily they adapt to their new home and, later, kindergarten. The accompanying photographs confirm and elaborate this message. The children are photographed in places that epitomise the ideals of Norwegian family life and kinned relatedness: in the company of grandparents and other relatives in ancestral places; at home on the ceremonial occasions of Christmas and major family anniversaries; on the national day; in the country cottage in the mountains, in the forest or by the sea, engaging in typical outdoor activities. In these photographs little or no concession is made to the child's country of origin. The clothing is relentlessly Norwegian, ranging from national costume on important occasions, to standard children's outdoor clothing. The message of these reports to the donor countries is that the children, despite their non-Norwegian physical appearance, are nevertheless changing into typical Norwegian children. The children's biological and social origins are backgrounded during this period.

The active kinning process continues through the first years of the child's new life. Adoptive parents tend to construct a life for themselves that derives its meaning from their understanding of the 'normal family life' that is lived around them. Indeed, they often seem to go beyond that of most normal (i.e. biologically made) families. Adoptive parents tend to be active in fora centred on children. They participate with enthusiasm in parents' associations at kindergarten and school and as support staff in various sports activities. They put a lot of effort into ensuring that the child becomes involved in and incorporated into a wider social as well as kin network. Studies have shown that adopted children spend more time with their grandparents than do biological children (Botvar 1994: 18). This may be interpreted as a deliberate way to incorporate the child into its parent's kinned trajectory, thereby ensuring them a kinned future. Through frequent social interaction with their own kin, the lack of biogenetic relatedness is rendered irrelevant.

Significance of Place: Planting the Child in the Adoptive Parent's Ancestral Land

Kinship brings people together in a shared temporal and spatial universe. Belonging to a place plays an integral part in personal narratives that are constituent in the make-up of Norwegian identity. Until recently, the Norwegian population consisted largely of small freehold farmers whose land was passed patrilineally from generation to generation. Most writers agree that a place of origin features strongly in Norwegian understanding of self and identity (Gullestad 1999, Kramer 1984). The family farm and its surrounding landscape is a social landscape, invested with signs and traces of kinned human action of the past and the present. Kinship viewed as a 'primary regime of subjectivation' (Faubion 2001, Howell 2003b), as a means of plotting – and of being plotted into – a life trajectory that is co-extensive within relationships with significant others, implies in the Norwegian case, that such plotting cannot occur without some reference to place of origin. Urbanisation only took off in Norway after the Second World War, and many writers (Larsen 1984, Witoszek 1998) argue that most Norwegians are still country folk at heart. Certainly, to be able to trace one's ancestry to a valley, a fjord, a remote district of some kind, and preferably to an old farm there, is highly valued by Norwegians. Not to be able to name a locality steeped in kinned history can be felt as a distinct loss. In light of this, the question for adoptive parents and their children becomes how to compensate for the absence of a shared history. To acknowledge and handle the fact of a past that occurred in a foreign land and with unknown foreign people, and at the same time render this irrelevant for their child's emerging Norwegianness, becomes a challenging project.

In light of this, it becomes very important for adoptive parents to emplot their adopted children's trajectories into their own kin reality. This involves engaging them in their own places of origin. One common method is to symbolically 'plant' their children in the soil of their ancestors. To place the child dressed in local costume in localities that are associated with kin is a common way to aid the transubstantiation. This attachment to locality is expressed most graphically in the local version of a national costume (*bunad*). There are more than twenty different *bunad* styles, each explicitly linked to a locality and, strictly speaking, one should not wear one that cannot be traced to a kinned connection to the locality. Those clad in the same *bunad* interact in a familiar manner even though they have never met each other before. This is noticeable on big public occasions when total strangers can be seen to approach each other because they wear a *bunad* from the same district. Many adoptive parents are quick to dress their new child in a *bunad* and to photograph them wearing it.

During this process, hardly a single reference is made to the place of origin of the child. As the children learn to speak Norwegian they also learn to be Norwegian. They eat Norwegian food, play Norwegian games, and learn Norwegian songs and fairytales. From the point of view of adoptive parents, their new child has 'come home'. This is the jargon employed by the adoption agencies. In their annual reports, they provide figures for how many children have 'come home' from the various countries that they adopt from. By 'coming home', they seem to be saying that the child finally has arrived where it was meant to have been all the time, thus backgrounding biological and national origins. The use of the term 'birth mother' as opposed to 'mother'[6] which is also used by the agencies, is further indicative of this. Through a linguistic sleight of hand, the biological parents in the country of origin are transformed into temporary caretakers.

Creating Origin Narratives

In certain contexts the special origin of the adopted child is foregrounded as something positive at the same time as the idiom of Norwegian-grounded kinship is confirmed. This is on occasions when adoptive families meet socially and when a shared sense of community is often created. At such times inter-family relationships frequently take on overtones of kinship. This sociality amongst adoptive parents is predicated upon one common feature only, namely the fact of adoption itself. Despite their avowals that they are 'normal' families, adoptive parents cannot altogether avoid facing the fact that in some profound ways there is a limit to their normality; their children are not their biological children. The most obvious manifestation of this is the fact that the children look quite different from the rest of their family and kin. While, through adoption, adoptive parents achieve their longed-for aim of becoming a family, with all that seems to entail, their bodies consistently deny the normality of the family. This creates a common bond between adoptive parents.

Adoptive families gather together at a range of social get-togethers that are organised either locally by the local branch of the adoption agency, or nationally though the annual gatherings of associations based on the children's country of origin. Thus, the annual national meetings of the India Association, the Columbia Association, etc. are arranged, and families travel from all parts of Norway to participate. They eat food from the children's country of origin; and they decorate the meeting place with artefacts obtained on visits to collect the child, or from return-visits. Whereas many dress their children in their own local version of Norwegian national costume, others use the occasion to wear clothes of their country of origin. At all such gatherings, they do not hide the abnormality of their family situations. The very fact of being different constitutes the families as 'normal' in the given context. The parents look like each other. They are all white, most are tall, blue-eyed and blond-haired. The children, on the other hand, despite their diverse origins, look more like each other than they do their parents. They are mostly dark-skinned, short, and have dark hair and eyes. The special quality of their shared situation in itself creates a sense of community between adoptive parents (Howell 2002). What is an emotionally charged space is filled with meaning by all concerned.

While most of the time adoptive parents tend to ignore the abnormality of their situation, in these contexts when adoptive families socialise, the fact of the child's different origins is emphasised and is made into a positive circumstance. And it is a circumstance that they all share, and which may be made the basis for normalising their situation, not only for themselves as parents but also for their children. As such, social gatherings of adoptive families may be viewed as yet another means towards the kinning of adopted children. These gatherings enable the children to observe other families like their own, all of whom behave just like gatherings of families who are made up only of ethnic Norwegians.

Those who have met during the preparatory period often forge close bonds with each other and they meet again at these events. Others who travelled and lived together when they collected their children often create a common history. The strange town, orphanage or hotel become shared places of origin for them. Adopted children and their parents have no other shared place of origin than the one where they first met. Other couples who 'gave birth' at the same place thus become participants in a

Figure 4.1 India Association on its annual gathering. Excursion in the mountains.

shared narrative of origins. Whereas maternity clinics do not take on a heavy symbolic loading for most biological parents, the orphanage, the town, the public offices they had to visit, become infused with significance for adoptive parents. Employees at the orphanage and the hotel, even the judge at the local court, become characters in the birthing drama. So when parents meet each other in later years, conversation returns again and again to those days or weeks when their child was being born to them. Thus, at such gatherings, a kind of meaningful past is jointly constructed; a past based on a shared experience of liminality. This may be derived from having shared in the temporal process of abnormal pregnancy and birth, or through the shared space of the foreign place where they collected their children.

Such families often go on meeting long after their children have arrived. Apart from participating in the frequent local, or annual national, get-togethers, many adoptive couples who have established a special rapport visit each other during the holidays, and they send Christmas and birthday cards to each other's children. Although the families have nothing in common beyond the fact of adoption, they maintain an active interest in each other's triumphs and tribulations and they talk of each other as being family. In maintaining these relationships, parents seek a resolution to the paradox of their special situation by engaging in Norwegian sociality in the name of Korean (or whichever) origin. Everyone knows that they are not real kin, but they interact in ways that are recognisably kin-like, and the get-togethers of adoptive parents can be interpreted as family reunions. Despite appearances to the contrary, what is celebrated on these occasions is not, I would argue, Koreanness (or Columbianness or whatever), but Norwegianness in general, and kinned Norwegianness in particular. These activities demonstrate what I call the adoptive family's dilemma, namely the desire for conformity while having to admit to non-conformity, a situation that gives rise to ambiguity regarding their identity.

It is common to hear adoptive parents explain that they participate in various fora and activities arranged for adoptive families because it is so good for the children to keep in touch with other children like themselves. It is, however, my strong impression that rather than being good for the children to interact, it is good for the parents to do so (see the next chapter). What has to be borne in mind is that, for parents, adoption is a project of some magnitude that they have embarked upon. It preoccupies them for life. For the adoptees, on the other hand, to be adopted is just part of their lives. The fact of adoption is in itself not a reason for them to get involved with others similarly adopted. One adopted woman I met, was suspicious of adoptive parents' motives for engaging themselves in these fora. 'Why do they absolutely have to force things Korean upon their children just because they were born in Korea?' she asked. She told me that she thought that many adoptive parents feel very special, and that they transmit this to their children. At the same time, for many adoptees, the knowledge that they participated when young in some form of joint activities with other adoptive families may contribute to their future sense of belonging.

Apart from the kin-like relationships that many such couples establish amongst themselves, adoptive parents also create an imagined community of all families with children adopted from overseas. According to Anderson, face-to-face relations are not a prerequisite for a sense of community, but may be established through a set of common symbols which results in what he calls 'imagined community'(1983). This is a relevant interpretation of most adoptive parents' experience of somehow being part of a community made up of families whose children have been adopted from overseas, even though they may never meet each other. The knowledge that there are many other families whose situation is like their own provides a bond as well as a confirmation of a pattern.

Paradoxes Inherent in Kinning of Transnationally Adopted Persons

Successful transubstantiation of the transnationally adopted child involves fixing it in a wider set of relationships. The overriding motivation to adopt a child is in order to create a family, to live a normal family life, and to establish new forms of relatedness with friends and family for couples that are unable to give birth. Although not being able to create one's own family in some profound sense reduces one's value as a man/husband and a woman/wife, once a child has arrived this lack is negated, and the individuals emerge as mothers and fathers.

As the above demonstrates, adoptive parents are very concerned with being 'good parents'. They are helped in this by the number of activities organised for them, primarily under the auspices of the adoption agencies. The mere fact of being adoptive parents in Norway makes them very self-conscious and reflexive about their status. It also leads to a very concerned and continuous examination of the child's development. Undoubtedly, the kinning of adopted children requires much more effort than does that of biological children. I suggest that adoptive parents are torn between wanting to be a 'normal family' on the hand, and taking account of the special circumstances of becoming a family on the other. This provokes a degree of ambivalence. During the child's early years, parents tend to ignore any potentially serious consequences of the special origins of their child and put their trust in efforts made at transubstantiation. But they must also heed the increasing demands from outside forces (adoption agencies, psychologists and other experts) to take full account of the child's difference and teach him or her a pride in their 'original culture'. Implied in this and similar expressions is an assumed natural desire to know one's roots, which finds its counterpart in discussions in the media and parliament. Successful incorporation of the child into its new family, social world and nation can only be achieved, according to present-day experts, by openly taking account of the duality of the adopted child's identity. (I return to this in the next two chapters.)

As the children grow up, many parents seem to be more open to acknowledging the non-biological quality of the relationship, perhaps because they feel secure in successfully having effected a transubstantiation. Now parents may begin to foreground the fact that the child has a biological and ethnic origin that they do not share. I wish to suggest that one solution to what may be called the adoptive parents' dilemma, namely to acknowledge the foreign biological and geographical origins of the child at the same time as engage in a kinning process, is found in family return visits to the child's country of origin. It is a solution that more and more families are taking advantage of. Arguably, this trend is in keeping with a growing focus on biological relatedness in society at large. It is noticeable that the adoption agencies have increasingly encouraged adoptive parents to learn about the donor country and to familiarise their children with its culture. However, the conceptualisation of 'culture' is here both reified and superficial, confined to certain cultural markers such as food, dress and artefacts, that are easily consumed without having to confront significant sociocultural differences. Rather, a folklorisation of the adoptees' cultures of origin takes place which, whether deliberate or not, renders it less threatening. Virtually no serious information is provided about social, economic or political institutions and conditions of the donor countries, and few parents that I interviewed expressed much interest in these aspects. It seems fair to ask on what basis the experts – the psycho-technocrats – make their recommendations, and how seriously they take their own advice. To what extent are all concerned paying little more than lip-service to the stated need to encourage a pride in one's 'original culture'? As I shall discuss later, return visits are, despite their increased popularity, in many cases little more than tourist trips. Although many parents (but not adoptees) claim that the return visit was one of the most significant events in their lives, little indicates a desire to really find out about the country. Viewed from a different perspective, these visits may be analysed as an aid to the kinning process; perhaps even its culmination. According to my findings, the majority of adoptees return fully confirmed in their Norwegianness.

To Conclude

Adopted children from overseas are 'sponsored' into existing kin-based networks and kinship histories by their adoptive parents. Faubion regards kinship 'as a system – or array of systems – of subjectivation, if perhaps many other things as well' (2001: 13). By subjectivation he follows Foucault and suggests that the term has a double meaning, 'all those processes through which individuals are labelled or made into subjects of one or another kind ...' and 'all those processes through which individuals make themselves into subjects of one or another kind ...' (2001: 12). This notion of subjectivation complements my analysis of parental efforts to make their children into Norwegian persons (subjects). The efforts of transubstantiat-

Figure 4.2 Double identity? Adoptees on 'motherland' tour to South Korea.

ing the transnationally adopted child into a person, whose identity is constituted through relationships with kinned Norwegian people, fix the child on a path of subjectivation. During this process, manifestations of difference are glossed over and, by and large, the biological parents emerge only as minor characters in the adoptees' personal trajectory. In the case of adoptive parents and their adopted children in the West, where kinship is constituted upon biogenetic relatedness, this process is much more visible, because the adoptees are incorporated into their parents' kinned trajectories by a sleight of hand, as it were. Indeed, adoption can be said to make sense of the biological relationship by throwing it into sharp relief.

Ever since Morgan (1871) it has been an anthropological truism to claim that kinship is a sphere where nature and culture meet in different ways in different societies. Nevertheless, a privileging of the natural as a point of reference has persisted in the discipline (Schneider 1984; Weismantel 1995). Only when M. Strathern (1992) studied some implications of the new biomedical research, including new reproductive technology, was 'nature' as an analytical category within kinship studies deconstructed. This does not mean, however, that for many people the category of nature is irrelevant.[7] Re-emerging in the guise of biology, genes and DNA, nature is certainly meaningful to most adoptive families. As I have tried to show, it is precisely the juggling act of keeping both biology and sociality as meaningful, but not hopelessly contradictory, that represents the main challenge for them. Through a process of kinning and transubstantiation, adoptive parents not only incorporate their children into their own kin, they also transform themselves into parents, thereby negating the separation between the social and the biological that is encountered elsewhere in society.

Notes

1. Changing gender patterns have also resulted in a public visibility of homosexual couples, who may enter into legally binding partnerships. Pressure groups representing them are demanding the right to adopt and the right to receive assisted conception.
2. Another interesting finding is that pressure from potential grandparents is being felt by many couples who fail to produce children. Only grandchildren can produce grandparents. Not having grandchildren similarly results in this generation also experiencing a sense of being deprived of something valuable, a relationship that has become socially necessary. According to recent studies, grandmothers, most of whom today are in employment when they achieve this status, spend more time with their grandchildren than did the grandmothers of the previous generation – most of whom were housewives (*Aftenposten* October 2003).
3. In Latour's terms we are thus in the world of hybridity, by which 'we moderns believe that we divide society from technology, culture from nature ... in a modernist attempt at creating distinctions, and yet, at the same time, we do not deploy these divides in the way we interact in and with the world' (Latour 1993: 10–13).

4. No figures exist as to the proportion of couples who undergo NRT before turning to adoption. According to my own questionnaires and interviews, it is my impression that more than half of those who adopted during the past ten years had at least one such attempt behind them.

5. According to my information, this is not usually the case. Allocation, by and large, follows a rota system.

6. Attitudes to the role of mother are highly complex and I cannot enter into a discussion of its ramifications here. See Melhuus (2003) for a detailed deliberation around its meanings in the Norwegian context.

7. As I was completing this manuscript, a study on the Norwegian royal family was published which contained one piece of information that sent shock-waves throughout the nation. According to the author (Boman Larsen 2004), King Olav V, the previous king who died in 1989, was not the real son of his father, King Haakon IV. The suggestion was that the latter's wife, Queen Maud (who was Queen Victoria's granddaughter), had been inseminated by the English royal surgeon, using his own sperm. Interestingly, an opinion poll carried out the day after the news was released, revealed that only one out ten of those asked thought that this fact was of significance for the status of the royal family. Perhaps Norwegians are more convinced by the force of kinning than had previously been assumed? (Melhuus and Howell unpubl. m s.).

Chapter 5

EXPERT KNOWLEDGE: THE ROLE OF PSYCHOLOGY IN ADOPTION DISCOURSES

When I first started to work on adoption cases more than thirty years ago, we thought that identity and personality development was a matter of 30 percent nature (*arv*) and 70 percent nurture (*miljø*). Today, research has shown that it is correct to turn these figures round.

> Norwegian social worker to a meeting in Adopsjonsforum, 1999

We felt that our daughter was born at Fornebu [Oslo international airport] on the day that she arrived home.

> Mother of a child adopted from Korea in conversation[1]

Adopted children are not born at Fornebu.

> Leader of the Association of Adoptive Parents, 2001

The Century of the Child

In this chapter I examine some theories in child psychology that were influential during the twentieth century, and try to elicit some effects they have had in society at large. My main focus will be on their effect on adoption policies and practice. Not without reason, the twentieth century has been termed the Century of the Child (Hulbert 2003).[2] It was a century that unified paediatrics and developmental psychology into a formidable body of expertise whose knowledge came to affect the lives of every family in USA and Northern Europe and, as the century moved on, those in other parts of the world also. The growth of psychological knowledge in Europe and North America led to the emergence of new professions, such as educationalists, paediatricians, child therapists and social workers; a group of experts that I label psycho-technocrats. As practitioners, they sought to apply psychological theories to practical action. Rose has termed the growth of this expertise the 'psy factor', and argues that it acquired a particular significance within contemporary Western forms of life, as we 'have come to celebrate values of autonomy and self-realizing that are essentially psychological in form and structure' (Rose 1999: xv). This ideological ascendancy of the autonomous individual has, as I have suggested, constructed and delimited our sense of what it means to be a human being. Bounded, and stripped of an analytical significance of sociality, the modern individual stands forth naked and alone, master of his or her destiny. Kinship and relationships became epiphenomenal, not constitutive. This view has taken on a status of universal truth. I shall argue that it has had profound effects on transnational adoption policy, and that it is in the process of being globalised.

Throughout the century, the 'psy' experts consolidated their position, and increasing attention was paid to their expertise by politicians and civil servants as well as by parents, primarily mothers. By focusing upon the growth and spread of the 'psy' discursive practices one may observe how the ideology and practice of governmentality became firmly established in Scandinavia. As the psycho-technocrats became increasingly influential in policy decisions at state level in matters pertaining to the well-being of its citizens, they empowered the state to involve itself actively, and in new ways, in matters previously thought of as private. The development of the welfare state entailed that matters relating to health and social welfare, education, childcare, family life and children's life more generally, became the responsibility of various ministries established in order to handle them. An upsurge in concern about children led to new legislation; and public child welfare agencies with the power to supervise family life and to take appropriate action whenever deemed necessary[3] were established.

Twentieth-century psychological discourses about child development, identity and cognition have had a strong effect on thinking not only about children and childhood in general, but also on the meaning of the family and kinship and, by extension, of adoption. Linked to questions of child development, there arose questions about the optimal conditions for children to grow up under, and how parents, and increasingly society, could ensure that these were provided so that children might develop into responsible and fulfilled adults. We have seen how, during the nineteenth century, the emergence of an idea of childhood as a special and vulnerable period requiring particular attention became an accepted truth. Children could no longer be left to themselves to grow up aided only by occasional practical assistance from relevant adults; they needed special attention and action, performed according to specific recommendations. Motherhood emerged as a role whose prime purpose was to provide the best conditions for children's growth. From an early focus upon hygiene and diet, the mother after the Second World War became expected to provide psychological nurture (Haavind, personal communication). Increasingly, popular parental handbooks published during the twentieth century gave practical advice at the same time as they were moralistically normative. They not only helped mothers to provide the best conditions for their children, they also enabled North American and European parents to assess to what extent they behaved according to expert know-how in their relationship with their children. The emotive significance of the biological mother–child bond could hardly be more valued. In such a cultural climate, the adoptee became somewhat of an anomaly.

As a discipline, Psychology was (and still is) based on an assumption of universal validity. As the twentieth century progressed, psychological understanding became accessible to all and encouraged everyone to have an opinion about selfhood. It is, I suggest, this diffusion of psychologically informed ideas that has lent such authority to the psycho-technocrats. They identified images of normality which could serve as a means by which individuals could themselves normalise and evaluate their lives, their conduct, and that of their children – developing, in Foucault's (1980) words, 'technologies of normalization'. Rose suggests that most knowledge of normality with regard to children has derived 'not from studying normal children [rather] it is around pathological children ... that conceptions of normality have taken shape' (1999: 133). This leads him to conclude that 'normality is not an observation but an evaluation' (ibid.). Morality and normality became fused, and further legitimated the supervisory role of the state in the expectations it levied at the mother. This observation may with benefit be borne in mind when one examines the received wisdom concerning transnationally adopted persons. Certainly, most studies on adopted children have tended to focus upon the maladjusted.[4] Psychological theories are applied in order to explain why some adoptees fail to settle down, develop severe behavioural difficulties, and/or experience problems of identity. Although they constitute a small minority, there is, however, (see Rose above) a danger that their findings are dominating the construction of the understanding of adoptive fates in general.

Following a brief consideration of the most influential psychological theories, I seek to elicit some consequences of this expert knowledge for Norwegian adoptees and their families. Mostly, the influence on adoptive families is indirect, disseminated through the adoption agencies. As a result of recent interest in the adopted children's pre-Norwegian background, two concepts have gained ascendancy in recent years that seem to help parents think about, and handle, problems that arise as their children grow up. These are the notion of the 'backpack', by which is meant that adoptees do not arrive as *tabula rasa*, but carry with them a backpack of early experiences, and, related to this, the concept of 'early emotional damage'. Bearing these in mind, I consider some findings from studies from Norway and Sweden on how transnationally adopted people fare in their new families and countries. The various theories and studies can, I suggest, best be understood in relation to the growing number of 'roots' visits that I shall discuss in the next chapter.

Competing Psychological Models

The early experts on child psychology did not agree amongst themselves; according to Hulbert, 'two poles have defined America's child-rearing advice from the very start ... and they still frame an underlying debate that sound[s] familiar' (2003: 365). Each generation of professional psychological experts, 'has featured a pair of presiding authorities who approached the questions from opposite directions' (ibid.) in what was popularly known as the 'nature versus nurture' debate. The protagonists are, on the one hand, those who emphasise the malleability of children, a position which promotes the significance of nurture and environmental factors, hence, they advocate parental authority and responsibility (the 'hard' approach). On the other hand are those who take the opposite position (the 'soft' approach), and argue for letting nature run its course. While the nurture position has been characterised as parent-centred, the nature one is child-centred. Its adherents advocate love, bonding and children's liberty (ibid.). What is noticeable about the debates of the early decades of the twentieth century is the way in which parents are brought into the discourse as active agents in the formation of their children. So, not only did the theoreticians give rise to new professionals who organised matters to do with children's health and psychological well-being on behalf of the state, these professionals also moved into people's homes and organised parent–child relationships. Representatives of both theoretical positions have claimed to provide a scientific understanding of child development and children's needs Ever since the 'soft' Hall and the 'hard' Holt (Hulbert 2003: 62), the first American paediatricians who, at the turn of the century made psychology an integral part of their popular guides in how to bring up children, the middle classes of North America and Europe have no longer been able to ignore psychological theories of good parenthood. Only the aristocrats of England and other European countries, and the poor working classes, were little affected by the theories. The former continued to leave the education of their children to nannies, tutors and boarding schools, and the latter had little opportunity to exercise choice.

The most influential expert on child-rearing was the American, Dr Spock. For forty or so years he told American and North European parents how to take care of their children and how to 'be' parents (Modell 1988: 151). His *Baby and Child Care*, first published in 1946,[5] has appeared in numerous editions and been translated into thirty-nine languages, making it perhaps the first manifestation of a globalisation of concepts and values regarding family structures and the ideal relationship between parents (mainly mothers[6]) and children. The first Norwegian translation appeared in 1952. Dr Spock occupies a middle ground between the two extreme positions noted above and this may, in part, account for his popularity. His was a sort of common-sense approach[7] and was based on attributing an unquestioned prime significance to a mother's physiological tie to her child (see my discussion on Bowlby below). Spock and other subsequent authors of 'how to' books on childcare do not address the situation of the adoptive parent–child relationship, though they do constitute a reference point for adoptive parents also. Books intended for adoptive parents began to appear in the USA during the 1950s. Dr Spock's model of natural love constituted a challenge to the viability of the adoptive relationship that the authors of such books could not ignore. They had to, 'replace physiology with symbols that are equally convincing representations of bonding, permanence and commitment' (Modell 1988: 156). At the same time they were unable to abandon the notion of nature altogether. The metaphor of flesh and blood hovers as a ghostly shadow in the background. However, rather than positing nature as the single cause of permanence of the parent–child relationship, the authors emphasise that adoptive parental love is as strong and as permanent as that which springs out of the biological bond. The element of chance, both in biological pregnancy and adoptive pregnancy, is emphasised; the paradoxical elements in the adoption discourse is evident (ibid. 180–82).

By the end of the twentieth century, 'the real scientific breakthroughs [heralded as imminent at the start of the century].... had converged on an unsettling recognition: there was far more complexity, and indeterminacy, in children's trajectories than scientists in the child development field had ever expected to discover – or had yet figured out how to handle' (Hulbert 2003: 316). This does not mean that the psycho-technocrats in Europe and North America (or elsewhere, see Chapter 9) have given up. Far from it. Postulated truths about children's nature and needs have affected child policies, and provisions for children at various stages in life, and trickled down to adoption discourse and practice throughout the century. They still continue to do so. In a case study investigating Norwegian social policy regarding the parent–child relationship, the developmental psychologist Andenæs argues that 'the discipline of psychology contributes to the construction of care and parenthood' and that, 'developmental psychology plays an important role in the various debates [about the balance between private and public contribution to children's lives and the balance between male and female parents' responsibilities] in the practice of social policy, family politics and family law'(2005: 212). I have no reason to believe that Norway is unique in this regard.

Biology versus Sociality and the Powers of the Psycho-technocrats

The fluctuation between explanatory models of biology and sociality used in the analysis and description of the adoptive relationship is directly linked to fluctuations in prevailing ways of thinking about human nature, identity and personhood in academic psychology. This again influences developmental psychology and the professionals who derive their expertise from it. The first quote at the outset of this chapter, taken from a Norwegian social worker who has spent more than thirty years working in the field of adoption, is apposite. Her statement was made as an introduction to a talk she gave to a gathering of adoptive and prospective adoptive parents in 1999. Far from using her statement as a springboard for establishing some kind of reflexive attitude vis-à-vis the validity of psychological research, she hailed the advances made in psychology. She displayed no hesitation in asserting that the current dogma concerning the relative contribution of natural and nurturing elements to the development of identity and personality is the truth. Not surprisingly, the audience was both taken aback and worried. As adoptive parents, this was not what they had hoped to hear.

Hers is a useful statement because it expresses very clearly three points that I wish to explore in this chapter. Firstly, it exemplifies the constituting power of expert psychological knowledge as a source for practice. Secondly, it exemplifies what may be called the trickle-down effect of such knowledge from academic psychology to practitioners with some psychological training which, in the process, renders it less nuanced. Thirdly, it shows how psychological models change over time. Those who increasingly are instrumental in constructing the policies are the professional practitioners such as educators, social workers, child therapists, adoption workers, and law makers. As acknowledged experts they exert considerable influence in the development of the welfare state and, by extension, gain power over the lives of children and adults. The original experts, the research psychologists, would probably not make such a gross statement as that of the social worker, but the users of psychological research need simple dictums that they may employ in their professional and practical life. So, politicians, social workers, bureaucrats, administrators working in adoption agencies, and adoptive parents, are all consumers of Psychology. Highly complex areas of knowledge, knowledge that is susceptible to changes in intellectual fashions, becomes increasingly reified and denuanced understanding in the hands of the practitioners. What most of these consumers of second-hand psychological knowledge seem to be unaware of is that the changes that have taken place within developmental psychology do not represent a steady progression towards an ultimate truth. However, the psycho-technocrats are not about to be disabused of this misunderstanding, not least because most of them have their own theoretical and professional agendas. In his study of the growth, and increasing influence, of the psychologically derived professions in Europe, Rose further argues,

The body of knowledge and expertise I term 'psy' is not merely a matter of language, and its objectivity is not merely a matter of discourse. The conditions of possibility of 'psy' knowledges to emerge are themselves practical and institutional, involving the collection of persons together in particular places, their organisation within particular practices and the grids of perception and judgment that are thrown over conduct and competencies as a consequence. (1999: xv)

In other words, psychological discourses have created psycho-technocrats who shape policies in fields that affect public involvement in the many matters that increasingly pertain to children. From their definitions of truth, parents have taken, and continue to take, their cues. One effect of the increasing authority of psychological explanations for behaviour resulted, amongst other things, in creating criteria of normality which in turn were naturalised. The nuclear family located in the family home was hailed as the moral ideal. Biological connectedness became the basis for kinned relatedness. The flesh-and-blood metaphors became firmly entrenched in scientific and pseudo-scientific discourses about kinship; those who deviated were assumed to experience severe problems. It became unquestioned reality that children are vulnerable and basically innocent beings who require special treatment in order to become well-adjusted adults. In line with an increasing intervention of the state in the private life of its citizens, the psycho-technocrats provide the legitimisation for state action. They laid claim to knowledge of children's nature and children's needs; claims that were put to good use throughout the twentieth century, such that 'the child – as an idea and target – has become inextricably connected to the aspirations of authorities' (ibid.: 123). This found its clearest expression in the legal provisions that were encoded during throughout the century, and the number of institutions that were established in order to ensure the application of these laws. In considering the various theories of personhood and child development, one has to bear in mind that the theories are not only of academic interest, but represent a conflict over what is or is not 'the truth'. Ultimately, it boils down to conflicting ontologies, different understandings of human nature, personhood, relatedness and emotionality and who 'is authorized to speak the truth and to whom' (Rose 1999: xix).

There has been a noticeable increase in the relative weighting given to biological versus social factors, exemplified most crudely by the statement of the social worker quoted above. Her insistence upon what 'research has shown' demonstrates a return to nature as a reference point. It confirms what I call an increasing biologisation of discourses about personhood and identity that we may witness in much of the modern Western world; and Norway is a good example of this. Recent research in medicine and genetics, which over the past years has received much media attention, is probably a major contributory factor in this growth of biocentrism. Effects are apparent in adoption discourses. The fact that the Adoption Act of 1986 (see Chapter 7) asserts the right to knowledge about biological parents is one example. Another is the 2003 law of Biotechnology that extends this right to children conceived by donor sperm. At the same time, noticeable fluctuations are discernible in how parents explain the nature of their relationship with their adopted children according to the relevance of the context. All involved tend to foreground the model of genetics (nature) in some contexts and that of sociality (nurture) in others.

The statement by the social worker is telling. So are the implications of the other two statements quoted at the beginning of this chapter. They concern the existential status of the adoptees and are in direct conflict with each other. It is very common to hear adoptive parents voice the opinion of the quoted mother, namely that their child was 'born' at the airport when they first encountered each other. Although said (partly) in jest, such utterances are indicative of the emotionality of the adoptive parents, rather than their rationality. They choose to regard their child as *tabula rasa*, as a person that may be transubstantiated and kinned. A new birth, a social birth, has been effected. Is it then, one may ask, not legitimate to say that the adopted child was born, or rather reborn, at this moment? In asserting – in the other quotation – that adopted children are not born at the airport, the leader of the recently formed Association of Adoptive Parents (see below) is, of course, directly denying the validity of such beliefs. Her statement is indicative of important changes in attitudes found elsewhere. She challenges the claims, even if made in jest, that an adopted child's life begins when it is united with its adoptive parents – when it comes 'home'. This she wishes to debunk as not only incorrect but, in light of recent experiences, damaging. The child is not tabula rasa, she insists, it has a biological and social past which must be taken account of. It was born to unknown parents in an unknown land where unknown persons have been involved, however briefly, in its becoming a person.

Increasingly, the adoptees' past is receiving serious attention from the various experts involved in transnational adoption. Consequently, adoptive parents are paying more attention to it also. Increasingly, I hear and read that children arrive with a 'backpack' full of past experiences. 'Angels who carry a heavy burden' is the front-page heading of a recent issue of the magazine published by one adoption agency. Although the amount of 'baggage' in the backpack varies with each child, the implicit message of this metaphor is that the past, however brief, will have consequences for the child's development in its new circumstances. The adoptees' pre-Norwegian past can no longer be ignored. Experts make a point of stressing that the past must be regarded as an integral part of the child's personality, laying the premises for future development and adaptation. The quality of the past is receiving particular attention in those cases where the adopted children fail to settle down in their new circumstances, and challenge their parents with unforeseen problems of various kinds. As a result of this shift in understanding, many parents are developing a new-found interest in the period before the child came to them. Previously they were concerned only about the child's physical health. Upon arriving in Norway, the children were, and are, submitted to a medical examination. Diagnosed medical problems are dealt with, but potential emotional ones are not addressed. Interestingly, in light of the escalation in the use of biological models for understanding individual behaviour and medical condition, there is virtually no discussion of the adoptees' genetic make-up as a source for understanding their condition. The focus is upon the environmental circumstances. In other words, medical, genetic, and psychological knowledge is applied selectively by those engaged professionally in transnational adoption – just as it is by the parents.

Psychological Theories of Child Development, Adolescence and the Formation of Identity

Psychological theories take as their analytical starting point the autonomous bounded individual and assume universal characteristics of human mentality, emotionality and development. This means that a conceptual leap is made from the individual to the universal, giving no analytic status to sociocultural factors. The consequence of such an approach is that, from a formal and psychological point of view, humans are identical regardless of their social and cultural environment, and '[t]hese values establish and delimit our sense of what it is to be a human being and what it is to have a life of liberty' (Rose 2000: viii). In effect, psychological research carried out in Europe and North America, where most such research is done, is made valid for humanity at large. Inappropriate consequences of this approach, which is clearly sociocentric, can be observed in its application in non-Western social settings. Such an approach fails to take account of what anthropologists take as a given, namely the fundamentally social nature of human beings. Humans create and transmit meaning about themselves and the world in which they live relationally and intersubjectively (Bråten 1998).

The above observations constitute a back-drop to my critique of the psychological theories of child development which have influenced the adoption discourse in Norway. I treat psychological theories about child development, childhood and identity formation as empirical data that may be interpreted on a par with other data. As such they are social facts. My aim is to bring attention to some consequences of the theories for values and practice of the psycho-technocrats. While they necessarily are normative in their quest for knowledge, I am interpretative of the knowledge that they use.

Research carried out in Norway on the adjustment and development of transnationally adopted children, is primarily informed by the theories on identity formation of the psychologists Erikson (e.g. 1968), Kirk (e.g. 1964), Marcia (e.g. 1966, 1980), who also influenced Brodzinsky (e.g. 1992) and Triseliotis (e.g. 1973), in their studies of adopted children in England (see below). They have not studied children who were adopted transnationally. The importance of environmental and nurturing factors in early infancy, was strongly argued during the 1960s and 1970s by all influential psychologists, and this argument was made good use of by those engaged in the adoption world. The statement by the Norwegian social worker cited above confirms its orthodoxy at the time. This was a period when it was more or less taken for granted that once the children arrived 'home' to their adoptive parents, were given Norwegian names, and integrated into Norwegian families and social life, they would rapidly become Norwegian children, indistinguishable in everything but appearance from Norwegian-born children.

However, while nurturing factors were certainly stressed, only those that occurred within a Norwegian setting were taken into account. Curiously, the pre-Norwegian nurture situation of the children received hardly any serious attention. This meant, in effect, that the work by another influential British psychologist, John Bowlby, whose writings on child development go back to the 1940s, was not brought to bear on the understanding of the situation of transnationally adopted children. Bowlby concluded that if a child was repeatedly separated from the mother during the first year, then this affected the development of the child's personality detrimentally. Such children, he argued, tended to go through a process that moved from anger to despair to apathy. The culmination of his researches were published in the *Attachment and Loss* trilogy (1969, 1973, 1980). Similarly, the famous paediatrician and psychoanalyst D.W. Winnicot argued that there is no such creature as 'a baby', there are only 'mother and child couples', or 'social environment of mother–child couples' (Katz 1990: 18, 28). While these ideas certainly were taken up in Norwegian psychological circles (Haavind, personal communication), it is curious to note that they were not applied to the situation of the transnationally adopted children once that practice had started. Given that most children adopted from overseas are between one and two years of age when they arrive in their new families, and hence have been separated from their biological mother at a critical stage, one might think that these theories would be regarded as relevant. The one certain fact about adoption is that the infant has been separated from its biological mother.[8] One possible explanation for the neglect could be that if these theories were taken seriously, they would, as it were, pull the rug from underneath the whole practice of adoption, whether domestic or transnational. The task would appear prohibitive to all but the most determined. 'How could one possibly consider taking into one's family a child whose development had been seriously damaged?', would be a relevant question to ask under the circumstances.

There are thus good commonsensical reasons for why the transnational adoption discourse in Norway focused so strongly on the beneficial aspects of the social and emotional environment. It might be thought counterproductive to seriously consider the fact that, not only were the adoptees separated from their biological mothers, they were also separated from their country of origin with its sounds, smells, and tastes – qualities that are held to be important for a baby's early life experiences. This neglect of important theories by adoption workers raises questions about selectivity in the applied use of expert knowledge.

The Turbulence of Adolescence

The experts' lack of interest in the adoptees' infancy contrasts starkly with the attention paid to their adolescence. This can probably be attributed to several factors. Firstly, transnationally adopted infants and children usually settle down very quickly in their new families. Parents are absorbed in transubstantiating and kinning them. At this stage, they are not interested in the child's life before he or she came 'home' to them. Secondly, with approaching adolescence, many adoptees themselves begin to question their own history. In-so-far as difficulties arise within the adoptive families, adolescence is the most likely time for this to occur. It is a widespread view that adolescence is a time of biologically derived turbulence (attributed to hormonal changes) that results in psychosocial challenges to the individual adolescent. Indeed, this has taken on the status of unquestioned truth and is a topic elaborated upon by the adoption agencies in their journals and their preparatory parenthood courses.

Psychological research claims to have revealed that adolescence is a period of trial and error, and that what a child has experienced in early childhood may give rise to serious conflicts during this critical stage. This has found a ready audience amongst adoption workers. Erikson argued that a successful process of identity formation includes the exploration of different life domains. This is a process supposed to start during adolescence and to develop in a social context. It may include deviant behaviour, and this needs to be handled in order for the youth to emerge a well-balanced personality able to form intimate ties with others (Erikson 1968; Irhammar 1997). Marcia (e.g. 1966, 1980) developed these ideas further and focused in particular upon the positive role of crisis. He identified four phases of identity status, namely: identity achievement, identity foreclosure, identity diffusion, and identity moratorium. Identity achievement is seen as the most mature and developed status since it is derived from exploration and a personal commitment (Irhammar 1997: 219). For an 'achieved identity' to develop, a person must have gone through a crisis during which s/he experimented with a variety of possible choices and which involved making some conscious decisions about future life (cf. Botvar 1999: 10–12). Brodzinsky, a pioneer in the psychological study of adoptees, builds on the work of Erikson and Marcia. His argument is that the healthy development of adoptees' identity must be sought in the degree of openness that they exercise with regard to their biological and ethnic background. He further suggests that those who form very close ties with their adoptive parents will remain in the stage of foreclosure, whereas those who have a bad relationship with them may never emerge from the stage of identity diffusion. In other words, the dice are not loaded in the adoptees' favour. Moreover, it is only when adopted children reach adolescence that they have the mental capability to understand the meaning of adoption and be able to reflect upon its consequences. This may lead to crisis (Irhammar 1997: 219). The work by Erikson, Marcia and Brodzinsky forms the basis for the psychologically orientated research undertaken in both Norway (Dalen and Sætersdal e.g. 1992) and Sweden (Cederblad e.g. 1994; Irhammar e.g. 1997) on transnational adoptees. Although their approaches vary, they all conclude that transnationally adopted children will meet tougher challenges in growing up than will their native contemporaries. They will experience difficulties in their self-perception and will have to resolve the assumed dilemmas of 'belonging to two cultures'. An early paper prepared as a submission to a 1976 White Paper on adoption in Norway, reflects this understanding. The author argued that we should not be surprised if children adopted from overseas, in spite of being adopted by well-educated, well-adjusted parents, meet problems during their adolescence, and experience a 'conflict of identity' (Seltzer 1976: 55).

Adolescence as biologically caused turmoil has become a cultural fact in the West – which in itself raises interesting questions about the relationship between biology, psychology and culture. Norwegian adoption workers accept it fully. One adoption agency has started courses for parents whose adopted children are approaching this stage. This is done so that parents may prepare themselves for this turbulent time. At a meeting of the Association of Adoptive Parents, the invited speaker (a therapist) told the adoptive parents that not only are the chances high that their children will have an extra-difficult adolescence, the chances are that it will last much longer than that of their Norwegian-born counterparts. Adoptive adolescents, I have heard another social worker tell an audience of adoptive parents, are likely to experience this period as particularly challenging. 'Their hormones fly between the walls, creating havoc', she said, and, 'puberty lasts twice as long and manifests itself twice as strongly in adopted young people as in those living with their biological parents'. One might ask if adopted hormones are qualitatively different from those of non-adopted ones, but nobody in the audience questioned their statements. But a quick perusal of ethnographic literature from many parts of the world that provide information about people in this age group, including most countries that send children for adoption to the West, would not support the argument that adolescence is universally a turbulent time or a time for evaluating options and making choices (e.g. Erikson 1968; Marcia 1980).[9] Cross-cultural psychological research is still in its infancy. Anthropological research on indigenous psychologies is rarely included in psychology courses. Until it is taken seriously, psychological theories with a Euro-American bias will continue to exert a hegemonic hold. Developmental psychology gives rise to a deterministic and inflexible understanding of children. How helpful current theories are for understanding the transnationally adopted youth as a category must remain an open question.

I cannot leave this discussion without mentioning one highly influential writer who appeals more to the emotions than the intellect of her readers, but is no less important for that. This is the American psychologist Betty Jean Lifton who herself is adopted and who has written several best-selling books (Lifton e.g. 1994) on the effects of adoption on the adoptees. She considers only domestic adoption in the USA, but her books are widely read by those with an interest in all kinds of adoption. The enthusiastic blurb at the back of her most recent book states: '*Lost and Found* has become a bible to adoptees and to those who would understand the adoption experience ... She breaks new ground as she traces the adopted child's lifelong struggle to form an authentic self' (1994). Lifton has a very negative view of adoption, but one, I suggest, that conforms to a widespread understanding of the practice and, more importantly, one that contributes to a continued focus upon personal crises, roots and biology. Her books are filled with quotable statements. Two will have to suffice. At one point she says: 'This sense of terrifying free-fall through the universe is a consequence of adoptees not feeling rooted in their own factual being and history' (1994: 28). And, in summing up the adoption experience for all concerned, she paints a frightening picture.

> In many ways this book is a ghost story, for it tells of the ghosts that haunt the dark crevices of the unconscious and trail each member of the adoption triangle (parents and child alike) wherever they go ... The adopted child is always accompanied by the ghost of the child he might have been had he stayed with his birth mother ... He is also accompanied by the ghost of the birth mother, *from whom he has never disconnected*, and the ghost of the birth father hidden behind her. The adoptive mother and father are accompanied by the ghost of the perfect biological child they might have had, who walks beside the adopted child who is taking its place ... The birth mother ... is accompanied by the ghost of the baby she gave up. (ibid.: 11 my emphasis)

Lifton's biocentric focus is far from unique. If one is to believe her, and many do, then adoption is indeed a practice doomed at the outset. It is certainly a practice that is inherently deeply problematic and which necessarily leads to many profound crises for all concerned, particularly the adoptees; but, as I shall show, the overall experience of transnationally adopted people in Norway and other Scandinavian countries does not validate her argument.

The Significance of the Adoptees' Early History and the 'Backpack' Metaphor

There has been a tendency in Norway to focus upon the idyllic aspects of adoption. The magazines of the adoption agencies were (and are, but no longer exclusively so) full of sunshine stories. Photos of children newly arrived 'home', the first day at school, confirmation and, increasingly, wedding photographs are appearing. The fact that not all children adjust equally well to their new circumstances has, until recently, been ignored by all but the parties directly involved. They have tended to keep it to themselves. While the majority of adoptions are successful, we are witnessing an increasing willingness to confront the fact that some adoptions provide serious challenges to all concerned. The publication of a book by an adoptive father in which he gives an account of two biological sisters who were adopted from Columbia and who failed to settle down in their new family provoked much debate (Øhren 1995). He told a story of endless strife, confrontation, lies and deceit, and finally alienation and the death of one daughter. During this painful period it emerged that the girls had experienced a very difficult time before coming to Norway. The father criticised the adoption agency for not providing information about the risk that transnationally adopted children may be seriously damaged by the experiences of their early years. The adoption agency on its part, accused him of sensationalising transnational adoption as a practice on the basis of his own very special case. This book was one of several contributing factors (another was the establishment of the Association for Adoptive Parents) that led to new attention being paid in adoption circles to the significance of roots, of genes, of original culture. Today, the question of whether one should ignore the adopted child's back-ground and assume that he or she will settle down as a harmonious kinned Norwegian, or whether one should take a serious interest in the adoptees' pre-Norwegian life, has become important for many. A related question is whether the adoptees should be encouraged to think of themselves as beings with a dual identity (Norwegian and for example, Korean).

What is becoming clear is that parents whose children, for whatever reason, have failed to settle down and have developed serious behavioural problems, have had to face the collapse of the dream of becoming a normal family. To make matters worse, most have had no one to talk to. Many who sought advice and help from the professionals in the public sector, met a wall of non-cooperation. Norwegian child care services are predominantly geared towards giving assistance to families where the parents in some way fail; where alcoholism, drug abuse, unemployment and/or violence are the most common causes. Social workers' theoretical apparatus and practical experience are little suited to dealing with middle-class families whose problems arise primarily from the child's own situation rather than that of the parents. The earlier emphasis placed on environment as the determining factor led most parents, especially those who adopted older children, to believe that entering a loving and well-appointed home would compensate for whatever early unhappy experiences the child might have had. If this turned out not to be the case, they felt bewildered and betrayed, and many experienced guilt-related reactions. Adoptive parents who try to do everything according to the books, but whose children suffer from behavioural and/or emotional difficulties, come to believe that

Figure 5.1 A typical Norwegian family activity.

they are somehow failing as parents. This can produce a powerful sense of guilt. The children may have severe learning difficulties at school, they may display various forms of hyperactivity, they may lie and steal and be violent towards other children, or they may have attachment difficulties at home. When parents turn to the various psycho-technocrats for help in coping, it is not uncommon to be met with unsympathetic reactions. Some are told that it was their choice to adopt from overseas and they must take the consequences when things do not turn out the way they had hoped. Meeting very little sympathy from their child's school or the local child welfare services, parents become bewildered, angry and exhausted.

Association for Adoptive Parents

The situation is beginning to change due, in part, to collective efforts engaged in by some parents. The recently formed Association for Adoptive Parents (AAP), whose leader is quoted at the outset of this paper, has filled a need. The members of the association are mainly parents whose children experience severe difficulties in settling down in their new familial circumstances. In this forum, parents are given the opportunity, many for the first time, to voice their anxieties, frustrations, unhappiness and feelings of guilt to others whose support may be counted upon.

The AAP organises meetings. They invite 'experts' from within the 'psy' professions to lecture on relevant recent psychological research which may help parents to understand more fully their children and the difficulties that they may be experiencing. In the search for explanations, a new concept, that of the 'backpack', is gaining ground. Far from arriving in Norway as *tabula rasa*, the adoptees are said to arrive with a backpack full of emotional and physical experiences, some of which may be extremely distressful and may help account for the child's failure to settle down. Parents are encouraged to unpack the backpack and examine its content, to get out of a 'state of denial'. It is argued that this may help them to gain some understanding of the reasons for their child's difficult situation today. The AAP give practical advice to parents on initiatives that might be helpful, and provide information on literature, their rights as citizens etc. They also arrange informal discussion groups in which parents are given the opportunity to exchange experiences and give each other advice. Some of these turn into mutual support groups that meet regularly over time.

The parents express deep satisfaction at meeting others with similar experiences, stating that this is the first time that someone not only believes their stories, but empathises with them on the basis of personal experience. Just as profound bonds were forged between adoptive parents during the pre-pregnancy and pregnancy stages, new bonds are forged between adoptive parents whose dreams of happy families have been shattered. The ensuing relationships between people from divergent socioeconomic backgrounds strike deep chords, and the shared painful life situation overrides whatever differences that exist, just as the happy circumstances of awaiting a child overrode social differences earlier. The types of relationship that arise during the AAP meetings appear to be of a somewhat different order than those formed during the pregnancy and birth periods, however. I have no indication that the parents establish kin-like relations in the same way as did many who met during the pregnancy and birthing stages. Their situations are perhaps too unhappy and disorganised for this to occur, and their children do not become friends in the same way. But they support each other emotionally at the meetings. Through sharing their experiences and giving vent to their feelings, they obtain sustenance, as it were, to continue in their daily lives. The employment of the backpack and baggage metaphors and the related diagnostic 'early emotional damage syndrome' (see below) seem to provide the parents with valuable insight into their children's behaviour. This helps them to gain a new understanding of their situation; their feeling of guilt is partially alleviated, and they may approach their children with a different outlook.

The Association for Adoptive Parents fights for a public recognition of the special situation of their children. They demand that the public social and health services take account of their children's backpacks and accept that, rather than placing all responsibility on the parents, they provide some post-adoption services for families that require assistance. Despite initial resistance amongst social workers and the adoption agencies, the AAP is beginning to be listened to. A few social workers are attending their open meetings and starting to engage in dialogue with the association. One effect of this focus on pre-adoption life that the adoption agencies do not like, is that the section in the Ministry of Children and Family that deals with transnational adoption increasingly argues that the older a child is upon adoption, the more baggage it carries in its backpack. They are therefore reluctant to grant permission for children over four or five years of age to be adopted. Adoption agencies argue against this, pointing to empirical examples when older children have settled down extremely well. In fact, the attitude of the agencies is highly ambivalent, for they fear that a focus on the possible negative consequences of adopting a child from another country may deter potential parents. They were initially very negative to the AAP, whose leader told me that during the association's first year she was refused space in their magazines to publicise their existence, and her offers to speak at meetings of local branches of the agencies were declined. However, the agencies have become more willing to acknowledge the backpack syndrome, and articles on this and related themes now appear in the journals. Indeed, the leader of the AAP recently wrote an article on the tense relationship between adoptive parents and the social services, which was published in the journal of one adoption agency (Talsethagen 2004: 12–16).

Early Emotional Damage Syndrome

In trying to handle this situation of disturbed adopted adolescents, we again encounter an ambiguous and ambivalent attitude among those professionally involved and the parents. The explanatory pendulum swings from biology to sociality and back when reasons are sought to explain serious difficulties. However, as stated above, in most professional fora today the newly arrived adopted child stands forth as anything but *tabula rasa*. Many scientific and quasi-scientific terms are bandied about. Apart from those of the backpack and baggage, a particularly well-received term is 'early emotional damage'. An article about this phenomenon was published recently in one of the agencies' magazines by a psychologist – himself the father of a transnationally adopted child. He has made a special study of these children. Basing his argument on ideas on psychosocial development by the psychologist Erikson mentioned above, he suggests that children develop during their first year a 'basis-feeling' made up of trust versus mistrust. According to Erikson, people go through life reproducing the particular basis-feeling created during early relationships in their subsequent relationships. With a background in frequent ruptures in the identity of their main nurturer, the author argues, the primary experience of adopted children is one of unpredictability, disturbances and chaos. This may be interpreted by the infant as rejection and lead to a general distrust of adults. It is this experience which forms the basis-feeling of these children who, in later life, seek to reproduce it. The child does this in order to recreate a sense of security which, perversely, is derived from an experience of rejection. It is this that is termed early emotional damage and which is held to affect the adopted child's behaviour in many adoptive families. Unconsciously, the child's behaviour becomes dictated by rejection, which it then reinforces in its new relationships, and '[t]hese children are usually "against" most things … They are so much "against" that they in many situations are unable to realise what is good for them. They act almost on principle "against" in order to recreate their sense of security' (Haarklou 1998: 5).

What we observe here is a return to the ideas of Bowlby and others who stress the importance of the early mother–child bond; ideas which, I suggest, have hitherto not been applied to the transnationally adopted child. The author of the article was invited to speak at a members' meeting of the AAP at which a large number of people attended. They expressed immense satisfaction with someone who put into words what they had experienced in their own families, and provided a sensible explanations for their child's behaviour. In such circumstances a rational (but not emotional) distancing from the child is observable on the part of the parents. They acknowledge the child's different origins and take account of this difference in ways that they earlier had sought to negate, and confront the child's as well as their own inability to cope. The backpack idiom, coupled to that of early emotional damage, becomes a helpful metaphor for parents' understanding, for forgiving and for reducing the pain. However, it remains an open question to what extent the metaphors help the adopted persons to understand their condition.[10]

The recent shift towards searching for causes embedded in the early history of the child thus finds a solution in these concepts. Psychology becomes a crutch upon which they may support their shattered lives. Through the diagnosis of early emotional damage they learn that attachment, security and trust are not part of their children's early experiences and that this may partly account for their later difficulties in their new homes. Another, better-known medical diagnosis that is commonly applied to these children is that of Attention Deficit Hyperactivity Disorder (ADHD).

In this arena of unhappiness, an analytical focus on environmental factors reigns. It is the early pre-Norwegian experience of the child, not the child's genetic make-up, that is made relevant for his or her personality and development when these show signs of maladjustment, Interestingly, despite the increasing preoccupation with biology in society at large, the adoptive parents rarely attribute their children's difficulties to genetic factors.

Studies of Transnationally Adopted Adolescents and Young Adults in Norway and Sweden

Due to reports of adjustment difficulties amongst transnationally adopted youths, including reported patterns of learning difficulties (Dalen and Sætersdal 1999), the adoption agencies as well as the governmental organ that oversees the procedure of adopting from abroad are beginning to acknowledge that transnational adoption may not always be a bed of roses.

The concept of the backpack is applied in order to understand adoptive adolescence. The received knowledge encountered today – that adopted children experience puberty more severely than other young people – some parents find extremely provocative, whereas others derive some comfort from it. There is, however, some evidence that indicates that puberty is a period during which transnationally adopted individuals confront the fact – and implications – of their difference; and some react strongly. A survey was undertaken by the Norwegian Central Statistical Bureau in 1997 on the relative proportion of Norwegian-born and transnationally adopted children who became involved with the local authorities' child welfare system (Kalve 1998). The statistics were broken down by sex, geographical place of residence, type of family and biological status of the children, and they revealed some interesting facts. Kalve found that overall there is a 'clear lower client rate of the adoptees'. Only 1.3 per cent of adoptees under the age of twenty received some kind of assistance from the child welfare services, whereas 1.7 per cent of Norwegian-born in the same age group did. However, the two groups showed a remarkably different profile. In the age group 0–6, no transnationally adopted children featured in the statistics whereas there were fifteen Norwegian-born children. In the pre-teen group (age 7–12) adoptees enter the statistics. Ten adoptees compared to twenty Norwegian-born per 1,000 of this age group have received some special action. But when we turn to the last two age groups (13–17 and 17–19), the adoptees overtake the Norwegian-born. The difference is most marked in the oldest group, where we find that the Norwegian-born children have declined to seven per 1,000, whereas the adoptees have increased to 22 per 1,000. Kalve draws some conclusions from the figures. First, he makes the point (made by myself above) that the socioeconomic background of the two groups vary dramatically. Most Norwegian-born children and adolescents who become involved with the child welfare services do so because of the conditions in their homes. Their parents are unable to cope. When we turn to the children adopted from abroad, the reason for their need for help is their own behavioural patterns. This, he concludes, gives grounds to suggest that the adopted adolescents themselves experience problems in connection with behaviour and coping (ibid.). However, Kalve also emphasises that these figures must be interpreted in the light of the fact that 98 per cent of persons adopted from overseas seek no assistance at all.[11]

While total numbers are low, and they represent only a small minority of adoptees, the figures are, nevertheless, indicative that transnationally adopted children may experience difficulties in coping during and shortly after puberty. Whereas the vast majority of the adoptees settle down extremely well – not least, I suggest, due to the concerted efforts engaged in by their parents to kin them and to involve them in the local community (Howell 2003b) – those that do not adapt seem to experience more than average difficulties. Interestingly, the study indicates that after the adoptees have reached the age of eighteen, most settle down in a way that is not the common pattern for seriously disturbed juveniles in the other groups studied. One might suggest that kinning goes a long way towards making life possible for transnationally adopted persons, but at certain stages in their lives, that is not always enough.

In this connection, I want to make a brief reference to a recent study undertaken in Sweden, published in *The Lancet* (Hjern et al., 10 August 2002: 443–48). The purpose was to 'assess the mental health disorders and social maladjustment' of transnationally adopted adolescents and young adults as compared to immigrants and Swedish born, including adoptees' siblings for the cohort born between 1970–79 (ibid.: 443). Data were obtained from Swedish national registers. Indicators of suicide death, suicide attempts, court sentences, discharges for psychiatric illness, and substance abuse[12] were compared. From one perspective, the conclusion is rather serious. For example, more than three and a half times as many adoptees committed suicide and attempted suicide. They were one and a half times as likely to commit a crime. The odds ratio for being admitted for a psychiatric disorder was 3.3; that of drug abuse was 5.2 and alcohol abuse was 2.6. These figures roughly paralleled those of immigrant children, but non-adopted siblings in adoptive homes showed a pattern similar to that of the Swedish-born.

Not surprisingly, this study provoked much interest and heated debate in Sweden. It was also widely discussed in Norwegian adoption circles. It raised questions about the significance of genetic make-up as well as the pre-adoptive period of the adoptees. A series of programmes were shown on Swedish television in the wake of its publication in which adoptees, psychologists and representatives of adoption agencies debated the findings. Like all large-scale statistical studies, this study also represents a challenge for interpretation, but the authors' stark conclusion, '[a]doptees in Sweden have a high risk for severe mental health problems and social maladjustment in adolescence and young adulthood' (ibid.: 443), may generate some anxiety amongst adoptees and their parents. But when we look at the actual numbers involved, the pictures becomes somewhat less disturbing.[13] They show that 0.3 per cent of adopted boys in the cohort and 0.1 per cent of the girls committed suicide, so suicide is, after all, a rare occurrence. Critical commentators have argued along these lines. For example, the study 'does not indicate maladjustment in the 84 per cent of the male and 92 per cent of the female intercountry adoptees in Sweden', findings that correspond to studies done in Holland and USA (Kim 2002: 423), and which indicate that the vast proportion settle down and adjust to their new life situation without major difficulties. Hjern et al. acknowledge this when they state that most adoptees are not affected, and they say, 'Our results could also be seen as further proof of resilience in children who start their early life in adverse circumstances' (ibid.: 446). The authors further make the point that, as a group, the intercountry adoptees displayed a similar profile to that of immigrant children. This is surprising in view of the low socioeconomic positions held by many immigrant families as opposed to those who adopt (ibid.: 447). Given that all the children adopted from overseas have experienced some degree of turbulence in their early life, one might suggest that had there been no difficulties in later life, then psychological theories of the child developmental cycle would be at risk of being invalidated. As it is, developmental psychologists might benefit from studying material on transnationally adopted persons in Scandinavia.

Swedish television concluded its series on transnational adoption with a panel debate in which a number of adoptees participated and voiced their opinion about the survey's findings and about being adopted from overseas. Many argued that transnational adoption produced psychological instability and that, for this reason, post-adoption services ought to be provided in an organised manner. Others claimed that the practice should be stopped altogether due to the posited detrimental effects. The debate became very heated, and provoked several Norwegian adoptees who watched the programme to react. In the weekend colour supplement to the largest Norwegian daily newspaper, the front cover features the photograph of a twenty-seven-year old freelance journalist who was adopted from Korea at the age of one and a half. The caption reads: 'Me, a ticking bomb?' Her article begins with a description of her reactions to watching the Swedish debate. She says that she was totally flabbergasted by what she saw. 'They quarrel. Loudly. With each other. Several shout and scream, make faces, roll their eyes. I who also am adopted … do not understand what is going on. And did not believe such harsh disagreements existed amongst adoptees' (Andersen 2003: 16). In particular, she was amazed by the angry reactions to one participant's claim that she had never felt any need to seek out her biological origins, nor to visit Korea. To make matters worse, and going against much accepted wisdom in adoption circles, the young woman insisted that she felt no such needs – even when she gave birth to her own child. Furthermore, she said that she was fed up with the expectations that as an adoptee one must undergo some kind of crisis of identity; that one has suppressed some kind of trauma and that it is only a matter of time before one will break down. Her statements provoked another participant (adopted from Ethiopia) to retort that 'To know one's biological roots and country of birth is a fundamental need in all human beings' (ibid.: 17).

As a result of watching the programme, the journalist decided to write about how it feels to be adopted – and to be pigeon-holed by either researchers or others. Referring to the Swedish survey and the dismal findings that had been publicised on the basis of it, she asks 'Am I a ticking bomb? Someone rootless without an anchor? And I who thought it was quite simple to be adopted'. In order to examine Norwegian expert opinion, she interviewed, inter alia, the head of the section dealing with adoption in the Ministry of Children and Family. He is a psychologist by training. He disagrees with her understanding of her own experiences and argues that all adoptees reach a point in life when they want to find out about their roots. He is also very critical of Follevåg's argument (see next chapter) that there is a biocentrism in adoption discourses. He asks her, 'Meeting other adoptees, don't you experience a sense of community?' Andersen replies in the negative. He asks if she feels that she has an attachment to Korea. Again she denies this. Undaunted, he insists that she probably does feel such an attachment, and says that without such anchors, 'we become rootless' (ibid.: 21). She also interviewed a man in his late forties who was one of the first Korean infants to be adopted by Norwegian parents following the end of the Korean war. His experiences have been uniformly positive. He does not associate whatever difficulties he has had in life with the fact of being adopted, but he is provoked by the number of people who, he says, expect adoption from overseas to be problematic (ibid.: 18). Finally, in order to give a balanced picture of the situation, she interviewed a young man adopted from Columbia who tells her how important it has been for him to meet his biological relatives. However, he adds that his brother, also adopted from Columbia, harbours no desire to search for his roots. The Swedish study and the various reactions to it are illuminating. By and large it supported a common understanding of the practice as inherently problematic by the public at large, as well as a number of relevant psycho-technocrats.

It is not easy to characterise those adoptees who used the survey to voice their own criticism of transnational adoption. They can be found amongst that small, but nevertheless highly visible and vocal group who reject their Norwegian situation and actively seek to associate with the country of their origin. Many feel confused about where they belong and may have failed to settle in their new homes. One expression of their dis-satisfaction with Norway can be seen in their choosing to abandon their childhood Norwegian-born friends in favour of seeking out same-age immigrants from the Third World. These adoptees often have a strong desire to meet up with biological relatives and may themselves take initia-tives to visit the country of origin, the orphanage, etc. Although I do not have any reliable statistics on this, it is my strong impression that many of those who embark on such an active search for roots arrived in Norway as slightly older children. While adoptees who experience difficulties in their new life remain a minority (see next chapter), they nevertheless receive a disproportionate amount of attention. Those who have settled down tend not to seek public attention. Those, like Andersen, who insist their experi-ences of growing up have, by and large, not been noticeably different from those of their contemporary Norwegian-born friends, and by so doing go against common expectations of what it means to be adopted – especially from overseas – meet resistance against being believed and taken seriously.

To Conclude

Psychological theories of child development and identity formation have been very influential in domains outside academia in which the welfare of children is on the agenda. In particular, debates about the relative signifi-cance of environmental and biogenetic factors have been especially rele-vant in adoption discursive practices where the professional technocrats consolidated their position as guardians of knowledge and morality. In Norway and other Western European countries their expertise has legiti-mated the state to take responsibility for defining and seeking to ensure what, at any given time, is held to be the best interest of the child. What seems to be evident in Norway is a renewed emphasis on the explanatory significance attributed both to bio-genetic connectedness and to the child's early months and years. What has emerged from my perusal of relevant psychological literature is that adoption is defined as problematic and requiring special measures. Because of this, I suggest that those adoptees who experience difficulties in growing up, and who attribute this to the fact of being adopted, find a resonance among both the general public and expert professionals. The few studies that have been undertaken on the fate of transnationally adopted children in Scandinavia may, like many large-scale statistical studies, be interpreted in both a positive and a negative way. In order to balance the picture, I turn in my next chapter to a further consideration of what the adoptees themselves think of their situation.

Notes

1. The statement about the airport is to be taken metaphorically to stand for the first encounter. With the exception of some Latin American countries who always insisted on adoptive parents collecting their children themselves, until recently most children met their new parents at the airport when they were escorted by an employee of the adoption agency. Today, however, the vast majority of adoptive parents choose to travel to donor countries in order to bring the child home themselves.
2. This diagnosis was first offered as early as 1909 by the Swedish feminist reformer Ellen Key, whose book by that title became a best-seller.
3. In Norway, the services of child welfare and child protection are organised in a single unit, not separated as in many other countries (Andenæs 2005).
4. Psychologically informed policies are clearly discernible in Norwegian values and practices in the fields of adoption and transnational adoption. From an early focus upon the power of a loving environment to ensure a happy and well-adjusted adoptee, we can notice a growing interest in the effect of the adoptees' pre-Norwegian experiences. I use the Norwegian empirical material in order to explore some ramifications of expert knowledge upon discursive practices of adoption, but, in fact, the influential psychological theories are not Norwegian in origin. They come mainly from Britain and America, thus indicating a globalisation of ideas and values within the Western world.
5. According to the Dr Spock web page, the book has 'sold more than 50 million copies, making it second in sales only to the Bible'
6. But as mentioned in Chapter 1, Norwegian state policy in recent years has been also to make the father's role an active one.
7. He told parents to trust their own instincts, to be guided by the love that he took it for granted that all parents feel for their infant, but insisted at the same on a fairly strict feeding regime in the early months.
8. Katz referred to above does make a reference to Winnicot in her book on inter-country adoption in Sweden. Her book is recommended by the agencies to prospective Norwegian adoptive parents. However, this topic has not been given much attention. Even when the parents are informed about possible effects of early life experiences on their children, they mostly ignore this. They are not receptive to such information at a time when euphoria is in prospect.
9. This does not mean that turbulent adolescence is not a social fact in the West. It does, however, raise questions about the relationship between mind and body, which cannot be dealt with here.

10. The topic of the adoptive parents' own baggage is not (as yet) addressed; nor the topic of parental personal difficulties after the child arrives. The effect on adoptees of, for example, parental divorce, or of the birth of biological siblings subsequent to the adoption, have not been seriously addressed.

11. An earlier study undertaken in 1995 showed similar findings. Five categories of children and adolescents who received assistance from the public child care services (both parents Norwegian-born, one parent Norwegian-born and one foreign, transnationally adopted, children of immigrants, refugees and asylum seekers), were compared for frequency of involvement in the child welfare system. This revealed that, overall, transnationally adopted people have the lowest client-rate (Kalve 1998). But again, transnationally adopted persons in the higher age group (18–19) score highest.

12. This is a unique study of such a magnitude. They examined 11,320 adoptees (8,700 born in Asia and 2,620 born in Latin America), 2,343 Swedish-born siblings in the adoptive families, 4,006 immigrants, and 852.319 Swedish-.born. 74 per cent of the adoptees were adopted at age 0–1 years None were older than seven years at adoption.

13. Suicide cases of adopted boys are twelve (0.3%) and of adopted girls four (0.1%). *General population:* boys: 326 (0.1%); girls: 120 (0.0% *sic*); adopted BOYS' suicide attempts: 44 (1.0%), girls: 158 (2.3%). *General population:* boys: 1,182 (0.3%); girls: 3,179 (0.8%); psychiatric disorders amongst adopted boys are 152 (3.5%), girls: 281 (4.0%). *General population:* boys: 5302 (1.2%) girls: 7,165 (1.7%). (Hjern et al. 2002: 445).

Chapter 6

WHO AM I, THEN? ADOPTEES' PERSPECTIVES ON IDENTITY AND ETHNICITY

I'm a coconut girl: brown on the outside, white on the inside.
                                        Swedish young woman adopted from India.

Children adopted from overseas are virtually indoctrinated and 'culture ter-
rorised' into believing that they must learn about their 'original' culture in
order to become 'complete human beings' with a complete identity.
                                        G. Follevåg, *Adoptert Identitet*

The Quest for 'Roots', and Return Visits

Whenever the topic of adoption, and especially transnational adoption, is
discussed in the media or elsewhere, some of the same issues crop up
again and again. Questions arise concerning the 'reality' of adoptive families and the relationship between an adoptee and his or her country of origin. The formulation of these questions derives from the Euro-American
distinction between biological and social kinship, and it is therefore important to investigate how transnational adoptees position themselves in relation to this dominant ideology. Part of the explanation for the public
interest may be found in an increasing attention being paid to the concept
of 'roots'; which dovetails into an increasing biologisation of discourses
pertaining to personhood, identity, human nature, issues of health, and –
kinship. The importance attributed to origins, descent and genealogy is
burgeoning in a number of different discourses on personhood and identity in Norway and elsewhere in Europe and North America. Several reasons may account for this. The Pulitzer Prize-winning novel *Roots*, written
by Alex Haley, was published in 1976. It was subsequently made into a
hugely popular film. The plot involves a seventh-generation descendant of

an African who was brought as a slave from what is now Gambia to the United States. His descendants trace the path back to the village where he came from. The book and the film alerted many American descendants of African slaves to seek their roots, or origins, in West Africa, and were a contributing factor to the rise of a new self-consciousness amongst American blacks. Roots has become a meaningful concept amongst many other migrant minority groups both in the United States and in Europe, including blacks in Britain (*Observer*, 26 September 1999) and children of North African immigrants in France (Iteanu unpubl. ms.).

Roots need not be necessarily be in an alien country. In Norway, as in many other north European and North American countries, there is a notable growth of amateur genealogists who are interested in tracing the

Figure 6.1 Poster at a hotel welcoming Norwegian adoptive families on 'motherland' tour to South Korea.

history of their kin and the kinned places associated with their ancestral past in Norway itself. In line with this, the concept of roots has found a place among the shapers of opinion in Norwegian transnational adoption circles. During the past decade, the two big adoption agencies have both appointed so-called 'roots officers' whose job it is to assist with the increasing number of applications they receive from adoptees concerning details of their early history. Some individual adoptees experience a desire to see the place where they originate from. Some also to try to find biological relatives. This may be the direct result of a personal crisis of some sort, leading them to embark upon a pilgrimage on their own. More interesting, from my perspective, is the fact that we witness an increase in the demand by families to participate in so-called return visits to their adopted child's country of origin. Such visits, also called roots visits or motherland tours, spring from different motives than the individual quests for roots. It is more often than not the adoptive parents – not the children – that want them. Moreover, the visits do not usually come about as the result of personal difficulties experienced by the adoptees, or their parents, but rather as a felt obligation on the part of the parents to enable their children to see their country of origin. One adoption agency used to arrange an annual tour to South Korea. More recently they have arranged three such tours each year, and the waiting lists are growing. The same applies to the organised return visits to India and to other countries of birth. While the popularity of these tours is increasing, there is also a noticeable ambivalence in the attitudes of those concerned. It becomes relevant to ask what existential status one should attribute to the adoptees' place of birth and the fact that they are born by unknown others (Howell, unpubl. ms.). I suggest, perhaps surprisingly, that these tours may be interpreted as a culmination of the parents' kinning efforts. The vast majority of adoptees return to Norway confirmed in their kinned Norwegianness, not, as might be expected, challenged as to its reality.

The reasons for the growth in such tours are complex but can, I suggest, be traced to opinions voiced by psycho-technocrats which have led to a shift in the adoption agencies' own thinking on the significance of the adoptees' backpacks. This is reflected in the topics taken up for discussion, and the literature distributed, during preparatory parenthood courses. Prospective adoptive parents are told that a visit to their child's country of origin is a 'must' if they wish the child to grow up into a happy and well-adjusted person and to feel at ease with what, more and more, is talked of in terms of their dual ethnicity, or of belonging to two cultures. On the home page of the Norwegian adoption agency Children of the World, the very first paragraph reads: 'To be adopted means being part of two cultures'. (http://www.verdensbarn.no/adopsjon.nml). What this might mean is not debated, but parents are admonished to respect their children's 'original culture', and instil in them a sense of pride in their country of origin regardless of their having arrived at a very early age. Most who express these opinions tend to reify culture, especially when they talk of an adoptee's 'original culture'. It should be noted that culture is becoming a euphemism for race in Norwegian adoption discourse; perhaps it is easier to acknowledge what after all is a patently obvious difference, through reference to culture rather than to race? (Howell and Melhuus forthcoming).

While many adoptive parents express an interest in their child's country of origin, their knowledge of its social and cultural traditions tends to be superficial, confined mainly to acquiring stereotypical cultural artefacts and the occasional visit to a restaurant that serves food from the country. Yet, they increasingly perceive their duty as adoptive parents to include a return visit at some point before the child leaves home. The twenty-six-year-old Norwegian doctoral student of literature, Follevåg, who was adopted from South Korea, is highly critical of such thinking.[1] He criticises those who maintain that culture is something one is born with. Unless one argues that culture follows colour of skin, he says, it becomes meaningless to suggest that the transnationally adopted children participate in the culture of the country where they happened to be born, but whose language they do not speak and whose sociocultural traditions and institutions they do not know (Follevåg 2002, 2003). He is equally critical of the increasing attention that is paid to questions of 'roots' in adoptive circles. Humans do not have roots, he says, only plants do. A plant removed from its roots is a dead plant. Does this mean, he asks rhetorically, that persons removed from their country and family of origin [their roots in current jargon] and adopted into a family in a foreign country are dead people? People who lack something ordinarily perceived as fundamental? (2003: 20). His views challenge those of influential psycho-technocrats, and are highly controversial.

Most of the children who participate in organised return visits are between thirteen and eighteen years of age. According to my interviews with families preparing for the Korea trip that I participated in, the children did not express much interest in going, whereas most of the parents were very excited about the prospect of 'seeing where my child comes from'. Similar differences between parents and children emerged from a questionnaire which I sent to those who had participated in return visits to India (Howell and Juvet Hermansen 2001). However, as the Korean-born travelled around Korea, visited the orphanage that they had come from and, in some cases, met their foster-mothers, the adoptees generally took a more active interest. Contrary to popular expectations, none of the adoptees I travelled with had any desire to meet with their biological parents. The same picture emerged from the India sample. Only a few declared a wish to meet biological relatives, and the reason given was almost invariably 'to see who I look like'. In Norway, people are always searching for shared facial features between infants and blood relatives. Observing this activity, many adopted children find the lack of such a search in their case disturbing. These are the moments when they are placed face to face with the 'unnatural' quality of their relationship with their family. At such moments many long for some proof of being biologically connected to someone. For many who have met biological relatives, the fact of discovering a physiological likeness seems to be the most pertinent and memorable aspect of the encounter. In fact, most are satisfied with one or two meetings. These are often highly emotional for all involved, but then the adoptees appear to be satisfied and many do not wish to maintain communications with their biological relatives afterwards. Many experience the encounters as confusing; they find – often to their sorrow- that they have little in common with their biological relatives (see below). In fact, the meetings may serve to confirm them in their Norwegianness and in their kinned relationship with their adopted relatives.

Contrary to the expectations of some, visiting one's country of origin does not provide an easy identity tag. Rather, it may be a highly ambivalent experience. The Korean-born young people who went on the return visit in which I took part, started to wear name-tags that stated their Norwegian name and the fact that they were on a 'Holt motherland tour' from Norway. They did this because they found it uncomfortable to be addressed by locals and having to explain their situation. They felt alienated from what was going on around them. Unlike a Korean-born adoptee in urban South Korea who, at first sight, is difficult to identify as an outsider, an Indian-born adoptee stands out like a sore thumb in India. Not only do they dress and behave differently from their Indian contemporaries; their whole deportment is different. In Norway they may be taken for Indian, but not in India. This produces some degree of confusion on the part of the adoptees. But, to judge from the responses to my questionnaire, such confusion is temporary and does not seem to have any serious impact on the people concerned.

Both the Korean and the Indian adoptees gave a clear impression of being well adjusted to their families and to their lives in Norway. They enjoyed the visits to their countries of birth, they liked seeing the country, and they especially enjoyed the visit to the orphanage. However, nobody indicated that the visit had had any effect on his or her sense of self or upon his or her life in Norway. To questions of whether they had hoped to meet some biological relatives – or if they would do so if they were given the opportunity later – the majority answered in the negative. Their reasons varied: they felt no need to do so; or it was too late by now and they felt sure that they would have nothing in common; or they did not want to meet totally unknown people who would want to be their relatives; or they already had a family and that was enough. The few who replied in the affirmative expressed, as stated above, a curiosity about appearances; they would like to see who they looked like. Others wanted to find out the reason why they had been given away. But very few gave the impression that it was particularly important to make contact with biological parents. On being asked if they planned to return to India in order to explore their roots further, no-one replied in the affirmative.

During the trip to South Korea, the Korean adoptees became more interested in things Korean, but their interest rarely went beyond that of tourists. At the end of the tour, several expressed a wish to learn Korean, or attend a summer school in Seoul organised by the Holt organisation that had arranged the adoptions. However, one year later such intentions had fallen by the wayside, and they were back in normal Norwegian life. All in all, the adoptees gave an impression of being at ease with their situation. The parents, on the other hand, were very exultant about the trip. It was, of

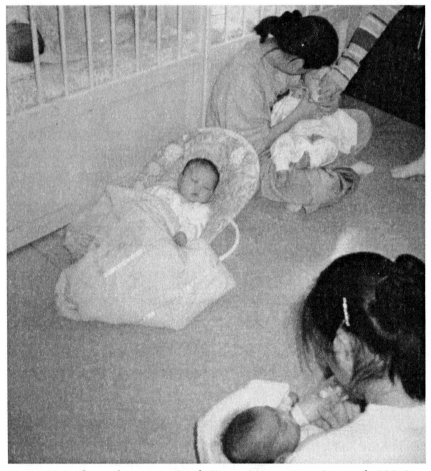

Figure 6.2 In the orphanage in South Korea. Norwegian adoptees hold babies awaiting their adoptive parents.

course, they who had initiated it, and they were unanimous in expressing the pleasure they derived from seeing their children's place of origin.

While the adoptees' reactions are representative of most transnational adoptees in Norway, not all have an equally relaxed attitude. There clearly exists a group of transnational adoptees that struggle in various ways with coming to terms with their fate, and experience a strong desire to make contact with their place and people of origin. My argument is that this latter group also tend to be more active in those fora that owe their existence to transnational adoption. This was confirmed at the Second International Gathering of Adult Korean Adoptees that was arranged in Oslo in 2001 and which I attended. One hundred and thirty seven persons from twelve countries between the ages of eighteen and the late forties took part. It was an emotional gathering with many individual adoptees expressing the difficulties they had experienced while growing up as adoptees. Two of the four Norwegian organisers who were interviewed in a national newspaper during the conference told the reporter that they had experienced many difficulties while growing up. In particular, conflicts with their adoptive parents were of such a serious nature that they no longer kept in touch. This gives a very slanted picture of transnational adoption, but one that the public is ready to accept (Howell in press).

That transnational adoption is problematic, and that the adoptees will want to search for their biological relatives, are part and parcel of many Norwegians' understanding. Such an understanding manifests itself in numerous fora; from deliberations in connection with legislation, to television programmes that document a search for roots, to articles 'from real life' in weekly magazines. Each incidence, each expression and utterance, confirms preconceived ideas. It is therefore important to balance the picture somewhat in order to let other, and actually more common, experiences of transnational adoption be aired. However, as argued in the previous chapter, whenever the critics speak, they are not listened to with equal interest. In another reportage from the international Korean gathering, a young woman who was planning to go on a return visit, stated that she thought it might be fun, but that she had never wished to seek her biological parents. She said that she was well adjusted to her Norwegian life. This was not well received by many at the gathering.

When asked how many at the gathering had been to Korea, about two-thirds put up their hands, and more than half of the group showed that they had actively tried to trace a biological relative. About half of these had been successful. This is clearly not a random sample and I would be extremely surprised if these figures are representative of the transnationally adopted young adults as whole. Nevertheless, those who express a desire to meet up with their biological relatives confirm a cultural stereotype in society at large, coupled to a biocentric bias in the construction of personhood.

Several documentaries about adoptees' searches for their roots and their biological relatives have been shown on Norwegian television over the past few years. Usually they document a successful reunion. This discourse bio- logical identity has been further fuelled by the advances made in DNA test- ing techniques and the legislation in Norway that allows a man to test whether or not he is the biological father of a particular child. As a result, biology has become even more the identifying criterion for personal identity, and the point is not lost on those who are adopted. In their case, biology and place of origin may become fused into one significant domain which they have to cope with. However, one documentary about a twenty-two-year-old girl adopted as a six-months-old infant from Bangladesh, gives a different impression. She felt no rapport with the culture she encountered, nor with her biological mother, father and sisters, all of whom she met. 'OK, so I've seen the country and I've met them, but I will never want to go back or have anything more to do with them. From now on I'll stick to package holidays', she concluded when filmed back home in her affluent parents' house.

This documentary provoked strong reactions. Several people I have spoken to about it felt that her reactions were unnatural. 'She must be sup- pressing something'. was a common verdict. Her story stands in stark con- trast to most other media reports of return visits. A popular Norwegian television series is called *Tore på sporet*[2] (Tore tracks them down). The show is immensely popular, and Tore Strømøy, the presenter, has been voted television personality of the year several years running. The format is sim- ple: members of the public request Tore's help in finding a long-lost fam- ily member, and the climax of each programme is the reunion between them. Several episodes have been devoted to people adopted from over- seas, and this makes for particularly dramatic and emotional viewing.

In 1999 the story of a young woman adopted from Ecuador was broad- cast. Tore had managed to find the woman's biological grandmother and some sisters of her deceased mother. There was an intense build-up to the dramatic and exultant encounter between the girl and her grandmother. The Norwegian film crew skilfully captured it, with Tore's excited com- mentary running throughout. Unlike the story of the girl from Bangladesh, this was a tale that conformed to most peoples' expectations regarding adoption and the supremacy of biological bonds. Many adoptees have told me that following one such screening, they were urged by friends and acquaintances to undertake the same kind of search; the implication being that this is a natural desire. Those who search expect the reunion to be a happy occasion, a moment when blood is manifestly thicker than water.[3] When the reality of an encounter turns out differently – as it often does after the first few meetings[4] – the disappointment may be profound. This, however, is never shown on television.

Reunion of adopted child and biological relatives tends to demonstrate conflicting cultural understandings about the meaning and responsibilities of kinship. The American documentary *Daughter of Danang* is shown regularly on American public television. It is about a woman who was adopted to the USA from Vietnam as a seven-year-old child following the end of the war.[5] Her father was an American soldier. Her mother, who had other children by her Vietnamese husband, heard rumours about the cruel treatment of mixed-race children and felt obliged to give her up. Years later, as a married woman with children of her own, the adopted girl wanted to visit Vietnam to meet her biological family. The film traces her journey. The expectations on both sides are very high. The meeting between biological mother and daughter is very emotional, as is that with her various siblings. At an early stage of the visit she says, 'I just hope that they understand I have been a hundred and one per cent Americanised. And I have no earthly idea of their expectation.' However, her worst fears are confirmed when she is preparing to leave and it all goes wrong. As would be expected in Vietnam from a well-to-do daughter, she is asked to contribute financial support for her aged mother as well as give substantial support to her sister who has been looking after the mother for many years. The adopted woman reacts very strongly against what she regards as attempts to exploit her. She feels repelled by bringing money into a relationship of this kind, a reaction that confirms my argument about Western notions of the immorality of money (Chapter 8). Much to the consternation of her Vietnamese relatives, she begins to cry and she is heard to exclaim, 'Don't know what to do! I just don't know. I wish this did not happen ... I wish the trip did not happen now, because I'm gonna leave with all these bad memories and all this bad feeling, and it's not how I wanted it to be' (transcript). Once back in the USA, she does not contact them again.

However, many of those adopted from overseas do not harbour such desires. In an open letter to South Korea, Follevåg continues his confrontation with many of his colleagues' interest in that country. He expresses how he resents always having been asked, 'When are you going back to Korea? When are you going to find your biological parents again?' And asks, 'Why do they think I do not belong in Norway?' His answer is, 'Because of you, South Korea, when they saw me they saw you....they did not see me as an individual' (2003: 21). In other words, his non-Norwegian looks mark his identity as far as the interlocutor is concerned¸ thereby enforcing a cultural reluctance to accept non-biological kinship as 'real kinship'. Similar sentiments were expressed recently in an article published in the membership magazine of a Norwegian adoption agency. A twenty-nine-year-old woman adopted from Bangladesh demands the right to 'be just a happy Norwegian' (Flydal 2003: 10). She argues that it is high time for Norwegians to accept that the Norwegian population consists of several thousand 'ethnic Norwegians' who are dark-skinned, and whose culture is Norwegian and sense of belonging is linked to Norway. Like Follevåg, she also resents what she characterises as everybody's assumed right to ask transnationally adopted persons questions about return visits, if they have knowledge of biological parents, and if their adoptive parents have been kind to them. She says, 'Personally, I am not interested in biological roots, but have experienced [throughout my life] that people I hardly know are very concerned about them on my behalf' (ibid.: 11). Although in my experience the sentiments expressed by Follevåg and Flydal – and Andersen mentioned in the previous chapter – are quite common amongst persons adopted from overseas, their voices are not often heard; and when they do speak, there is tremendous resistance to what they have to say. Such opinions do not conform to popular understanding of the adoptive status.

Adoptees' Perspectives on Identity and Ethnicity

'I am a coconut girl: brown on the outside and white on the inside'. said a young Swedish woman who was adopted from India as a two-year-old.[6] Such a characterisation of themselves is fairly typical of transnationally

Figure 6.3 The right to just be a happy Norwegian.

adopted young persons and adults. I have heard many Norwegian adoptees make statements like, 'I'm Korean [Indian, Ethiopian or whatever] on the outside and Norwegian on the inside.' These statements raise questions of identity and ethnicity which are far from easy to answer.

The Norwegian pedagogues Dalen (e.g. 1992, 1995); Sætersdal (e.g. 1999) and Ryggvold (e.g. 1999) have been conducting a longitudinal study of factors involved in identity formation of a group of adoptees from Vietnam and India and, more recently, from Columbia. Originally they were interested primarily in researching how the adoptees cope at school. Recently, they extended the scope of their enquiries to map young adult adoptees' appreciation of their life situation (Botvar 1994, 1999. Brottveit 1996, 1999).[7] From their findings, as well as from my own fieldwork, it is fair to conclude that the vast majority of transnationally adopted Norwegians are comfortable with their sense of self, and that they primarily identify themselves as Norwegians. By and large, they are accepted as such by the Norwegian population. For this reason I do not agree with the proposal that transnationally adopted people in Norway should be regarded as a new ethnic (or cultural) group or category (Sætersdal and Dalen 1999). However, from the point of view of self-ascription, it is useful to distinguish between different categories of belonging (cf. Brottveit (1999: 67). At the same time it is important to avoid a unitary analysis of selfhood, and allow for different self-ascriptions according to context. Individual adoptees may, and probably do, activate a variety of interpretations of their own sense of Norwegianness in different contexts. Thus adoptees, just like their parents – and most people for that matter – will in some circumstances emphasise one aspect of their personhood, e.g. gender, age, skin colour, or place of origin. In other contexts, yet other aspects take precedence, e.g. being a boy scout, a high school pupil, a granddaughter, adopted from China, or whatever. There is no evidence to suggest that adoptees, unless they are experiencing psychological problems, understand these various statuses and roles as somehow peculiarly shaped by the fact of adoption.

Immigrants? Norwegians? Double Identity?

One consequence of the popularity of the backpack metaphor has been that the discourse about 'roots' has taken on a more profound significance, and the concept of 'double identity' is now being encouraged. During the early decades of transnational adoption neither concept was much in evidence. Rather, it was assumed that the 'power of kinship' would produce Norwegians – albeit Norwegians who looked different from the majority of the population.

While not denying their foreign origins, most adopted children I have met insist that they are not immigrants. It seems to be the case that by far the largest majority do not, in most contexts, identify themselves either with their country of origin or with people who come from that country. This is in marked contrast to the situation in the USA, where the presence of large communities of immigrants from countries from which children also are adopted has given rise to ethnic categories such as Korean-American, Columbian-American etc. Many American transnational adoptees categorise themselves along similar lines, and many experience an affinity with the immigrants who originate from the same country as themselves (American adoption worker in conversation). This is not the case in Norway. Non-Western migrant communities are of recent origin (see discussion at the end of this chapter) and only to a limited extent do the countries coincide with those from which Norway adopts.

In a survey that sought to establish how transnationally adopted young people in Norway define their ethnicity, Botvar found that 62 per cent of those asked stated that they regard themselves fully as Norwegian, while 22 per cent would partially agree with this. At the same time, 59 per cent answered in the affirmative to the question: 'I am proud to have connection to two different countries'. These answers led Botvar to suggest a schema of categories which he divides in the following manner:

Exclusive Norwegian belonging/identity	35%
Double belonging /identity	20%
Foreign belonging /identity	15%
No belonging /identity	15%
Uncertain /identity	15%

Source: Botvar (1999: 67)

Botvar does not distinguish between boys and girls here, but he comments that there is a tendency for boys to emphasise their Norwegian belonging more than girls. Moreover, people adopted from Columbia are more oriented towards their country of birth than are those from Korea. The age at time of adoption does not appear to be significant.

It is difficult to know how much reliability to attribute to these figures. The samples are small and questionnaires sometimes contain leading questions; but they may be regarded as indicative of certain trends. Brottveit's investigation of thirty-six adoptees from Korea and Columbia (whose average age was twenty-five and whose average age at adoption was three), found a wide variation in attitudes towards their origins, their own appearances and the importance they gave these factors. He makes the anthropological point that ethnicity is best understood as relational, i.e. made in interaction with others and in contrast to others. He suggests, nevertheless, that three categories along ethnic lines may be discerned. The first category he characterises as 'Norwegian', i.e. those who identify themselves unequivocally with their Norwegian family and society at large. Secondly, there are those that he characterises as 'double ethnic', i.e. those who, as young adults, begin to take an active interest in their origins and background which may at times lead to a stronger identification with their country of origin. A third category is that of the 'cosmopolitan'; i.e. those who do not concern themselves with ethnic markers as part of their

Figure 6.4 Two cultures? Korean born adoptee and her ethnic Norwegian husband dressed in hired traditional Korean wedding costumes.

own identity. They take a more open-ended view and reject most attempts at classifying them (Brottveit 1999: 64–65).

The adoptees may, and probably do, fluctuate between the various categories of identity, without this presenting a real problem. My findings have shown that it is primarily others, not the adoptees, who expect an identity and/or role dilemma. This is not to deny that transnationally adopted children have to face a somewhat more complex situation in the emplotting of their personhood than do those born into the same biological, social and racial group that they grow up in. What is clear from my own, and others', studies on transnationally adopted people in Norway, is that, in most cases, they are not much concerned about the 'falseness' or otherwise of their kinned relationship with their adoptive parents and other relatives. Most adoptive parents succeed in incorporating their children into their own social and kinned community, and the vast majority marry native Norwegians. That children tend to emphasise similarities with their Norwegian-born family and peers and ignore differences, has been characterised as 'rejection of difference' (Sætersdal and Dalen 1999). This rejection of difference does not entail a rejection of the fact of adoption itself – most families speak openly about this from the beginning. Rather, the children, as well as their parents, tend to insist that the fact of adoption does not entail any special consequences for the adoptee. At the same time, others are highly critical of such a reaction, arguing that the adoptees suppress important aspects of their identity, that in effect, they labour under what might be termed false consciousness.

How the transnationally adopted people perceive themselves in term of nationality is unproblematic. They all became Norwegian citizens upon the completion of the adoption procedure. How they perceive themselves culturally, socially and ethnically is, however, more complex. As I discussed in Chapter 4, the adoptive parents work extremely hard at 'planting' their adopted children into their own kinned soil. During the symbolic pregnancy and birthing stages that the parents construct for themselves, the biological origins of the adoptees are not much elaborated upon. The social quality of kinship takes strong precedence, without this being said in so many words. The same applies to the first few years after arrival when, I argue, the child's essence is being transubstantiated into that of a Norwegian kin-person. The body, of course, is not transformable, but physiological differences are 'rejected' as insignificant by parents who encourage a strong and positive self-image in their adopted children. They do not explicitly remark upon the difference in looks between themselves and their children (although dressing them in typical Norwegian clothing, including national costumes, may be a way of changing their outer appearance as well). But many have told me that they speak in positive terms about the fact that their children do not have to spend hours sunbathing in order to get a tan, about their beautiful dark eyes and hair etc.

Whether because of this, or for other reasons, the researches by Botvar have shown that both male and female transnationally adopted young people have, on average, a more positive attitude to their own bodies and the way they look than do their Norwegian-born contemporaries; but that boys are more satisfied than the girls. Given the fact that many have reported some form of teasing and harassment during childhood because they look different, this is an interesting finding. Botvar suggests that it may be because adopted boys are more actively engaged in sports activities than are the Norwegian-born. This may give them a positive bodily self-image and compensate for the fact that most of them are noticeably shorter than are Norwegian young men (Botvar 1999: 60–63).

There is therefore little evidence to suggest that adopted people deny their origins. They acknowledge the fact of adoption and their different skin colour and different looks (ibid. 64). For the majority, however, this difference does not constitute a basis for creating an alternative sense of identity and does not have sufficient detrimental effects for them to suffer from a negative self-image. At the same time, most resent having their different racial features commented upon by outsiders.

Imagined Community?

To what extent the adopted children experience a sense of community, imagined or otherwise, amongst themselves is a question that occupies many adoption workers and experts. In light of recent experiences of attempts to establish fora just for them, it has emerged that such offers do not meet a felt demand. Most adoptees are resistant to having the special nature of their existence pointed out. They have no wish to be thought of as different from their Norwegian-born peers.

Whereas a large proportion of adoptive parents share a sense of community amongst themselves, the adoptees generally do not. Their parents, however, assume that they do. When the children are small they accompany their parents to the various gatherings of adoptive families. They are too young to realise the special quality of their situation. When they get older, however, to the disappointment of their parents, most lose interest. The following statement, made by an adopted adolescent girl who did not want to attend one such gathering, is fairly typical. She said, 'I thought it was idiotic [to attend]. Mum said it was o.k. that I did not go, but then I would have to come up with a good reason for not going. That was really daft. I could not think of a good reason so I had to go. I kept thinking, "what am I doing here?" We did not have anything in common. I just looked at them. Some of them were really dark-skinned' (quoted in Brottveit 1999: 47). Such a reaction goes against the grain of parents and adoption agencies alike.

Adoption agencies have tried for many years to encourage the adoptees to join together in associations. It is thought that they will benefit from meeting others in the same situation as themselves and be able to discuss common problems. In other words, that they, like their parents, have a need for this kind of community. However, experience shows the opposite.[8] In 1997 an organisation calling itself Network of Transnational Adoptees in Norway (*Nettverk av utenlandsadopterte i Norge*, NUAN) was formed. Its purpose was to provide a forum for adoptees between the ages of eighteen and twenty-five. At its first general meeting, about 140 young people from the whole country attended. The project was initiated by the two large adoption agencies, which gave financial support to the conference.[9] The stated aim of NUAN is to provide a common forum; a forum in which to discuss common experiences, share thoughts, anxieties etc. and, whenever necessary, support for the transnationally adopted young people. When a second meeting took place the following year, only twenty-five people attended. The membership is not growing. By March 2000 there were about eighty members and, four years later, the organisation had virtually ceased to exist. The adoption agencies are considering whether to make another attempt at getting it off the ground (personal communication). Given that several thousand transnationally adopted people within the age group live in Norway, it seems fair to conclude that Norwegian transnationally adopted young people do not feel that they constitute a community. The fact of being adopted does not represent a sufficiently important aspect of their self-perception for them to actively engage with other adopted young people. Perhaps they feel more confident about their kinned status than do their parents and the adoption agencies?

If transnational adoption by itself does not constitute a sufficient criterion for communality, then being adopted from the same country might. Several adoptees have told me that they feel some common bonds with those who originate from the same country as themselves, more than they do with transnationally adopted generally. To my knowledge, two such organisations exist: one for people adopted from South Korea, the other for people from Columbia. They distribute information about the countries, give classes in local cookery and, from time to time, language courses. Depending on the leadership at any given time, the associations may be active. But even at its most active, their membership represents only a small percentage of the potential. This is the same in Denmark. In a country where more than 8,000 children have been adopted from Korea, the Danish Korea Club had, in 2001, only 120 members (personal communication by the leader of the club). What is apparent is that, in most cases, transnationally adopted individuals are not much concerned about the reality, or otherwise, of their kinned relationship with their adoptive parents and other relatives. While some may, at times of adolescent turbulence, shout at their adoptive mother, 'you are not my real mother', such reactions are not usually deep-felt, and do not suffice as a basis for a shared communal feeling with other adoptees. In a survey conducted amongst the members of the Danish Korea Club, the researchers found that many did not experience any special ethnic identity as children, and that their Danishness was described as either 'good' or 'fairly good'. About half of those who responded had visited Korea, and expressed an interest in 'roots', whereas 25 per cent were not interested. The conclusions drawn are that the Danish adoptees have a generally good relationship with their adoptive parents, but that to explore some implications of their Korean-ness made a difference to those whose sense of self was uncertain. These findings correspond broadly to the findings made in Norway by Dalen and Sætersdal, Botvar and Brottveit .

Race and Colour as Criteria for Inclusion and Exclusion

Ethnic boundaries are increasingly being drawn in contemporary Norway. In the present context, two categories of foreigner are relevant: children adopted from the Third World and the former Soviet bloc, and migrants and asylum seekers who come from many of the same countries in search of a better life – whether economic or political. These two groups began to arrive at about the same time: during the late 1960s, early 1970s. Both keep increasing in number. The waves of immigration from poorer countries in the South has contributed towards new discriminatory sentiments and practices, and has placed questions of racism – if not race – on the agenda. The relationship to, and integration of, non-Western immigrants into Nor-wegian society has become a fraught political issue, and the tendency has been to discuss differences between 'us' and 'them' in terms of culture – such as culturally foreign (*fremmed kulturell*) and the multi-cultural society (*flerkulturelt samfunn*). Only indirectly have notions of race and colour been confronted – as in the slogan 'yes to a colourful community' (*ja til et farg-erikt fellesskap*).While the term race is hardly ever used in Norwegian dis-course, I argue that culture has become a euphemism for race and, as a result, the two categories of foreigners are viewed very differently. Whereas the adoptees – who look very different from their new kin and parents and who come from unknown countries – will be transformed and transubstantiated in order to be subsumed within Norwegian kinship and culture, most immigrants from outside Western Europe and North America remain outside mainstream Norwegian social and cultural life.

As mentioned, Norwegian adoptees do not identify themselves with non-Western immigrants groups in the country. In fact, they actively resist being associated with them. At a talk given to a meeting of a local associa-tion of one of the adoption agencies, the then leader of Network of Transna-tional Adoptees in Norway made the following statement, '[w]e may look like immigrants, but we do not feel we have anything in common with them. Inside, we are Norwegian'. As far as they are concerned, the boundaries that separate immigrants from Norwegians are clear-cut. Indeed, some may express more hostility towards immigrants than do their parents or their native Norwegian peers. So, far from feeling bonds with these other 'new' Norwegians, they deliberately distance themselves from them. Far from feeling an ethnic solidarity, they may feel that immigrants represent an ethnic 'role handicap'. (cf. Brottveit 1999: 91). In fact, many blame these groups (their numbers and behaviour) for themselves being stereotyped and made the victims of racism (Howell and Melhuus forthcoming).

Whereas the category of native Norwegian includes transnationally adopted children, it excludes immigrants and their children. A kind of colour-blindness operates regarding children adopted from outside Europe, and they are fully accepted by all as the son/daughter of farmer Hansen, doctor Olsen, etc. As the adoptees leave home, however, they may encounter strangers who assume that they do not belong to the Norwegian cultural reality that they themselves feel they are part of (Sætersdal and Dalen 1999). They experience this as a shock. Almost all the adoptive parents interviewed in a recent study expressed anxiety about their children's future in terms of racism. Their main concern is that casual strangers would not distinguish between their children who 'really are Norwegian' and the children of immigrants (Brottveit 1996: 133). Again, a complex picture emerges when we consider the identity of transnationally adopted persons. Adoptive parents are confident that the adopted children will become theirs in the sense that they will be like them in every way except bodily appearance. During the early years of transnational adoption, people assumed that children who looked 'foreign' were in fact adopted and treated them with benevolence. As more and more immigrants from the South entered Norway, such an assumption could no longer be taken for granted, and adoptees risked being the target for racist remarks. While the vast majority are successfully transubstantiated and kinned into their families and incorporated in their local social environment, their status is more ambiguous when it comes to being Norwegian. Because of their different looks they will always remain non-ethnic Norwegians and, as such, anomalous. This indicates that there are limitations to what kinship may do for a person.

In order for there to exist a meaningful category of 'foreigner' there must necessarily exist a meaningful category of 'native' or 'local'. The meaning and value attributed to each is generated in the interface between the two. The degree to which foreigners are treated as outsiders must be dependent upon the extent and strength of the values attached to being native, and how much the foreigners retain their 'differences'. Difference is mainly manifested through religion, food, clothing and sexual politics. Hence, the construction of 'us' and 'them' has direct consequences for the relationship between those perceived to be on the outside and those who are enclosed within. My argument is that the more Norwegians are able and willing to extend imagined sameness (Gullestad 2002: 45) to the foreign persons, the more likely it is that they may cross the boundary and not be regarded as trespassers. To some extent inclusion and exclusion are dependent upon context. Parliament recently debated whether to perform DNA tests on all non-Europeans who apply to enter Norway on grounds of family reunion. This is in sharp contrast to the rules regarding children adopted from overseas by ethnic Norwegian couples. So even biology becomes an ambiguous criterion for inclusion.

The following incident exemplifies some perceived differences in Norway vis á vis the two categories of recent immigrants, and demonstrates the conceptual links that are made between birth, blood, place and nationality. The increasing interest in genealogies noted earlier is accompanied by an increasing interest in place of origin, which, in turn, leads to a new-found popularity of national costumes (*bunad*) to be worn on special occasions. The *bunad* is largely a product of the mid-nineteenth-century Romanticism which found its inspiration in nature and life in the country-side and, as such, is an example of the invention of tradition. Nevertheless, it has taken root in the imagination of Norwegians and is incorporated into a sense of themselves (Witoszek 1998). As already mentioned, only those who can make a legitimate claim to descend from a particular region may wear the national costume associated with it.

In connection with the celebration of the National Day in Oslo in 1999, these values were challenged.[10] A woman immigrant, born in Pakistan, but with Norwegian citizenship, was one of the very few foreign-born members of the Oslo City Council. She was appointed to head the arrangement committee for the celebration of the National Day. This position involves leading the huge procession of school-children who wind their way through the centre of the city. Waving Norwegian flags, singing national songs accompanied by numerous school bands, the procession reaches its culmination in front of the Royal Palace where the royal family greets its whole Norwegian 'family'. Some thought that it was most unfitting for 'a Pakistani' to lead this procession, and she received anonymous letters trying to dissuade her. The question arose as to what she should wear on the day. Other Norwegians would, as a matter of course, wear a *bunad*. Many adopted children also wear them on this day. In contradistinction to ethnic Norwegians and adoptees, however, the woman councillor could lay no claim to the Norwegian fjords and valleys. She was therefore not entitled to wear a *bunad*; yet if she had chosen to wear some form of South Asian national dress – *a salwar kameez* or *sari* – many would have found this also to be provocative.

By a happy coincidence, the city of Oslo, which hitherto did not have *bunad*, had commissioned one to be designed in connection with the city's one thousand years' jubilee the following year. She was invited to inaugurate this on the occasion of the National Day. This was much less controversial. The Oslo *bunad*, like the Pakistani-born woman politician, is without history in Oslo and Norway. Or rather, together they initiated a historical trajectory. Both the Pakistani politician and the Oslo *bunad* are linked to Oslo the place. However, they are both newcomers in terms of Norwegian identity and do not fit into the larger order of things. Symbolically, the event marks a new fact of Norwegian social life. A previously homogeneous and mainly rural population must give way to a heterogeneous and increasingly urban one. Wearing a *bunad* – the ultimate symbol of belonging to a place, but in this case, one without tradition – she signals the advent of a different future. The event marks a future where immigrants have come to stay and to participate in Norwegian social and cultural life; a population who share place, but not history. What the incident demonstrates is the strong associations made in Norwegian cultural life between place of origin, kin relatedness and identity. Claims to Norwegianness can be put forward only within a discourse that privileges a temporal kin-based connectedness extending back in time and linked to a place. Personhood is achieved through both shared substance and shared essence. Only the idiom of kinship can provide such a connection. The new Oslo *bunad*, however, provides the opportunity, as it were, for accommodating new citizens to both the city of Oslo and the nation state of Norway. Kinship without genealogy is acknowledged through belonging to a place. In an oblique sort of way, the example highlights the problem that is faced by adoptive families.

However, unlike the Pakistani immigrant who could not make any claim to a temporal or spatial link to Norway beyond her own personal history of arrival, adopted children from overseas are 'sponsored' into existing kin-based networks and histories by their adoptive parents, who make use of whatever measures are available to them to transubstantiate their children's subjectivity. One method many use is to dress adopted children in a *bunad*. In contrast to the Pakistani immigrant, it is unlikely that anyone would regard adopted children in *bunad* on the National Day as illegitimate. Being adopted, kinned and transubstantiated, they are from a formal, as well as emotional, point of view equal in every way to biological children. This further highlights the question of sameness and otherness. With regard to adopted children, otherness is negated, and an 'imagined sameness' is achieved which is not similarly achieved with regard to immigrants. In this case, kinship may usefully be thought of as 'a regime of subjectivation' (Faubion 2001). Through the processes of transubstantiation and kinning, adoptive parents negate a separation between the 'social' and the 'biological' encountered elsewhere in society. This enables the children to develop their sense of self and personhood as an integral part of their relatedness to non-biological relatives.

Norwegians are highly reluctant to enter into discussions of race or racism, although race often figures as an implicit understanding specifically with regard to questions concerning discrimination (Howell and

Melhuus forthcoming). Recently, the growth of neo-Nazi organisations has rekindled a racist discourse, and both racist and anti-racist sentiments are heard in the public arena. In 2000, the murder by a neo-Nazi activist of a teen-age boy, whose mother was Norwegian and father African, caused a public outrage. The murder in 1999 of a seventeen-year-old boy adopted from India similarly shocked Norwegian society. Attempts by the small political party 'White Alliance' to place race on the agenda by announcing its intention to 'send back all immigrants and sterilize the transnationally adopted' led to the Party leader being charged and tried under the Racism Act. All these events have alerted adopted families to the potential dangers facing their children. Just because transnationally adopted children in Norway have, by and large, not suffered serious racism, does not mean that they completely escape, nor that they will do so in the future. The case of the killing of the boy adopted from India indicates that all is not well in Norway, and reports of random harassment by police against Norwegian

Figure 6.5 The power of kinship. Norwegian girls of different origins wearing *bunad*.

non-white adoptees (mainly young men) appear from time to time in the media (e.g. *Aftenposten* 4 November, 2003).

That transnational adoption necessarily means that the resulting families are 'mixed race' is not an issue in Norwegian public debate about adoption. This is in sharp contrast to the situation in the UK and USA, where many of those involved in the process express hostility to white parents adopting non-white children. The argument is that mixed-race families provoke confused formation of the adoptees' identity, which, in turn, leads to confused identification with either racial group. In the USA, where there still are many non-white children available for adoption domestically, to place them with white parents has even been described as genocide (Russell 1995: 188). In fact, the American National Association of Black Social Workers reaffirmed, in 1994, its 1972 resolution that 'It is the right of a child to be raised in a permanent, loving home which reflects the same ethnic or racial group' (ibid.). Russell, a black American social worker, is a forceful and influential opponent of mixed race adoption, be it domestic or transnational. She insists that, not only are black and white cultures very different [in USA], but a strong and unequal power relationship exists between them, and she asks, 'How then … can a white family and community raise a Black child to become a Black adult? At best, he can only become a well-fed, well-dressed, well-trained person, but a psychological mongrel – a new spelling of neo-colonialism' (ibid.: 193). Such arguments continue to be ignored in Scandinavia (see also Irhammar 1997), but they are influential in England. From a pragmatic standpoint, it might be suggested that this difference in attitude may be accounted for by the ethnic make-up of the populations. Minority groups in Scandinavia form small and recent enclaves, and children from immigrant communities have, so far, not been made available for adoption. However, I suggest that there are more complex reasons for the differences between the situation of Scandinavia, the UK and the USA which reflect deeper differences in social, economic and cultural life.[11] Thus, the issue of mixed ethnic/racial identity of parents and adopted children, which has become an important debating point in the UK and North America during the past decade, finds no counterpart in Norwegian discussions on adoption.

Sætersdal and Dalen have suggested that adopted people in Norway may be described as 'a new cultural category in Norwegian society' (1999: Chapter 10). They argue that the adoptees have 'double-marginality' – status as adopted and status as having a different racial and ethnic origin from their adoptive parents – which means that they are neither Norwegian nor immigrants (ibid.: 156). This is a somewhat different argument from that of Brottveit (above). His category of 'double-ethnic' is, in my view, less problematic because it is derived from the adoptees' own identifications, and I wish to raise several objections to the proposal of double marginality. Firstly, this concept implies that the adoptees are doubly outside Norwegian society, a fact my material contradicts. Secondly, how to define 'cultural category' is highly problematic. One might be tempted to think that this is an attempt to avoid an even more problematic category, namely that of race. Thirdly, what criteria should be employed, and who is qualified to apply them? Fourthly, the category is externally imposed; my material shows that it is highly unlikely that this is a categorisation that the majority of Norwegian transnational adoptees would confirm. For a social, cultural or ethnic category to exist analytically, it must exist empirically in the sense that it is acknowledged as such by its members and, ideally, but not necessarily, attributed a corresponding status by outsiders. In the case of transnationally adopted people, it would be difficult to find arguments that support any of these criteria. If, minimally, a community must exist in the minds of its members (Cohen 1985: 98) then there is no community of transnationally adopted people in Norway, as evidenced, for example, by the failure to establish interest associations. While the parents are firmly inside the Norwegian community, their transnationally adopted children might be thought to occupy a more ambivalent position. But kinship and relatedness are much more than biology. Having been kinned to their parents by intersubjectively engaging in the creation of their sociality, the vast majority of the transnationally adopted young adults feel comfortable in their social worlds, predicated as these are upon kinned sociality. And, as anthropological theories of ethnicity assert, identity and ethnicity are established relationally and socially, not individually (cf. Barth 1969). Minimally, ethnicity must be understood as a question of boundaries and shared criteria for inclusion and exclusion. In the case of the transnationally adopted persons, they achieve their sense of who they are through processes of kinning and through social interaction outside the home, not through joining with others whose personal history is similar to their own.

To Conclude

Finding a comfortable place in Norwegian society involves more work for adopted children than for their Norwegian-born peers. Being the non-biological children of their parents, they are in the cross-fire, as it were, of various experts, and they have to negotiate a path, at times difficult, towards their own sense of personhood and identity. During this process many have to confront a series of conflicting concepts and categories. Firstly, in a cultural setting in which the dominant metaphors for relatedness are those of shared flesh and blood, questions of biology cannot be ignored. Biological origins have somehow to be squared with their adopted kin status. Secondly, different cultural reference points have to be sorted out. Increasingly, in adoption circles, culture is naturalised as well as reified. The concept of an 'original culture' to which the adoptees somehow are expected to develop a positive attitude, does not find resonance amongst the adoptees themselves. However, the very fluidity between self-imposed and outside-imposed values militates against any one identity being made consistently relevant in all situations. Adoptive parents and adopted children are, no doubt, confronted with paradoxes more frequently than biological families, but this is something most handle with seeming ease and according to the demands of a particular context. It does not, in most cases, seriously impinge upon their understanding of who they are, or the quality of their kinned sociality. Ultimately, I wish to suggest that the 'power of kinship'. the fact of being emotionally and socially (and permanently) related to others – not the handling of an autonomous self – may largely account for how people experience their personhood, be they adopted or not.

Notes

1. He expressed this view when he was the invited speaker at the annual meeting of the association for families who have adopted from China. As a result of his talk, many adoptive parents changed their view about the meaning of roots and the necessity for undertaking return visits.
2. I was approached by his assistant with a view to take part in one programme and to comment on the popularity of such quests. I requested the chance to interview Tore ahead of the programme. After a couple of hours' conversation, we agreed not to include my comments on his programme.
3. Perhaps the story of the Prodigal Son may account for this expectation? It is known by all school hildren brought up in a Christian cultural tradition and exemplifies parental love. Upon the son's return, the father embraces him and orders his servants to 'bring the fatted calf and kill it and let us eat and be merry, for this my son was dead, and is alive again; he was lost, and is found' (Luke 15: 24). I have no evidence that transnationally adopted persons have this story at the back of their minds when they set out on a search, but it might be one contributing factor.
4. True, the first encounter is usually highly emotional. However, subsequent meetings are often anticlimaxes when the parties realise they have very little in common; see the story of the Daughter of Danang below.
5. In 1975, a controversial evacuation programme known as Operation Babylift was instigated whereby large numbers of Vietnamese infants and young children were sent for adoption to American couples.
6. She made her statement as a member of a panel of young adults adopted to Europe from India at a conference on adoption held in Delhi in 2002 (see Chapter 9).
7. Botvar and Brottveit used data collected by Dalen and Sætersdal. Earlier questionnaires were followed up by in-depth interviews with adoptees as young adults, their parents, and, in some cases, their teachers.
8. Parents' and children's situations are radically different. The parents have made an active choice to adopt and appear to need to justify this. The children, on the other hand, have been passively adopted.
9. This further demonstrates the active part played by the agencies in shaping attitudes.
10. Norwegian National Day, 17 May, marks the signing of the Norwegian Constitution in 1814 and the subsequent separation from Denmark. It is a public holiday and commonly referred to as Children's Day. It is a festive occasion when every town and village celebrates with flags, processions of schoolchildren, brass bands, public speeches and parties.
11. They have, inter alia, to do with a history of colonialism, slavery and imported labour – none of which affected Norway, and only marginally Sweden and Denmark.

PART II

Governmentality and the Role of Psycho-technocrats

Chapter 7

BENEVOLENT CONTROL: ADOPTION LEGISLATION IN THE USA AND NORWAY

Because of the profound effects that adoption has on personal, familial and economic relationships, adoption laws and practices are among the most interesting and complex manifestations of government regulation of the lives of private citizens.

J. Hollinger, *Adoption Law and Practice*

The birth of a child is a political event.

W.P. Handwerker, *Births and Power*

The child – as an idea and a target – has become inextricably connected to the aspirations of authorities.

N. Rose, *Governing the Soul: The Shaping of the Private Self*

Bringing Up Non-biological Children as One's Own in the USA and Norway

I turn next to a consideration of some legal provisions that seek to regulate the practice of adoption. Laws, and debates surrounding the formulation and passing of them, often provide an important window through which to view contemporary values concerning the topic under negotiation. This is definitely so in the case of legal provisions drafted to safeguard and promote the well-being of children. Laws reflect current ideas and values at the same time as they seek to modify or change these in a particular direction. What at any time is thought to constitute an improvement also reflects reigning values. Laws are thus descriptive as well as normative. In European jurisprudence, justice and fairness are two major principles that have accompanied the development of democracy. Detailed laws that regulate the private family life of a country's citizens are relatively late arrivals in Europe. In particular, laws that regulate the life of children did not appear until the turn of the twentieth century. From that time onwards, however, childhood has been more and more regulated until, arguably, it has become 'the most intensely governed sector of personal existence' (Rose 1999: 123). As the new category of childhood, perceived as qualitatively different from that of adolescence and adulthood (Ariés 1962, Cunningham 1995), became entrenched in people's thinking, children and childhood emerged as prime targets for state intervention. During the second half of the twentieth century the dictum of 'the best interests of the child' took hold in influential circles in Western Europe and North America, and affected legislation pertaining to all matters affecting children (Caiani-Praturlon 1991: 205). Adoption, a practice that challenges the very foundation of nineteenth- and twentieth-century biocentrism of European kinship and emotionally-based relatedness, seems to represent the ultimate practice for the development of benevolent control by the state authorities.

The law is a prime technology of government. Family forms can be said to be crafted through laws (Sterett 2002: 223) and an examination of changes in adoption legislation brings this point out clearly. According to Foucault, 'governmentality' is a certain mentality that has become the common ground for all forms of modern thought, a way of thinking about the problems that should be addressed by the state and its various authorities (cf. Miller and Rose 1990: 76). In laws, this mentality has the opportunity to represent itself and lay down premises for action. Moreover, the drafting of laws dealing with family and children provides a prime opportunity for the relevant expert professions – the psycho-technocrats – to have their voices heard.

Two levels of governmentality may be observed to exist within the legal domain of adoption: firstly, the national level where each country codifies basic premises for adoption and issues legally binding directives for the practice. Secondly, the global level where legislation on adoption is codified in international treaties or conventions. In the next chapter, I shall argue that a normative project of deliberate globalisation of Western morality and rationality – deriving its legitimacy from the human rights discourses – may be observed in the formulation, codification, execution and monitoring of relevant multilateral conventions. Given that these conventions are between contracting states, I shall argue that governmentality in this case may be expressed as state-sponsored globalisation. Today, most countries have some kind of adoption laws, whether these refer only to domestic adoption or are extended to cover transnational adoption as well. In this chapter I shall look at some pertinent aspects of adoption legislation in Norway and North America.

I shall seek to demonstrate how the changing ideology concerning children and parents has affected national legislation in the two countries.[1] What must be borne in mind when interpreting the various laws, regulations and conventions of children in general, and adoption in particular, is that they reflect changes that have occurred in ideas and values amongst

Western educated classes. A kind of triangular dynamic has been brought about between the aspirations of the middle class, those of the various experts who provide the premises for action, and of politicians in their roles as law-makers. While the ideological principles underpinning the laws are in line with a liberal and idealistic approach toward governing society in order to achieve the best interest of its subjects (cf. Miller and Rose 1992), they are also normative and universalising. They emerge as not only good, but somehow true.

The characterisation of man as an autonomous individual being finds a clear expression in contemporary family law – both in the USA and Norway. Indeed, Nussbaum has suggested that in order to be normative it is necessary to maintain the centrality of the individual (2000). It is the 'best interest of the child' that is placed in focus in legislation, denuding him or her of any constitutive significance of sociality. From such a perspective, kinship – and kinning – is not perceived as part and parcel of being human, but rather as epiphenomenal. Ultimately, the individual remains the bearer of his or her fate. Rights are grounded in the individual. Current influential pedagogic thinking advocates that the individual child has to be empowered to exercise his or her agency. Such a philosophy has wide-reaching consequences when it is introduced to parts of the world whose ontology and epistemology are predicated upon very different understandings.

There are two reasons why I have chosen to focus upon the USA and Norway in my study of the legal situation regarding adoption. Firstly, the two nation states arguably represent two extreme poles of political and social ideology and organisation in the modern Western world. The USA adheres to a liberal market ideology that gives great freedom to the individual to organise his or her private life; and American citizens, by and large, resent much interference from the state. Norway, by contrast, has developed a welfare state based on an ideology of 'imagined sameness' and equality (Gullestad 2002: 45) in which the state, with the approval of its citizens, has increasingly taken charge of people's private lives. While Americans are suspicious of state authority and tend to distrust it, describing its activities in the social and private domains as 'interference', Norwegians feel comfortable with the way the state increasingly controls their lives, trusting it to look after their best interest on the basis of equity. According to Vike, 'The modernization of Norway, more so than most other western counties, has nourished a shared sense of politics as a collective activity and as the privileged tool for the realization of humanistic goals' (2002: 57). From the 1930s onwards, psycho-medical technocrats have provided the premises for political debate, and contributed importantly to the drafting of social, medical and family legislation. These factors provide an interesting contrast, and I shall try to elucidate some consequences of the differences when we examine the legal-administrative system that has grown up in each country with regard to adoption. My overall argument will be that we may discern a high degree of governmentality in Norway and a low one in the USA. A further reason for focusing on the USA is that it has been an important disseminator of psychological expert knowledge, and a major contributor to the psychology of adoption.

Most commentators on the history of children and families in Europe and the USA agree that before and during the Middle Ages it was common practice for children to be brought up by relatives or strangers 'as if they were one's own' (Cunningham 1995, Gillis 1996). Depending to some extent on regional differences, the practice continued until the end of the nineteenth century. As already discussed, the abandonment and wet-nursing of children was not uncommon in Europe, and did not give rise to moral condemnation until the late nineteenth century. It was, however, an informal practice, one that was not regulated in the legal framework. Mostly, the practice of fostering and adoption was carried out for the benefit of the adults concerned. For reasons of poverty or illness, many biological parents were unable to support yet another child and looked to others to do so. Couples who either could not have children of their own, or who needed more labour on the farm or in the business, looked for children to resolve the situation. Whereas affectionate relationships might develop between the children and the adults in question, this depended on circumstances and was not the reason for entering into such an arrangement. With the emergence of a new social value (endorsed by religion) placed upon the nuclear family, with the new image of the child as vulnerable and innocent and in need of long-term protection and guidance, coupled with a rapid growth of industrialisation which led to child labour in the factories – often under extremely tough conditions – a new concern about the fate of children began to emerge in the industrialising countries.

As the nineteenth century progressed, the child – as an idea and a target for control -became inextricably connected to the aspirations of the authorities. By the end of the century, legislation regulating child labour and welfare began to be passed, and adoption laws appeared in most European countries during the first decades of the twentieth century. Laws that regulated adoption usually came in the wake of more general legal provisions that regulated the living conditions of children. This was not the case in the USA, but here adoption was brought into the legal system much earlier. I therefore start by considering adoption legislation in America.

Adoption Laws and Practices in the USA

Domestic Adoption

The legal situation of adoption in the USA developed somewhat differently from that in Europe – not least because adoption laws appeared earlier. But the political, social and cultural situation in the United States was also, historically, very different from that of European countries, and this had an effect upon attitudes and practices with regard to abandoned – uncared for – children. The nineteenth and first half of the twentieth centuries was a time of rapid expansion in North America, demographically as well as industrially and economically, and European immigrants settled throughout the vast country as the native population was decimated. The American legal system is not homogenous throughout the nation. Whereas the Constitution from 1789 forms the backbone of the US legal system,[2] individual states maintain a high degree of autonomy. Following the Ninth and Tenth Amendments to the US Constitution, state governments are considered the proper domain for the enactment of family, property and succession laws. This is the reason why we may observe major differences in various states' laws regarding marriage, divorce, death sentence, abortion – and adoption (Hollinger 1992: 1–4).

Today, each state has enacted its own adoption law. Despite some common themes and some identical provisions, these laws are not (and have never been) uniform, nor are judicial interpretations of them consistent from one jurisdiction to another (ibid.: 1–145). Attempts to bring the practice of adoption under one federal law have been unsuccessful, and this is unlikely to be achieved in the near future. In the USA, a cultural adherence to the overarching right of the individual person and family to sort out its own affairs remains firm.[3] Nevertheless, as state regulations of family and individual relationships have become more pervasive in the USA, adoption has increasingly become an activity that requires judicial supervision in line with principles of child welfare. This in turn has led to an intensified conflict between 'traditions of family privacy and autonomy and government commitment to promoting children's welfare' (ibid.: 1–51). In other words, the active involvement of the state in the private sphere seems to meet more resistance in the USA than it has done in Norway and other European countries. But the very heterogeneity of the American legal situation makes it difficult to make generalizations about the theme.

Adoption law must ensure that the three parties involved – the biological parents, the adoptive parents and the adoptee – each receives fair treatment. However, there has been a noticeable shift in the adoption laws of both the USA and European countries during the past century, from aiming to satisfy the needs of adoptive parents, to favouring the needs of the adoptee (Caiani-Praturlon 1991: 206, Melosh 2002: 52–53).[4] Recently, as manifested in demands for open adoption, the needs of biological parents are receiving more attention. In what follows I shall draw attention to those aspects of US adoption laws that I regard as particularly pertinent in highlighting the significance that is attributed to biological connectedness, and the involvement of the state in the process of adoption.

In his famous study of American kinship, Schneider argues that 'the cultural universe of relatives in American kinship is constructed of elements from two major cultural orders, the *order of nature* and the *order of law*' (1968: 27, original emphasis). Whereas relatives in nature share heredity (biogenetic substance), those in law are bound only by law and custom. He further suggests that biological kinship symbolised by the metaphor of blood is perceived as superior, and that the Cinderella story demonstrates this. The stepmother is related by law, but not by nature and is therefore 'able to cruelly exploit the child' (ibid.). Modell is faithful to this analysis. She argues that a reason for the chaotic and contradictory nature of the adoption laws of the various states 'stems from a cultural resistance to the idea that blood can be severed and replaced by contract' (1984: 20), and that, '[t]he thrust of adoption law and adoption policy is to pretend that blood is there; a fictive kinship is just like a biological relationship'. Moreover, there is a general notion that 'artificial kinship disrupts the true course of nature' (ibid.). While on first reading I was convinced by this argument, I now wish to suggest that this interpretation may reflect more recent attitudes to the nature of kinship and relatedness rather than a historical tradition.

As discussed in Chapter 3, pre-nineteenth-century Americans did not set much ontological or moral store by the flesh and blood metaphor, any more than they did on the home as the bastion of the biological family. According to Gillis, '[p]rior to the nineteenth century, whose child you were depended more on circumstances than on biology' (1996: 39). Carp makes a similar point when he compares English and American attitudes towards the practice of adoption. English common law did not recognise adoption, and the legal opposition to the practice stems, he argues, from 'a desire to protect the property rights of blood relatives ... a moral dislike of illegitimacy, and the availability of other quasi-adoptive devices such as apprenticeship and voluntary transfers' (Carp 2002: 3). By contrast, American colonists were less preoccupied with the primacy of biological connectedness within family groups, which often meant that they practised 'adoption on a limited scale' from the beginning of the migrations, and that 'the fluid boundaries between consanguine and non-consanguine families in colonial America led in some cases to informal adoption of children, particularly in Puritan Massachusetts and Dutch New York)' (ibid.). If we return to the three motivations to adopt identified by Goody (see Chapter 3), namely:

- to provide homes for orphans, bastards, foundlings and children of impaired families;
- to provide childless couples with social progeny;
- to provide an individual or couple with an heir to their property;

then the motivations in the USA can be said to be a mixture of all three. I suggest that a fourth reason may be added, namely a felt need to provide an individual or couple with the means to improve their economic prosperity. I have in mind here the rapidly growing need for labour in nineteenth century America which found one answer in child labour and in the adoption of children in order to use them as cheap labour – whether on farms or in industry.

A large new class of urban poor, made up primarily of the massive influx of immigrants, led to many parents being unable to support their children. This in turn led to flocks of abandoned children on the streets in the rapidly growing towns of North America. Informal transfers of children to substitute parents meant that many children were 'adopted' by owners of sweatshops and could be seen to lead hard lives. What has been called 'instrumental adoption' dominated nineteenth century child exchange. The main purpose of the transaction was the child's labour, and older children were preferred to infants (Melosh 2002: 12). From the mid-1850s to the early 1910s, the Children's Aid Society of New York collected abandoned children found on the streets of the city and transported them to the 'supposedly more salubrious environs of Midwestern farms' (ibid.: 13). These 'orphan trains' had fallen into disrepute by the First World War when new and progressive thinking on childhood was beginning to take hold. However, the old sentiments persisted in parts of the country, as evidenced by a letter written in 1918 by the mayor of Bagalusa, Louisiana, to the above-mentioned society. He requested 'some white babies ... a carload ... by a carload, mean about thirty to fifty. We do not care to know anything about their antecedents of parentage. All we want to know is that they are healthy ....' (quoted in Melosh 2003: 12). The mayor further stipulated that he wanted about half and half of Catholic and Protestant children, indicating, according to Melosh, a continuation of the practice of apprenticeship which involved a kind of religious nurture or supervision.

These factors may account for the fact that adoption legislation came relatively early in the USA compared to Europe. The first adoption law was passed in Massachusetts in 1851. According to Hollinger, this law did not 'create' adoption, but 'legitimised the numerous informal transfers of parental rights which had been taking place for a variety of reasons since colonial times' (Hollinger 1992: 1–20). For an adoption to become legal, this law required an agreement approved by a judge, the written consent of the child's biological parents, its unwed mother, or a legal guardian, and that the adopters should demonstrate that they are 'of sufficient ability to bring up the child ... and that it is fit and proper that such an adoption should take effect' (ibid.: 1–23). From then on, all rights and responsibilities were transferred from biological relatives to adoptive parents. Other US states rapidly followed suit. By 1929 all existing states had a law of adoption. Some ambiguities remained, however, especially concerning the status of the biological tie from the point of view of inheritance. In fact, questions pertaining to the transfer of property were an important reason for instigating adoption laws in the first place. Whether an adoptee should have the right to inherit from his or her adoptive parents' blood relations remained unclear in some states until recently (Hollinger 1992: 1–29). Most early adoptions were entered into as a result of economic considerations. Because of this, the cases were heard in probate courts, not, as might be expected, in family courts. This is still the case in several states, including New York state.

The new adoption laws both enhanced the parent–child relationship and subjected this relationship to the scrutiny of the state. A distinctive feature of America's first adoption law was a stated requirement to serve the best interests of the child. But, according to Hollinger, little was done to 'breathe life into this requirement' until well into the twentieth century. In so far as any concern with the child's well-being was made explicit it was phrased more in economic rather than in psychological terms (ibid.: 1–34). Unlike the situation in several European countries (Scandinavia as well as France) where legislation to promote and safe-guard children's welfare preceded legislation on adoption, this was not the case in the USA. Thought-provokingly, in both England and the USA, laws regulating the treatment of children were introduced in the wake of legal regulations concerning the treatment of animals. Not until 1889 did cruelty to children become a criminal offence in England. This was almost sixty years after cruelty to animals had been outlawed (Franklin 2002: 6).

'By the end of the nineteenth century, farmers in Kansas and business men in Boston were adopting children' (Modell 1994: 23). Moreover, they were no longer predominantly adopting blood relatives (as had tended to be the case), but complete strangers. Adoption laws enabled the state to take upon itself the right to break the moral and exclusive force of blood ties, by allowing non-biologically related children to enter into an as-if kinned relationship with as-if parents. At the same time, the state gave itself powers to negate existing blood-ties whenever it deemed these to be faulty. Modell argues that a general principle came to underpin the organisation of domestic American adoption, namely the responsibility of the state to supervise 'the moving of a child from one kind of family ('unfit') to another ('fit'), and from one kind of home ('unstable') to another ('stable')' (Modell 1994: 28–29, 41–42)[5]. Thus, in 1938, the state of Pennsylvania, invoking an act from 1887, removed a child from her father's house (Modell 1994: 27). In the words of the presiding judge, the rights of parental control are natural, but not inalienable. The state has a right to intervene if the parents are 'corrupt or incompetent' (ibid.). However, opinions varied, and continue to vary, as to the rights and responsibilities of parents as well as those of the state in family matters.

With the adoption laws, the state implemented an ideology of civic responsibility for children. Although the spirit of adoption was to ensure permanent relationships, several state provisions were in fact unclear about the duration of the relationship. For example, in New York, adoptions could be 'abrogated' for abuse of a child, or, more sinisterly from the adoptees' point of view, if the child committed 'any misdemeanour or ill behaviour'[6]. This provision was not abolished until 1974 (Hollinger 1992: 1–39).

While statutory penalties for advertising available babies and children (in effect for sale) did not appear until the 1940s and 1950s (ibid.: 1–49), this – as noted earlier – has not prevented the buying and selling of sperm and egg from being legal in the present day. Many Americans demand the right to choose their adopted child. A documentary broadcast in 2000 on Norwegian television showed how the state authorities in one state seek to find adoptive families for a group of children deemed unadoptable due to age, colour, intelligence or handicaps. They organise an annual 'fair' to which prospective parents are invited to inspect the children on offer. Couples are allowed to take them home for a trial period. Few of those interviewed expressed any ethical scruples about the practice. The children presented a picture of what may best be described as 'dejectedly hopeful' as they were scrutinised for possible virtues and faults. Such a practice would surely not be allowed in a Western European country.

Although many adoptions have been effected via state-endorsed agencies staffed by professional social workers, adoptions outside such agencies equalled or outnumbered agency placements throughout the twentieth century, except for a few years during the post-war period. As infertile couples began to adopt in order to fulfil emotional needs and to enable them to create families, they were interested in keeping the transaction a secret. Moreover, they disliked social workers' inspection of them and their homes. Similarly, unwed mothers wished to conduct the birth and adoption as circumspectly as possible in order to avoid the social stigma attached to illegitimacy. It was therefore in the interest of both parties to keep a low profile. However, in 1951 the state of Delaware required agency involvement in adoption (Melosh 2003: 40). Not all states followed suit. Today many domestic as well as transnational adoptions are conducted privately. The finalisation of an adoption must, however, go through the courts, although until very recently the records were kept sealed.

Open Adoption

Secrecy about the adoptive relationship was not thought important in the early days of adoption and there was no restriction on access to court records. Original birth certificates, if they existed, were available to the adoptees – and to anyone else who might be interested.[7] But as prospective adoptive parents began to desire infants rather than older children, and to do so out of an emotional desire to have a child, they also began to desire a complete rupture with the biological parents and the child's origins, and insisted upon withholding their identity from them. Once an adoption was finalised, the transaction left no visible public traces (Modell 2002: 3). Adoption records were sealed off and access denied. This was in line with the notion that the adoptive relationship should replace the previous biological relationship; in my terms that kinning could, and ought to, occur. Adopted children were 'as if begotten' (ibid.). While secrecy about the adoptive relationship was prevalent during the1940s, 1950s and 1960s, as soon as transnational and transracial adoption got under way, and children were adopted who could not be passed off as biological children due to their different appearance, secrecy generally became less imperative. At the same time, as discussed in Chapter 3, an adoption rights movement emerged in the1970s, indicating, I suggest, a lack of conviction about kinning of non-biological relationships. Partly influenced by writers like Lifton – who argued that adoptees were somehow lacking an important part of their identity and that they all desired to be reunited with their biological mother – many adoptees gathered in support groups that soon turned into activist groups. They demanded the right to know the identity of their biological parents (primarily mothers). At the same time, some vocal birth mothers demanded the right to be reunited with their estranged children. Following a referendum, the campaign for open records resulted in Oregon becoming in 2000 the first state to give unlimited access to once-sealed records (Melosh 2003: 275).[8] Open adoption is becoming the preferred practice in the USA. Thus one of the seven principal attributes of American adoption identified by Hollinger (1992:1–8/17), namely confidentiality, is abandoned.

Transnational Adoption in the USA

Domestic adoption in the USA reached a peak in 1970 (Melosh 2003: 4). Due to a number of factors, such as the general availability of contraception and abortion and the decline in the social stigma attached to single mothers, healthy white infants began to be in short supply here as in Europe.[9] This led many in need of a child to look overseas to fulfil their desire, and transnational adoption grew rapidly. Bartholet argues that the laws of the United States and most foreign countries 'operate[s] significantly to impede or prevent international adoption' (1992: 10–36). Despite the large number of prospective adoptive parents, and the large number of prospective adoptees in the Third World, the legal barriers erected by law to such adoptions are so formidable, she says, as to allow only a small trickle of transnational adoptions actually to take place (ibid.). Certainly, there are many more abandoned or orphaned children in Asia, Africa and Latin America than are made available for adoption; but the reasons for this are more complex than just a matter of law (see Chapter 9).

American legal provisions for transnational adoption are, just as those for domestic adoption, embedded at the state level and, as a result, requirements vary considerably (see Bartholet 1992 for an overview of the social and legal situation in USA). Transnational adoption anywhere is legally complex, largely because it is subject to the laws of at least two different jurisdictions: those of the donor and recipient countries. But in the USA a third jurisdiction is involved, namely that of the individual state. Each jurisdiction has its own set of requirements and they may be contradictory. Thus, for example, the state of California allows homosexual adoption, but many other states do not. Some states may consider single individuals as adoptive parents whereas others insist on heterosexual married couples only. Furthermore, the upper age limit for applicants will often vary. At the same time, different donor countries operate different criteria with regard to marital status and age. No country so far is prepared knowingly to give a child to a homosexual couple. Thus a prospective adoptive person, or couple, needs to choose a country most amenable to their particular personal situation. They may also have to change place of residence within the USA in order to relocate to a state that allows adoption by people like themselves. Moreover, immigration laws may prevent children from some countries from entering because they do not meet the restrictive definition of 'orphan', and some countries whose laws fulfil American requirements do not release children for overseas adoption (Bartholet 1992: 10–36).

In terms of sheer numbers adopted from abroad, the USA by far outstrips all other adopting countries.[10] Many agencies are small and have little experience with cultural practices and legal systems outside the USA. This can lead to complications in inter-country relations. Whereas federal law regulates immigration and naturalisation of children adopted from overseas, the remainder of the transnational adoption process is governed by state law (Bartholet 1992: 46). Just as American-born children may be handed over in adoption directly by one or both of their biological parents, who may or may not be assisted by a third party or a state-licensed public or private agency, so children born overseas may be adopted by direct contact with biological parents. This is known as private adoption and is not allowed according to the Hague Convention. Adoptive parents may work through an intermediary, through an American adoption agency which has agreements with agents in donor countries, or through a public or private adoption agency in the country of origin (Hollinger 1992: 1–64). American prospective parents of a child adopted from overseas must, in most states, undergo a home study that assesses their suitability as adoptive parents. But, unlike the requirements in Norway and elsewhere in Europe, in the USA this is often organised by a private adoption agency, and the couple have to pay a substantial fee for the service (Bartholet 1992: 10). Under the circumstances, it is, critics claim, difficult to remain objective.

A large number of private adoption agencies operate in the USA. They may be non-profit making, some are religious foundations, but many are straightforward businesses. Most charge substantial fees for their services.

As demonstrated by the commercial transactions in connection with donor eggs, it appears that there is less concern about ethical implications in the USA than in Europe. It appears that more American individuals and agencies have been involved in scandals in various donor countries than have European ones. This has given rise to accusations of 'child purchasing' and to bribery. Local institutions and lawyers in some donor countries are particularly prone to being bribed. Since the USA has no overall federal agency to oversee the practice of transnational adoption, and the country has not ratified the UNCRC or the Hague Convention, it is difficult to control what actually takes place in the different agencies and countries.[11]

The notion of the benevolent state ensuring the best interests of its citizens has met with, and continues to meet with, profound suspicion in America. Rather, to many Americans, a benevolent state is a state that leaves them alone to decide for themselves. This is in sharp contrast to attitudes in Western Europe. It is from these perspectives that I now turn to a consideration of Norwegian adoption laws, thinking and practices.

Adoption Laws and Practices in Norway

A major difference between legislation on adoption in the USA and in Norway is that the latter has one legislative system that is applicable to the whole country and one centralised state authority that supervises all transactions of transnational adoption, and issues all approvals according to identical criteria which are encoded in law. A second major, but related, difference between Norwegian and American society more generally is that Norway is a prime example of the welfare state. In the present context, the main implication of this fact is that the Norwegian state has been playing an increasingly active role in organising more and more aspects of people's lives. For example, since the Second World War, both education and health services have been the exclusive responsibility of the state.[12] The Norwegian political system is a prime example of a state whose purpose is not just to ensure law and order and supply basic infrastructure, but to actively ensure the general well-being of its citizens. Moreover, what at any time constitutes well-being is decided by the state through legislative measures. Policies are based on advice sought, and given, by various experts drawn from the relevant professional bodies. Thus, Norwegian governmental and state order may be said to be built on an attitude that incorporates the idealistic principles of governmentality as outlined in this book. Norwegians are more willing to be regulated than are Americans, and they reject the legitimacy of the free market in matters of personal and family relations. This means that the bureaucracy established in Norway to ensure that the letter of the law is followed is organised according to identical principles and procedures throughout the nation. It also means that Norway has ratified both the UNCRC and the Hague Convention.

These factors do not, however, mean that the various actions initiated by the Norwegian state are uncontroversial. This is far from the case. Norwegian society is also highly individualistic.[13] Diversity of opinion is noticeable in debates about policy for adoption and new reproductive technology. A number of ambiguities concerning the relationship between adopted children, adoptive parents and biological parents are observable in Norwegian thinking and cultural practices. Some of these ambiguities are clearly evident in White Papers on adoption preceding legislation, in Parliamentary debates and in the actual adoption laws. A historical examination of adoption laws therefore provides a good means by which to observe changes in Norwegian understandings, values and priorities about kinship, family, parenthood and children.

The 1917 Adoption Act

The first Norwegian adoption act, entitled To forge a link (*At knytte et baand*) was passed in 1917; fifty-nine years after the first American law on adoption. It was nine years ahead of the first English legislation on adoption and amongst the first in Europe. Private bills about adoption had, however, been submitted to Parliament as early as 1883 and 1886, demonstrating a felt need to regulate the relationship between foster parents and foster children; but nothing had come of this. The background to the Adoption Act of 1917 was the inter-Scandinavian committee on family law that worked between 1910 and 1912 on common issues pertaining to marriage, divorce and adoption. On the basis of this, Norway and Sweden both obtained their adoption laws in 1917, and Denmark got one in 1923. As part of their work, the committee gathered information on legal provisions pertaining to adoption from several other European countries. Common to all of these was that the adopted child obtained the surname of its adoptive father and rights of inheritance from him. Ties with the biological family were severed following adoption. However, apart from Italy and France, all countries allowed the adoptive parents to negate the relationship (Ingvaldsen 1996: 11–12).

The main purpose of the 1917 Act was to meet a need arising out of involuntary childlessness of well-situated couples, which was stated as 'a desire to see their name and family continue'. Thus, the practice may be regarded as a response to Goody's second and third points, namely to provide a childless couple with social progeny and an heir to their property. At the same time, it was also understood, but not much elaborated, that adoption should benefit the child as well. Paragraph 8, for example, states that '[permission to adopt] must not be given unless there is good reason to assume that it will serve the interest of the child'. Relevant children at the time were mainly illegitimate children whose prospects otherwise, especially in the rapidly growing urban areas, were pretty grim (Ingvald-sen 1996: 10). Most commentators agree that the 1917 Act catered primarily for the needs of the adoptive parents and their biological kin. Having said that, there were some ambiguities as to who the Act was really intended to protect – the child or the parents.

The 1917 Act and the ensuing amendments, as well as the new Adoption Act of 1986, all came in the wake of acts regulating the state's responsibilities towards children. The 1917 Act came in the aftermath of more than two decades of codifications of a series of laws that sought to protect the weak groups in Norwegian society. A concern for the plight of illegitimate children resulted in a series of Children Acts at the beginning of the twentieth century – the so-called Casberg Children Acts, named after the politician responsible for formulating them. These acts became a model for subsequent acts in other European countries and were acclaimed for their liberal attitudes. Of the six separate acts that made up the Children Act, four were concerned with children born outside wedlock. Mothers were made legally bound to name the father of their child who then was held responsible for economic support. But given the extreme difficulties encountered in extracting economic support from men identified as fathers, many mothers were more or less forced to give up the child for adoption. Much of the debate surrounding these laws was concerned with the right of an illegitimate child to bear the father's name and to inherit from him. The opponents feared that the name- and inheritance rights would undermine marriage and family life. Others objected to the public interference into private life that this law was seen to represent. One commentator stated in 1915: 'When the state decides about the most intimate aspects of the most intimate relations, then soon our home will not longer be our own but the state's' (Ingvaldsen 1996: 10). This view is similar to views expressed in the USA today; but whereas the notion that the private sphere should remain outside public control has persisted in the States, in Norway that view was soon abandoned.

The parliamentary debates surrounding the first Adoption Act centred around legal aspects concerning the adoptee's surname and about inheritance rights. Until the 1979 amendment of the Naming Act of 1964, surnames in Norway followed the agnatic principle whereby a legally married wife and the children of the marriage automatically took the husband's and father's surname.[14] Surnames, of course, are *par excellence* about relatedness and relational identity. Particular names denote not just the parent–child relationship, but also the wider kin both lineally and laterally. The public naming of a newborn child is perhaps the most graphic step in the kinning process. As was discussed in Chapter 4, the place of origin, often linked to a family farm (in Norwegian called 'kin farm' (*slekts-gård*) plays an important part in the constitution of personal identity. A surname is frequently the name of the kin farm. To share in a surname –

also known as 'kin name'(*slektsnavn*) was – and still is – part of a person's identity and a part of a kinned group's identity. The kin name denotes belonging, with all the moral connotations that this involves.[15] The question of the adopted child's name was, not surprisingly, problematic. The 1917 law clearly reflects a strong belief in the importance of a biological basis for kin ties that are reckoned in the agnatic line. By conferring his surname on a child, a man's paternal status is confirmed. Indeed, the right granted to adoptees to revert to the surname of their biological father, reflects this. In practice most adoptees took their adoptive father's surname, but the right to revert was considered sufficiently important for it to be safeguarded.

An implicit understanding about the meaning of kinship upholds the biological connection as primary (Ingvaldsen 1996: 17). Thus, adopted children did not cut their legal links with their biological parents. They kept all rights to equal inheritance from them.[16] By extension, the biological parents had rights of inheritance from the child that they had given up for adoption, and some right towards financial support. By the same token, the law gave priority to biological children if there were any, and adopted children could only inherit a small portion of their adoptive parents' property. To equate an adopted child with a biological one was not even debated in the preamble to the 1917 Act. But the responsibility for the adoptee's upkeep was passed to its adoptive parents. At the same time, the adoptive parents did not have rights of inheritance or rights to maintenance from their adopted child. Property was to be kept within the blood line. Blood was clearly perceived as thicker than water in the eyes of the law. In 1923 a minor amendment to the 1917 Adoption Law was passed that removed an adoptee's automatic right to revert to his or her original name, making the break with biological relatives complete. If the adoptee desired to use that name, he or she had to apply for permission.

However, a reluctance to accept that an adopted person could be truly kinned into his or her adoptive kin network is demonstrated by the fact that adopted children were placed in a legal relationship with their adoptive parents only, not with their parents' kin. Moreover, a special right, *Odelsrett*, which gives a male in direct line the right to inherit or reappropriate the family farm in cases when it has gone out of the family, was not extended to adoptees until 1974.[17] The right to *odel* was a descent, not a family, right. This is made abundantly clear in a letter from 1950 from an adoptive mother living on her husband's *odel* farm to a committee deliberating revisions to the 1917 Adoption Act. She writes, 'I can well see that my husband's siblings like the boy [her adopted son] and admire him because he is clever, but this does not prevent them from regarding him as a stranger – almost like a cuckoo that has ended up in a nest where he does not belong – and they can't wait for an opportunity to drive him away from the home that he, of course, regards as his' (cited in Ingvaldsen 1996: 62). At the time, many argued against changes in *odel*, basing their arguments on the pre-emptive rights of (biogenetic) kin, and the committee did not find sufficient reason to change the law. The Norwegian law of *odel* was not changed until 1974, when both biological daughters and adoptees could claim the right. The Adoption Act of 1986 reconfirms this, and biological bonds were no longer regarded as preeminent for kinned relatedness.

Amendments in 1935, 1948 and 1956

Amendments to the original act of 1917 were passed in 1935, 1948 and 1956, but it was not until 1986 that a complete revision of the act was undertaken and a new adoption act came into being. That act was subject to some amendments in 1999. The different weighting given the perceived needs and rights of the three parties involved in an adoption – the biological and adoptive parents and the adopted child – have changed throughout this period, but it is fair to say that an overriding concern with biological connectedness has framed, in some way or another, the debates and the formulations of the legal provisions.

The preoccupation with the rights of parents is manifest in the amendment of 1935 when two kinds of adoption were made legal: the so-called 'weak' adoption whereby the adoptive parents might revoke the relationship if the child was unsatisfactory, and 'strong' adoption whereby revocation was made impossible and all legal ties with the biological family were severed. This decision must be viewed in relation to debates about eugenics and 'racial hygiene' that were prevalent in Norway during the first half of the twentieth century. There was a strong concern with containing bad genes and encouraging good ones. Poverty was to some extent linked to an idea of bad genes (Roll-Hansen and Broberg 1996). Many were on the look-out for the manifestation of bad genes in an adopted child, and the weak version of the adoption law was meant to provide a let-out for adoptive parents should this become necessary.[18] A revised adoption law was passed in 1944 which enabled the revocation of an adoption if it was discovered that the child was chronically ill or handicapped (Ingvaldsen 1996: 20). In line with an ongoing Scandinavian co-operation on family law, this was confirmed in 1948 (O. tid. 1948: 408–9). Such 'deficiencies' had to date back to prior to the time of adoption, and submission to revoke had to be made within five years of the adoption itself. This provision was not abolished until the Adoption Act of 1986. At the same time, the 1948 amendment opened the way for adoption even if a couple had biological children, but were deemed good parents. Moreover, the duty to support biological parents was repealed. This amendment reflected both a backward glance (the best interest of the parents) and a forward one (the best interest of the child). The next amendment came in 1956 when strong adoption became the only type allowed – a practice that by this time had become the norm.

No versions of the Norwegian adoption law specified, or encouraged, secrecy about the adoptive relationship. In the period preceding and following the 1917 Adoption Act there was full acknowledgement of the non-biological status of the relationship. However, by the 1950s it had become common practice to pretend that the adopted child was one's own biological child. This was a time characterised by an explanatory shift from the determining significance of biology (nature) to environmental factors (nurture). It was also a time when the family and family life were idealised and the model of women as mothers, housewives and homemakers became dominant. Motherhood was the manifestation of one's success as a woman. Indeed, psychological literature of the 1950s explained childlessness in women as the result of psychological abnormality (Leira 1996: 133), thus putting enormous pressure on the women concerned. Many who failed to produce a child tried in secret to find a child to adopt.[19] Adoption thus became a shameful activity, and the fact of adoption was a well-kept secret even from the adoptees themselves. With transnational adoption such pretence was not possible; the children very clearly did not look like their parents. Openness about childlessness and adoption resulted, and the stigma that had attached to this was largely removed and adoption came out of the closet, as it were. During the postwar period the social and environmental aspects of adoption became emphasised. The term 'social parents' was introduced for the first time in the 1956 amendments, marking an acceptance of the overriding significance of environmental factors in bringing up children. At this time the state took upon itself a more active role in family politics and childcare. To find suitable parents for unwanted children became a public responsibility.

The 1986 Adoption Act

The first major reconsideration of the 1917 Adoption Act resulted in a new Act of 1986, following the Children's Act of 1981. The reason for a new law was the decline in infants available for domestic adoption and the near explosive growth of transnational adoption that was taking place in Norway during the 1970s and 1980s. The authorities saw it as urgent to bring transnational adoption under ordered and regulated control. Curiously, despite the concern about transnational adoption, the practice receives little explicit attention in the final Act.

The 1986 Adoption Act is interesting from many different perspectives. A reading between the lines reveals (yet again) a tension between biological and sociological thinking. This is a tension which, I suggest, reflected the thinking of the bureaucrats and others who worked with transnational adoption. The ambiguity is clearly reflected in the 1986 Act. Both biology and sociality (nature and nurture) receive attention in different sections of the text to the exclusion of each other. For example, legally speaking, adopted children are from now on to be regarded as in every way equal to biological children. The assumption is that adoptive parents will love and treat their adopted children as if they were their biological children. At the same time, the postwar practice of anonymity regarding biological origins of adoptees which had led to a virtual taboo on the topic, was replaced by a stipulation that gave the right of adopted children to be told (should they so wish) the identity of their original parents upon reaching the age of legal maturity. In other words, adoptees both are and are not equivalent to biological children. This provision indicates a new emphasis being attributed to the relationship between biological relatives. However, at the same time, a change in the terminology used indicates a change in thinking – from an exclusive biological set of values to a more sociological one. The words 'own children' (*egne barn*) and 'real parents' (*virkelige foreldre*) used in earlier laws, were substituted with 'born children' (*egenfødte barn*) and 'original parents' (*opprinnelige foreldre*). Henceforth, no differentiation was to be made between born and adopted children.

Despite the fact that by 1980 transnational adoption had become the most common form of adoption in Norway, and that this fact provoked a new law, it does not feature much in the actual White Paper, the hearings to the bill, nor in the final text itself. Indeed, the most debated point, which concerned the right to know about biological origins, hardly applies in the case of transnational adoption; actual information about a child released for adoption to another country follows the stipulated by-laws of the country of origin. Frequently, biological parents are not known and, in many countries, even if the identity is known, the orphanage is not at liberty to divulge the information. The new Norwegian provisions thus have little practical relevance. This situation has not deterred the relevant parties from heatedly debating whether it was important for a person to know his or her biological origin in order to become a harmonious being. The debate is revealing about the contemporary climate of opinion.

The political parties differed as to the importance they attributed to knowing one's origins. The Labour Party was most adamant in positing a human need to know one's roots in order to develop a sense of belonging. They argued that, in the rapidly changing present-day society, there is a particularly strong need for people to have knowledge of their biological and genetic make-up. While the Labour Party focused on adoption, the Christian Democrats and other parties chose to widen the discussion and drew parallels between adoption and the rapid growth in assisted fertilisation. Interestingly, the Biotechnology Act of 1994 specified the anonymity of sperm donors. This was revoked in the revised Biotechnology Act of 2003.

In arguing their case for openness about biological origins, several politicians drew a parallel to the situation of adopted children, and claimed that many had their lives ruined by not knowing 'who they are'. They stated that it was wrong to 'build one's life on a lie' and that not knowing the identity of the sperm donor who had given them life would mean this.[20] The conceptual joining of adoption and assisted conception is further made explicit in the 2003 law, where when it is made obligatory to inform those who apply for assisted conception treatment about the option of adoption.

Adoption legislation, like all legislation dealing with family and children, is controversial and subject to much debate. Despite signs of some degree of liberalising the criteria for becoming adoptive parents, the norm, however, remains a highly conservative stereotypical model of the married couple with a settled way of life and established economy. The question as to who can adopt was much debated in the hearings preceding the 1986 Adoption Act and it was readdressed in the preparations to the 1999 amendments. Much of the debate hinged on who may be allowed to adopt. As mentioned in Chapter 3, Norway is surprisingly conservative and restrictive when it comes to procreation.[21]

To Conclude

Norway and the USA represent two extreme positions in the attitude towards the state's involvement in the family. The Norwegian welfare state operates according to an ideology that has increasingly supported public involvement in family life in general and adoption in particular. Legislation is national, uniform and restrictive. It is practised fairly stringently, and displays a clear intent to control and regulate in order to ensure not only the child's best interest, but that of citizens more generally. The fact that private adoption is to all intents and purposes not allowed in Norway, and that only three adoption agencies are licensed to arrange adoption on a non-profit-making basis, further enhances the non-market aspect of the transaction. The government has ratified the Hague Convention on Intercountry Adoption and seeks to adhere to its various rulings.

In the USA we find a much more heterogeneous situation. The criteria for adoption of a child from overseas vary from state to state and, within states, from agency to agency; but they are much less stringent in general than they are in Norway – or in most other European countries. Private adoptions abound in the USA as do profit-making agencies. There is little supervision of practices in donor countries. Not having signed the Hague Convention, it is difficult for American state or federal institutions to insist on adherence to its decrees. The authority of the professional psycho-technocrats also varies. Many individuals choose to bypass their scrutiny as far as possible and, because they may hire their own private social worker to undertake an evaluation of them, the room for manoeuvre is much larger here than in Europe.

The welfare state represents a special type of involvement of the state in the life of its citizens. It can be characterised by a high level of ambition vis-à-vis the number and range of institutions and projects that it initiates for people's benefit. From such a perspective, it may be argued that the Norwegian state's engagement in transnational adoption represents an achievement. Because adoption is an activity that is easily defined and delimited, general ideals of family, parenthood, and children may be achieved through legislation drafted on the basis of advice from the psycho-technocrats. Rules and procedures for conducting transnational adoption are perceived to be highly rational and directly tailored to meet the needs of the children and parents concerned in the most efficient, fair and humane manner. By contrast, the situation in the USA is not informed by the ideals of a welfare state, and the ideals of governmentality as an approach are not developed. The value attributed to the market and to individual free choice, coupled to the majority's wish to keep the private, family sphere within the control of families themselves, have led to a very different approach here when it comes to adoption and transnational adoption. The recent fashion of open adoption is more the result of spontaneous pressure groups of individuals with a particular agenda, than the result of changing notions in the expert professions. Nevertheless, the fact that a number of states have altered their laws in order to allow open adoption can, I suggest, be traced back to the ideology of the right to choose, the right to know, the iconic status of the autonomous individual, and the increasing emphasis being placed on the biological rather than the relational quality of personhood.

To what extent these different approaches have been pursued on the international stage will be the topic of the next chapter.

Notes

1. In the next chapter I examine international legislation, and also undertake a more thorough discussion on the growth and global diffusion of the 'rights discourse', and in Chapter 9 I examine the adoption laws of some selected donor countries.
2. Federal law takes care of military and international matters, citizenship, weights and measures, currency and postal services as well as laying down principles regarding the organisation of education, health and crime protection.
3. This can even be said to be reflected in the insistence of the individual state io regulating and supervising proper behaviour within its area of jurisdiction and not relinquishing this to the federal system.
4. Modell (1994) gives a detailed exposition of the various factors involved in the passing of the American adoption laws. I base many of my comments upon her exposition, supplemented by Hollinger's monumental treatise *Adoption Law and Practice* (1992), and Melosh's (2002) study on the history of adoption in America.

5. In a study of adoption by white couples of North American Indian children, Strong shows that a similar principle was at work, although not codified in the same way (Strong 2001: 17). During armed conflict between the early settlers and Native American groups, children were often spared and adopted by settler families; families, it was assumed, where the children would receive a far superior upbringing. Furthermore, various missionary groups mediated the removal of hundreds of Indian babies and infants from their biological families and brought them to white American couples for adoption. The practice has been seen by Native American activists as a way of imposing hegemonic white middle-class principles of reproduction, child rearing and family life upon peoples whose social and cultural values diverge. In 1972, American Indian activists fought to make orphaned children remain on the reservation in Indian foster or adoptive homes, so 'that they might associate themselves with their own race and learn their own culture' (Melosh 2002: 175).

6. The possibility exists for returning children adopted from overseas if they turn out to be less than desirable, (see the case mentioned in Chapter 2).

7. This was due not to a deliberate policy, but more to the incompleteness of records (Hollinger 1992: 1–38).

8. Advocates of open adoption are gaining ground in the USA. A study in 1993 of thirty-five adoption agencies showed that thirty-two discouraged confidential adoption and thirteen of these advocated full disclosure (Grotevant and McRoy 1998 in Melosh 2002: 278).

9. In another respect, the American situation is, however, somewhat different from the Scandinavian one. Despite the ideological focus upon the individual's right to decide his or her fate, abortion is highly controversial in the USA, and the 'pro-life' lobby appears to be gaining some ground. Extensive poverty in certain regions and amongst the lower classes also means that many children are abandoned by parents (mothers) unable to look after them.

10. This means that an American presence in donor countries tends to overshadow other recipient countries and this, in turn, leads to occasional resentment – both by the other countries seeking adoptable children as well as by some donor countries.

11. Legislation to enable ratification by the USA had been signed by President Clinton in 2002 and ratification was expected to take place within a couple of years. However, with the change in government, this has now been put on ice.

12. Some private schools are allowed for special reasons, but they receive up to 80 per cent public funding. A few private medical clinics are also allowed.

13. One manifestation of this is perhaps that in a population of four and a half million, seven political parties are represented in parliament.

14. This was in line with the *pater est* rule whereby a child born to a married woman automatically becomes the legal child of her husband. With contemporary DNA tests, this is about to be changed.

15. According to the 1979 Amendment, a child had to be registered with a first name and a surname within six months of birth. The mother's or father's surname were both acceptable. If no registration was made, the child would be given its mother's surname.

16. In most cases this was a fictive right as the vast majority of children being adopted out were either illegitimate children of poor women or one child too many in a poor family, hence there was not much to inherit. Adopted children usually underwent a significant upward economic and social mobility. The true basis for this legal provision is probably more to be found in the vested interest of the kin of adoptive parents who wished to secure their rights in future inheritance.

17. Goody calls this right *retrait lignager* (or the linear purchase of right) and says that it existed in England and France, but was abolished several centuries ago (Goody 1969: 123).

18.   The ideology of eugenics had a stronger hold in Sweden than in Norway. Sweden passed an extended sterilization law in 1941.

19.   Although the ideal of a nuclear family lost some of its appeal in the 1970s and 1980s, much indicates that it was on the way back in the 1990s (see Chapter 3).

20.   Several adoptive parents have given as an argument for not choosing to adopt from Russia or Eastern Europe that if their child looked Norwegian the relationship might appear deceitful. With a child who clearly could not be mistaken for their biological child, such a situation could never arise (Roalkvam, personal communication).

21.   The standard requirement is that prospective adoptive parents should be married. Single women may in special circumstances adopt; homosexual couples may not. However, the Minister for Family and Child Affairs gave in 2003 dispensation to three lesbian couples to complete a step-child adoption of the child of one of the partners from a previous heterosexual relationship. The same criteria for eligibility for adoption are applied with regard to assisted conception.

Chapter 8

BENEVOLENT CONTROL: INTERNATIONAL TREATIES ON ADOPTION

The UN Convention on the Rights of the Child has established a near global consensus (American and Somali objections notwithstanding) concerning the minimum necessary rights for children; rights to provision, protection and participation – the 3 'Ps'.

> Bob Franklin, *The Handbook of Children's Rights*

Is the category of childhood general, let alone generalisable? These are difficult and highly charged questions. All too often professionals, activists and policy makers get so caught up in the pain, distress and needs they work with that the answers to these questions are either assumed, or dismissed as irrelevant to practice.

> E. Burman, 'Local, Global or Globalized?
> Child development and International Child Rights'

In the liberal democracies of the Western world the ultimate repository of rights is the human person. The individual is held in a virtually sacralized position. There is a perpetual, and in our view obsessive, concern with the dignity of the individual, his worth, personal autonomy and property .

> A. Legesse, quoted in K. Van der Wal
> 'Collective Human Rights: A Western View'

Global Governmentality: The Case of Transnational Adoption

In this chapter I shall examine two international conventions, the UN Convention on the Rights of the Child (UNCRC) from 1989, and the more specialized Hague Convention on Protection of Children and Co-operation in Respect of Intercountry Adoption (Hague Convention) from 1993. In each case I identify some of the points that emerged as controversial during the drafting stage, and seek to reveal the many explicit and implicit values that went into the formulations of the various provisions. In this connection I provide an examination of some constitutive, but largely unexamined, principles such as the 'best interest of the child' and 'children's rights'. I also include a brief presentation of the African Charter on the Rights and Welfare of the Child from 1990. This, I suggest, may be interpreted as a counter-proposal to the UNCRC which, in some quarters, was regarded as an attempt to apply Western values about childhood and parenthood on a global scale. I conclude the chapter by raising some questions concerning Western ambivalent attitudes to money, in which certain categories of exchange are held to be morally outside the monetary sphere. The transfer of rights in people, especially children, falls into such a category.

The promotion of international policies, and legislation, to ensure the quality of children's life, is a prime example of governmentality on a global scale. As an indirect mechanism of rule by state powers, govern-mentality is primarily concerned with 'the conduct of conduct', that is with the ways in which human conduct is directed by calculated means (Dean 1999, quoted in Gupta 2001: 111). As I showed in the previous chapter, Norwegian child and adoption legislation and associated infrastructure are the manifest expressions of national governmentality. Similarly, international conventions and guidelines and the establishment of a global infrastructure to supervise the implementation of these, are the manifest expressions of global governmentality. In both cases, psychologically informed discourses, voiced and managed by the psycho-technocrats who work both nationally and internationally, legitimate practice.

The shift in control over children – from the family to public authorities – that took place in Europe during the second half of the nineteenth century, and was consolidated throughout the twentieth century in legislation, is now happening on a global scale. Global law about children (in the form of international conventions) seeks to ensure the 'best interests of the child' by transferring authority not only from the family to the state, but also from the state to the international level. This is very explicit in the case of transnational adoption.

The UN Convention on the Rights of the Child and the more specialised Hague Convention on Intercountry Adoption both spring out of the UN Declaration of Human Rights (UNDHR) of 1948, and their prime aims are to safeguard the 'best interests of the child'. The initiative for both conventions was taken in Europe, and the principles and values upon which they are formulated derive their impetus from Western values as these are expressed in child, family and adoption laws. Thus, local Western notions of childhood have subsequently been globalised, or they are actively sought to become so. The responsibility for overseeing that the conventions are implemented in the various countries that have signed and ratified them is placed in the hands of national public agencies in each country, who carry out their duties under the beady eyes of the West. Furthermore, the locus of control and monitoring of the implementation of the various edicts are located in the West: at UNICEF headquarters in New York in the case of the UNCRC, and in The Hague in the case of the Convention on Inter-country Adoption; locations which, in a broad sense, coincide with those to which children are adopted. At the same time, aid projects aimed at children in Asia, Africa and Latin America are formulated, established, supervised and evaluated by governmental or non-governmental organisations from Western countries and reflect the values of the two conventions. The overarching principles of the best interests of the child, children's rights, agency and empowerment, are normative and express predominant contemporary Western values and practices. There is thus an intentionality built into the globalisation of (Western) rationality and morality, that is perhaps more explicit than in the case of economic and technological manifestations of globalisation. The globalisation of Western notions of childhood springs out of a genuine desire on the part of the wealthy nations to safeguard and improve the lives of unprotected children. As such, it may be viewed as a continuation of the 'the white man's burden' of the nineteenth century (Howell 2003a).

In regulating the life of children – in the domains of family, education, labour, adoption, inheritance – these international conventions place responsibility for the implementation of the regulations in the hands of state authorities. For example, the Hague Convention displays a clear abhorrence (e.g. Article 22) towards so-called private adoptions, i.e. those that are carried out without the involvement of publicly endorsed bodies in both donor and recipient country. Less and less power is left in the hands of the family, to such an extent that it has been argued that children today are the most controlled category of humanity (Rose 1999).

This transfer of authority from family to government is very explicit in the case of transnational adoption. As a practice of the state, transnational adoption involves two levels of control: the national level and the international. Transnational adoption is a transaction carried out between two, in principle, sovereign nation-states: the donor and the receiver country. Each has its own laws and jurisdiction which have to be accommodated. This may give rise to procedural stumbling blocks as well as to conflicts of interest. Adoption is a sensitive issue in most countries, and adoption of a country's own children to countries overseas is particularly sensitive. Because it manifests an inability to look after its own abandoned children, many a donor country feels embarrassed about this, and regards it as shameful. Adoption to overseas is therefore a practice that, in many cases, the nation-states themselves wish to be seen to control, as will be demonstrated in the next chapter. Moreover, in an attempt to ensure that adoptions are carried out in a manner that is morally and legally acceptable, to some extent the two international conventions superimpose their injunctions upon the national legal system.

Both conventions allocate the task of monitoring to national institutions; but under supervision. The UNCRC obligates participating nations to provide factual updates on the legal, material, health, family and educational circumstances of children living within their national boundaries, and UNICEF arranges meetings of all signatories once every ten years. (For detailed up-to-date information see http://www.unicef.org./crs/.) The follow-up on the progress of the Hague Convention is more sporadic, but several meetings have been held, manifesting a clear intention of global supervision,

Given that the conventions are between contracting states, governmentality in this case may be expressed as state-sponsored globalisation emanating from the West. Before I enter into a consideration of these two international treaties, I wish to examine some basic concepts, in particular that of the 'best interest of the child' that underpin the discourses.

From the Best Interest of the Child to Children's Rights and Empowerment

Most commentators argue that the contemporary normative definitions of children and childhood are – overtly or covertly – Western, and that these have been extended to include children and childhoods everywhere (Burman 1996; Penn 2002; Stephens 1996; Scheper-Hughes and Sargent 1998: 37–41). Indeed, Burman questions whether the category of childhood is general or generalisable, and suggests that 'all too often professionals, activists and policy makers get so caught up in the pain, distress and needs they work with that the answers to these questions are either assumed or dismissed as irrelevant to practice' (1996: 46). This point is worth bearing in mind when examining the international treaties which, after all, were drafted in order to protect a category of humanity deemed incapable of protecting itself.

As argued throughout this book, at the root of the Western definition of children and childhood lies the unquestioned constitutive assumption of universal man perceived analytically as a bounded individual. According to the French anthropologist Louis Dumont, the reverse side of such an analytical (and moral) centrality of the individual is the universal (Dumont 1979: 792). From such an understanding, he suggests, developed the notion of universal rights. In itself, this ontological starting point gives rise to a whole series of beliefs and assertions, the consequences of which can be far-reaching, especially in those cultural settings that do not share the same premises. The extent to which alternative cultural understandings are manifested in the drafting of international legislation is minimal. Political discourses on rights can be traced to the eighteenth century and the work of French and English philosophers, and their values came to the forefront in the UNCRC and the later Hague Convention. These express currently reigning values amongst influential groups in the Western world[1] pertaining to the constitution of human beings, personhood and human rights in general, and children and their rights in particular. As discussed in the previous chapter, the relationship between morality and law is far from arbitrary. Laws are not neutral tools for the regulation of practice. Laws both reflect established moral values and practices, and are normative in-so-far as they seek to influence these in a particular direction. This applies equally to international conventions which reflect predominant Western moral values and practices, and, in the case of the two considered here, they explicitly seek to influence the rest of the world to adopt them. At the root of the enterprise lies the unquestioned idea of the universal person, perceived as a bounded autonomous individual whose sociality is epiphenomenal rather than an integral part of his or her being. Penn argues that leading North American educators have claimed that 'children are pretty much the same everywhere and the people teaching them have pretty much the same ideas'; that the stages of growth and development and the accompanying practices are assumed to be the same everywhere; and that '"culture" produces only minor variations' (Penn 2002: 124). With such an understanding, universal implementation of procedures is unproblematic.

The principle of the 'best interest of the child' underpins the two conventions, but it is a principle that has received minimal debate. The use of the singular form of the noun is not, I suggest, accidental. The focus is upon the autonomous child with his or her embedded rights. National adoption laws, as well as the sections of UNCRC that deal with adoption and the Hague Convention, all state in their various preambles that this consideration is the basic starting point for the articles that follow. However, few attempts are made at defining what this might mean in practice. It is so taken for granted, so naturalised, that those concerned do not seem to think it necessary to debate its meaning. Who in their right mind could possibly argue against such a goal? Nevertheless, what participants of one cultural tradition might deem obvious, those of another would not necessarily agree with or, at any rate, prioritise. By reading between the lines and by identifying scattered sentences throughout the documents one may elicit some understanding of what the law-makers have in mind – however implicitly. For example, there is no disagreement about the statement that the best interest of a child – as a universalised category of individuals – is to grow up with his or her biological mother and father in a family home. Far from being modified in response to increased knowledge about the variety of kinship ideologies and practices, such an understanding appears to be hardening. This I attribute to an increasing Western biologisation of discourses on the meaning of personhood, relatedness and family. And yet, as I demonstrated in my explorations of historical and cross-cultural variety in the attributed meanings to concepts such as kinship, family, parenthood and children, very little, if anything, can be taken for granted about these concepts.

I now wish to take the issue further by examining the genealogy of 'the best interest of the child'; for then to suggest that this concept was incorporated, and further developed, into a discourse on children's rights, and then, more recently, narrowed even further into a demand to acknowledge children's agency, and to 'empower' them to participate in formulating their future. I have already shown how the desire to ensure the 'best interest of the child' features in early American adoption laws (although it did not influence practice) and that it is mentioned, but treated as subsidiary to the interests of the adults, in the first Norwegian adoption law. In Norway, it was not until the Adoption Act of 1986 that this was stated as an unequivocal underpinning principle. However, what might actually be the best interest of the child is left undefined in the law.[2] Possibly the vagueness itself is useful in that it allows politicians, administrators, and psycho-technocrats to make their own interpretations when using it as reference for intervention. Recently, a conflation is observable between the demands for a child's best interest and a child's rights. For example, when the abolition of the rule that safeguards the anonymity of sperm donors in Norway was debated in parliament in 2003, the majority who voted in favour couched their arguments in terms that a child has the *right* to know his or her biological origin and that to know this would be in their *best interest*.

No clarity about the concept emerged on the international level either. No consideration was given to any possible diversity in the meaning of the overarching aim of Article 3 of UNCRC, namely that 'the best interest of the child shall be a primary consideration'. Cantwell[3] suggests that it names a solution without saying anything about what the solution consists of and concludes that 'like [the more recent] "children's rights" in the Eighties' it still remained – and remains? – a concept in search of definition' (2002b: 2). The concept, he says, has been invoked in various European countries to justify a variety of interventions by the state authorities, notably those of removing a child from his or her family. To most European and North American delegates it implied that the child's best interest is to be with his or her biological parents – unless the conditions on the home front are so abysmal that the authorities regard it as necessary to step in. Cantwell points out that it was hardly debated and went unchallenged as to its meaning and ramifications throughout the drafting process of the UNCRC. Nevertheless, the concept is central in the UNCRC. It appears as a guiding principle in the Preamble, is confirmed in Article 3 and is reaffirmed or underlined at various points throughout the text; in the provisions concerning, e.g. juvenile justice, parental responsibilities and situations requiring substitute care. Cantwell makes what for me is a most significant observation: that, throughout the text, the child's best interest is stated as a *primary* consideration, except once when, in discussing adoption, it says that, 'the best interest of the child is *paramount*' (my emphasis). In other words, to remove a child from its biological parents, and to transfer its permanent care to other parents is regarded as the most severe form of intervention. This reflects European practices. When a child is forcibly removed from its parents in Northern Europe and the USA, fostering is preferred to adoption; the underlying hope being that, one day, the parent(s) will become able to look after their child. This may further be attributed to a lack of conviction regarding the potential force of kinning.

Cantwell argues that the concept of best interest was deliberately left vague, and that the concern expressed by the Venezuelan delegate at the last meeting of the UN Working Group preceding the final Convention in 1989, that the concept lacked juridical precision – was not heeded. Very often, he says, it is interpreted as concerning material well-being.[4] He further points to a new development that has arisen out of the UNCRC. From now on 'children have the *right* to have their best interest taken into account' (Cantwell 2002b: 3; my emphasis). As such, the claim has to be seen in relation to other codified human rights. This new focus has not, however, helped to clarify what precisely is at stake, he argues. While the best interest of the child is now a right of the child, it is in no way equivalent to the rights of the child. Although the latter is also open to manipulation, '[it] constitutes in effect a "last-resort" guarantee that human rights will be applied to the advantage of those who are to benefit from them' (ibid.: 4). The Hague Convention is similarly formulated upon an unproblematised assertion that '[a]doption must be in the best interest of the child'. Both conventions endorse the idea that for the 'full and harmonious development of his or her personality, the child should grow up in a family environment, in an atmosphere of happiness, love and understanding'. Furthermore, the responsibility to ensure such conditions for every child is placed upon the state.

Child advocacy organisations have played a major role in the adoption, ratification and implementation of the UNCRC, thereby further extending their influence (*Childhood* editorial 1999: 403). However, a recent change in attitudes may be observed. Increasingly it has been argued that to pursue a policy of best interest is paternalistic and that it should be replaced by the principle that children have a right to express their views and have their wishes taken into account. For example, according to Franklin, the English Children Act 1989, 'carefully straddles the divide between protectionist (paternalist) and participatory rights' (Franklin 2002: 4). Such thinking is evident in the international community as well and is reflected in the UNCRC. Articles 12, 13 and 14 state the child's rights to form his or her own views and to express them in matters affecting him or her. Moreover, children have the right to be listened to. One Indian commentator confirms (approvingly in this instance) the replacement of needs by rights, and says,

'Looking at adoption from a "Rights Framework" rather than a "needs" approach is essential' (Mehta 20002: 8).[5] These provisions may provide the impetus for the more recent emphasis given to the concepts of empowerment and agency in the international community of professionals. The stress placed on empowerment and participation is in line with the focus given these terms in development discourses generally. The World Bank defines empowerment as: 'In its broadest sense, empowerment is the expansion of freedom of choice and action. It means increasing one's authority and control over the resources and decisions that affect one's life' (World Bank Poverty net). They recently produced a sourcebook on the theme entitled *Empowerment and Poverty Reduction; a Sourcebook* (2002).[6] Norwegian Save the Children has in recent years changed its focus from 'poverty alleviation' to 'rights based' programmes in the Third World (Berre 2004: 3).

The Committee on the Rights of the Child was set up in the wake of the UNCRC to oversee the progress made in all member countries. Here one may notice a growing attention being paid to this new concept. Indeed, at a two-day seminar that I attended in 2002 (organised by the Save the Children as part of the preparatory work for the Norwegian delegation to the planned conference later that year at UNICEF headquarters in New York), several invited speakers from various countries stressed precisely how the work they were engaged in was directed towards encouraging the empowerment of children and instilling in them an awareness of their own agency. In the Convention jargon, participation is now added to the '"P"s of protection and provisions' (Cantwell 1992b; Franklin 2002: 6). More recently, the preoccupation with participation and empowerment has meant that actual aid projects are being directed at encouraging these aims at the expense, perhaps, of more practical concerns. In a study of Save the Children Norway's activities in Ethiopia, Berre (2004) shows how the right of children to participate has become central to their activities. She examines the introduction of projects intended to ensure a children's participation (CP) into 'a local context where generally there is little participation and few or no individual rights', and concludes, 'it was not the Ethiopian children who were empowered …' [rather] 'empowerment seemed to happen to the concept of CP itself '(2004: 166).

So, important changes in attitudes and priorities concerning the treatment of children took place towards the end of the twentieth century. From being perceived as helpless and vulnerable in the post-war period, by the end of the century children have become regarded as individuals with rights on a par with those of adults; and the task of experts has become one that facilitates their agency through empowerment and participation. This principle pf participation further expresses an ambiguity in the meaning of childhood (Roche 1999: 475). These particular changes in values have not filtered through to transnational adoption practices.

UN Convention on the Rights of the Child

A watershed in international relations was reached with the UN Declaration of Human Rights of 1948. From that time onwards we have seen a proliferation of charters specifying a number of rights with an increasingly specific focus. The rights of children was a relative latecomer, but the UN Convention on the Rights of the Child was adopted in November 1989, and since that time has 'dwarfed all previous international human rights treaties' because the rate and speed of ratification was unprecedented and the Convention could enter into force the following year (Franklin 1995: ix). Apart from the USA,[7] only Somalia and East Timor have failed to sign the UNCRC. According to Franklin, the reason for this acceptance is not difficult to find. It is, he says, because 'it has a vision. It expresses some basic values about the treatment of children, their protection and participation in society'. In my view, however, to suggest that the Convention expresses some globally shared values about the treatment of children is highly questionable. As noted in Chapter 2, 'the child' as a universal being envisaged by the Convention, belongs to a conception of childhood that implies the becoming of a socialised adult (Ennew and Morrow 2001: 10). Contemporary ideas of childhood that stress domesticity and dependence, and romanticise childhood as a time of innocence, are largely of recent Western origin (Boyden 1997: 191; Cunningham 1995, Chapter 7; Stephens, 1995: 9–12) and are not shared by people in many other parts of the world. And the same applies also to the notion of agency.

The UN Convention on the Rights of the Child came about largely as a result of the UN Year of the Child, which took place in 1979, to be followed by the International Youth Year in the mid-1980s. Active participants during the Year of the Child were particularly concerned about child labour and the growth in the number of street children. Media in Europe drew attention to concrete cases where, it was argued, the interests of children were ignored; and questions concerning children's rights were raised. According to Ennew, Western thinking holds strongly that childhood should take place inside a home, inside a family, a private dwelling, and those that do not conform to this do literally fall outside – outside society, outside childhood (Ennew 1995: Chapter 15). One of the most provocative issues to many engaged in work in connection with the Year of the Child was precisely the street children. Ennew argues that they represented the starkest challenge to the Western notion of modern childhood, which, she states, has been globalised through colonialism and later through 'the imperialism of international aid' (ibid: 202, see also Boyden 1997: Chapter 7; Burman 1996; Stephens 1995,). According to Nieuwenhuys, in order to gain funds and legitimacy, the NGOs have 'found one of their most important allies in a particular kind of child – *street children*' (1999: 41, original emphasis).

Unlike its precursors – the Geneva Declaration on the Rights of the Child from 1924 and the Declaration of the Rights of the Child which was adopted by the UN in 1959 – the UNCRC is not just a statement of good intentions, but is legally binding upon the ratifying countries. Whereas the two early declarations 'announced young people's entitlement to adequate nutrition, free education and medical care as well as rights against exploitation and discriminatory practices', the period leading up to the UNCRC was characterised by a concern for 'children's moral and political status, as well as their social and welfare needs' (Franklin 2002: 6). In so far as the Convention seeks to guide the practices not only of legislatures and courts, but also of parents, police, social welfare agencies, health care professionals and others who work with and have responsibility for children, it may be characterised as a tool for effecting state control. Moreover, the Committee on the Rights of the Child urges governments to educate their publics about the rights of the child. Reports on progress must be submitted regularly, and a conference is held every ten years to review the situation and propose future work.

In the Preamble to the actual articles of the UNCRC, we can read some unquestioned assumptions upon which the articles were formulated. Some of the relevant ones in the present context are:

- 'Recalling that in the Universal Declaration of Human Rights, the UN has proclaimed that childhood is entitled to special care and assistance'.
- 'Convinced that the family, as the fundamental group of society and the natural environment for the growth and well-being of all its members and particularly children ...'
- 'Recognizing that the child, for a full and harmonious development of his and her personality, should grow up in a family environment ...'
- 'Considering that the child should be fully prepared to live an *individual* life in society' (my emphasis).

The diversity of cultural understanding receives a nodding acknowledgement at the end of the Preamble, when it is stated, 'Taking due account of the importance of the traditions and cultural values of each people for the protection and harmonious development of the child ...'.

However, the implications of this are not pursued in the actual articles of the final Convention, or in the subsequent monitoring reports. By making the bounded individual the basic unit at the expense of an analytic understanding that persons are constituted through the particularity of their sociality – whose meaning in each case is derived from local cultural and social ideas and practices – a conceptual leap is made from the individual to the universal and the global. In effect, humans are desocialised and deculturised. As in the Preamble to the Convention, lip service is paid to the significance of cultural values by many who are actively engaged in such work. It frequently appears, however, that this is not informing practice. The fact of cultural plurality continues to be ignored when it comes to the actual formulation and execution of bi- or multilateral treaties and conventions. Rather, as I have witnessed on a number of occasions, sociocultural factors are regarded more as a nuisance – to be acknowledged only to be dismissed. I suggest that one reason for the reluctance to accept the profound relationship between cultural values and practices is that the representatives of Western countries simply fail to realise that they are also products of their socio-cultural backgrounds; that the values that they cherish and feel a moral duty to propagate are not necessarily true and right in an absolute sense. Moreover, given the fact that the various human rights conventions are predicated upon the unquestioned supremacy of the autonomous individual, diagnoses of failures, and suggestions for remedying these, are invariably sought in individuals. Occurrences that elsewhere might be regarded as profoundly social are not treated as such.[8]

Representatives from forty-three nations worked on the formulation of the UNCRC. It was a challenging task to articulate worldwide moral standards for the treatment of children. Not surprisingly, debates were fierce. It was the product of ten years of negotiations amongst government delegates, intergovernmental organisations, and NGOs; although only a small number actively participated (Freeman 1996: 53). In his analysis of the processes involved in drafting key articles in the UNCRC about which there was serious dispute, Johnson argues that conflicts tended to be avoided through the use of minimal texts or general formulations in the final wording, rather than coming to clear resolutions (Burman 1996: 52).[9] According to Freeman, it proved difficult to obtain consensus in five main areas. These were: matters pertaining to freedom of thought, conscience and religion – which provoked several delegates form Islamic states; inter-country adoption – about which many Latin-American countries expressed reservation;[10] the rights of the unborn child – which produced splits along religious lines and between developed and developing countries; the need to respect and take account of traditional practices – which was strongly voiced by several African counties, particularly with regard to female circumcision; and, fifthly, the need to specify the duties of the child not just the child's rights. This last point was raised by Senegal and other African countries.

A major change in approach and focus took place during the decade of deliberations – due not least to a rapid increase in transnational adoption (Cantwell 2002a: 1). The original draft proposed by Poland in 1978 contained no mention of adoption. The revised 1980 draft contained an injunction that States 'facilitate' adoption, but the final version of 1989 specified the need for 'protection', especially regarding transnational adoption (ibid.). Articles 20 and 21 of UNCRC deal with adoption, both domestic and transnational. These articles form the basis for the subsequent Hague Convention. The UNCRC articles, however, are left deliberately vague due to the controversial nature of the practice, and many delegates thought that adoption would not be included because of this (Lehland, in conversation).

The responsibility for caring for 'children temporally or permanently deprived of his or her family' is, in Article 20, placed firmly on the shoulders of the state. Such care, it is stated, 'could include, *inter alia*, foster placement, Kafala or Islamic law [see below] adoption or, if necessary, placement in suitable institutions ... [d]ue regard shall be paid to the desirability of continuing in a child's ethnic, religious, cultural and linguistic background' (Article 20: 3). Article 21, which deals explicitly with adoption, begins by reasserting the authority of the State Parties who shall: 'Ensure that the adoption of a child is authorized only by competent authorities ...' Further, it is recognised that 'inter-country adoption may be considered as an alternative means of a child's care, if the child cannot be placed in a foster or an adoptive family ... in country of origin'. Finally, and this, according to many, is the rub, each country is required to '[t]ake all appropriate measures to ensure that, in inter-country adoptions, the placement does not result in improper financial gain for those involved'. This last point was subject to heated debate during the discussions of the Hague Convention and it is still not resolved.

According to most commentators, the UNCRC has been instrumental in globalising a Western middle class view of 'the child' and childhood, making the concept of 'the world's children' meaningful.[11] Stephens argues forcibly that there has emerged a consciousness of children at risk, identified primarily as children of lost innocence, of leading lives outside the home, and as being out of control. Moreover, she argues that the role of the child has become central to our understanding of modernity and that we need to understand 'the global, political, economic, and cultural transformations that are currently rendering children so dangerous, contested and pivotal in the formation of new sorts of social persons, groups and institutions' (1995: 14). One might argue that, without a global acceptance of the Western notions of 'the child', a global acceptance of human rights and Western morality and rationality will be severely impeded. The UNCRC with its monitoring committee becomes a powerful tool to ensure that this does not happen.

The Hague Convention on Protection of Children and Co-operation in Respect of Intercountry Adoption[12]

The Hague Convention on Intercountry Adoption was finalized in 1993 and came into force in 1995. The background to the work on the convention can be traced back to 1988 when Italy proposed to the permanent

Bureau of the Hague Convention the establishment of a committee to 'prepare a convention on adoption of children coming from abroad...because substantial numbers of children from economically developing countries are being placed for adoption with families in industrialized countries'. (Van Loon 1994: 15, 17).[13] By that time, the practice of transnational adoption was well-established and growing in scope and scale, and a need to regulate and supervise the practice was felt.[14] As discussed above, Article 21 of the UN Convention deals with adoption, both national and transnational, but it is vague on procedure. The main points that are reiterated throughout are that adoption shall ensure the best interest of the child, and that 'competent authorities' must take charge of the process. The Hague Convention builds on Article 21 of the UNCRC and elaborates on the implications of it. A major concern during the drafting of the UNCRC was to prevent the practice of 'improper financial gain for those involved', a point that also was, and remains, important in the Hague Convention.

Discussions on the draft text started at the time when Romania was experiencing major problems in preventing malpractices in the adoption of children to foreign couples. Reports of this in Western European and North American media, coupled with information about appalling conditions in many orphanages and children's homes, soon took on a sensationalist slant (see next chapter). According to Cantwell (2002a: 1), the issues raised by the situation in Romania, and subsequently in Russia and other Eastern European countries, greatly influenced the tone and emphasis of the final texts. A need to establish legally binding standards, and a need for a system of supervision in order to ensure that these standards are observed, were the main reasons for initiating the Convention (Parra-Aranguren 1994: 179).

The Hague Convention was not received with the same general acclaim as was the UNCRC. While most of the countries who receive children – with the exception of the USA – have ratified the convention, many of the key providers of children for adoption, such as South Korea, Ethiopia, Guatemala, have not.[15] The Hague Convention provoked much more debate than did the UNCRC but, as I shall show, compromises were found in most instances. Explanations given by Western bureaucrats for the failure of donor countries to sign (that it is only a matter of time, or that a particular country has no tradition of signing international treaties) may not be fully adequate. In many countries, adoption to the wealthy countries in Europe and North America, many of whom are previous colonial powers, is a highly sensitive political issue and there is not always consensus within the country regarding the practice. Disagreements exist as to whether the country should engage in transnational adoption at all, and, if they do so, what are the most appropriate ways to handle it.

The proposals for the Convention were universalistic, intended to be generally applicable. Whenever disagreements arose, these were primarily between donor countries on the one side and recipient countries on the other. By and large, it seems that the values of the recipient countries prevailed. Nevertheless, because of the seriousness of some conflicts of interest, certain compromises were reached on the most controversial points, or they were left deliberately vague. A Norwegian delegate to the proceedings told me that he attributes the success of the Convention to the fact that controversial issues are left open-ended. At the same time, the potential for conflict remains. Western countries that receive children remain irritated by some donor countries' reluctance to accommodate their demands, and some donor countries object to what they regard as the Western countries' high-handedness in issuing demands. I have heard those donor countries who have ratified the Convention described by citizens of recipient countries as 'good countries', whereas those who have failed to do so are talked of in terms of 'having a lot of problems'.

Five main principles form the basis upon which the Hague Convention is developed:

1. Adoption must be in the best interest of the child.
2. Only central authorities and accredited bodies shall control all inter-country adoption.
3. The subsidiarity principle must be adhered to, i.e. adoption can only take place when efforts have been made to place a child with close family or in a family-like environment in the country of origin must be adhered to. But '[i]ntercountry adoption may offer the advantage of a permanent family to a child for whom a suitable family cannot be found in his or her state of origin'.
4. Co-operation shall be established between the countries in order to ensure that children's best interests are looked after and that their basic rights are not violated.
5. Proper procedures shall be ensured in both donor and recipient countries.

Even though many countries have not signed or ratified the Convention, it has received 'an unusually high and rapid response' (Cantwell, talk 2002). By the end of 2002, fifty State Parties had ratified it in addition to ten signatures. According to Cantwell, who was active in drafting both the UNCRC and the Hague Convention, 'every word, every comma had to be negotiated' (ibid). He was particularly proud of having made the 'subsidiarity principle' into a rule.

Bones of Contention

When we consider that adoption practices exist in some form or another in most societies, and are firmly entrenched in the whole social fabric of a society and integral to the kinship system, it is not surprising that customary adoption and fostering practices in non-Western societies have not easily been strait-jacketed into Western models. In many instances, local practices continue as before, despite new Western-inspired laws. This became clear at the first Australian Conference on Adoption held in 1976. The representatives from Papua New Guinea, from various Pacific islands, from Maori in New Zealand and aborigines' groups in Australia voiced dismay at the proposal that adoption would entail permanent alienation – not just from the 'immediate family, but from the wider kinship network, as adoption of the child [it was argued] diminishes the family group and is a loss for the wider society' (Van Loon 1994: 24). In former French colonies of West Africa, on the other hand, the introduction of the *Code Napoleon* during colonial times included provisions of so-called 'simple adoption' (*adoption simple*). This does not lead to a complete severance of bonds with the biological family and may also be revoked. As such, it corresponds more easily with local practices of fostering (cf. E. Goody 1982; Bledsoe and Isingo-Abanike 1989). Similarly, in Latin America where local legal codes were based on the Spanish counterpart of the *Code Napoleon*, simple adoption, being in line with many local practices, eased the transfer from customary law to the modern judicial system. However, this is an option that the Hague Convention has rejected, insisting on the strong version of alienation; biological ties are replaced by adoptive ones. As a result, many of the countries that practise some form of 'simple adoption' have declined to ratify the treaty. This is the case of, for example Thailand, which, nevertheless, sends children for adoption to the West.

Islam presents an obstacle to strong adoption since it is not recognised by Islamic law and therefore most, but not all, Muslim countries forbid it. Tunisia, which changed to secular law in 1958, Turkey, which also adheres to a secular legal system, and Indonesia (not a Muslim country although the majority of the population is Muslim), all allow adoption out of the country.[16] Other Muslim countries such as Egypt and Syria do not extend their family law provisions to members of other religions. This means that Christians may adopt, but only children born of Christian parents. The Convention's insistence on strong adoption was thus perceived as problematic by several Muslim states. The Kuwaiti representative, for example, stated in connection with an early draft of the UNCRC that, 'While some features of adoption are to be found in our laws, they are included in the system of foster care (*kafallah*) which performs its role in the psychological, health, social and educational care of the child … [but] In compliance with the Koranic injunction "Call them after their true fathers", a child cannot change its name while in foster care'[17] (Van Loon 1994: 26, 27). In other words, artificial filiation bonds are not tolerated. It follows from this that full adoption is not permissible within the Muslim legal system.[18] Strong adoption was hotly debated during the formulation of the text. In the end, the majority voted for no exception, which resulted in the Muslim countries remaining outside.

Other disagreements that arose during the debating stage also originated from donor countries. Although the Philippines has ratified, they insist on a trial period before finalising the adoption. The topic of a trial period received several days of debate. Those countries which insist upon a trial period want to safeguard themselves against malpractice in the receiving country. An example illustrates how the Philippines was vindicated. One Norwegian family had adopted four children at the same time. This proved too much, and they felt obliged to give up three to be placed with foster parents. A high-ranking official from the Philippine authorities insisted on checking out the situation for himself. He took the opportunity to express his misgivings about the irrevocable nature of adoption. Norwegian officials, on the other hand, suggested that perhaps the Philippine decision to give four children at the same time to one couple might have been inadvisable.

Yet another controversial issue was the question of biological parents' anonymity versus releasing information about the child's biological background. A heated debate arose between donor and receiving countries about this. As discussed, adoption laws in most European countries and Canada (the situation in the USA varies depending upon the laws of each state) give the legal right to an adopted person to know his or her biological origins upon reaching legal maturity. This is presented as a human right. However, during negotiations, many donor countries did not agree – primarily out of a concern with protecting the biological mother, but also because the knowledge of biological origins was not regarded as particularly important. Article 16 represents a compromise solution. It states that: '(1). The Central Authority of the State of origin shall … prepare a report including information about his or her identity, adoptability, background, social environment, family history, medical history including that of the child's family.-…' but (2). '… Taking care not to reveal the identity of the mother and the father if, in the State of origin, these identities may not be disclosed'. In other words, in this case, attempts to establish hegemony of Western values were defeated. India, for example, was one country that did not agree to disclose. They still do not. When I interviewed the director of the Indian Central Adoption Agency (CARA) in 2002, he was adamant in his conviction that the birth mother's identity must be protected. One reason was that, while abortion is not confidential in India, adoption is. This means that many unmarried girls who find themselves pregnant may opt for secret adoption.

The role of the States Parties is, in the UNCRC, unequivocally given all authority; but it is left deliberately vague in the Hague Convention. No uniform law of adoption is laid down, and 'the Convention is neutral on the question of jurisdiction', i.e. whether the authorities in the donor or recipient country should have the right to determine whether an adoption should be made (Duncan 2000: 44). A division of responsibility is the compromise solution. One of the most difficult questions to resolve during the negotiations was the role of independent specialists in donor countries, such as doctors and lawyers. Should they be allowed to make arrangements for adoption overseas, or simply act as expert advisers during the procedures, was a question that aroused much debate. The reason for the controversy was that it concerns the payment of fees to individuals. While this is allowed in the USA, as well as in several donor countries, it is forbidden in other recipient countries. Again, a compromise was reached. Article 22 states that non-accredited persons or bodies may make arrangements for inter-country adoption within its own territory, subject to supervision by the competent authorities of the state, if they 'meet the requirements of integrity, professional competence, experience and accountability of the State' (ibid.: 45). The issue is not resolved, and the question of financial gains reappears at every follow-up meeting (Cantwell 2002a).

Like the UNCRC, the Hague Convention meets irregularly to discuss problematic issues. Controversial questions continue to arise about the responsibility of bodies other than central authorities; i.e. agencies, orphanages and agents for private institutions. Related to this are concerns about accreditation criteria. In 2003 several delegates raised questions about how to ensure that consent to adopt was freely given by biological parents. This was in response to persistent reports and rumours that babies and infants are kidnapped in order to be sold to adoptive parents; or, even worse, under the guise of being adopted, they are sold for use in organ transplants.

There is no disagreement amongst the various globalising agencies (multi- or bilateral alike) about the meaning or desirability of the overall ideology of the conventions. The *inherent* rightness of the various declarations on rights is not debated. From their perspective, the purpose is to alleviate the pain and distress of children in poor countries. Consideration of the variety in sociocultural values and practices regarding family, kin and adoption is irrelevant. By the same token, non-Western countries might argue that Western values and practices are irrelevant for them. Thus Burman's question, 'Is the category of childhood general, let alone generalisable?' (1996: 46) becomes highly pertinent. But despite the many objections that were phrased in terms of cultural plurality by non-Western countries' representatives, most nationstates ended up signing and ratifying these treaties. However, alternative conventions are occasionally formulated by non-Western countries in order to circumvent particularly objectionable sections in global conventions. One such is the African Charter on the Rights and Welfare of the Child.

The African Charter on the Rights and Welfare of the Child

Reservations voiced by some African countries during the drafting of the UNCRC resulted in a special charter that was intended to give voice to African values and to contrast them to some of the UNCRC. The Organisation of African Unity agreed in 1990 on the formulation of The African Charter on the Rights and Welfare of the Child (ACRWC), (see Ojo 1990 for a discussion of the background to the Charter). It is a document that I interpret as an act of resistance on the part of the African states against what they perceive as the attempted imposition of Western values.[19] The ACRWC entered into force in 1999 after receiving the required fifteen ratifications (Amnesty International Index: IOR 10/001/2002). The Charter starts by affirming its adherence to UNCRC, but also to the African Charter on Human and Peoples Rights (in force 1986). The charter does not diverge from most of the paragraphs of the UNCRC, but makes a strong argument for the need to take account of African practices and values and to regard children as integral members of their communities, not as isolated individuals. The quote by Legesse given at the outset of this chapter, in which he criticises the Western 'obsessive, concern with the dignity of the individual, his worth, personal autonomy and property' makes the point forcefully.

The objections to the UNCRC, as I read them, are directed at the unquestioned assumption of the Convention that its definitions of what is right and proper are universally applicable. In other words, while the Convention employs the language of universality, the African critics insist that it frequently expresses values and assumptions directly attributable to a contemporary Western view. In order to balance this trend and to make the provisions more in line with 'African values and practices', the Preamble states: 'Taking into consideration the virtues of their cultural heritage, historical background and the values of the African civilization (sic) which should inspire and characterise their reflection on the concept of the rights and welfare of the child...' And making the point that rights should not be isolated from responsibilities, they continue, '[c]onsidering that the promotion and protection of the rights and welfare of the child also implies the performance of duties on the part of everyone'.

The Africans are critical of what they regard as the failure of the UNCRC to perceive children as constituted as persons through their relationship with others: their parents and members of the wider kin group. In other words, the expression of extreme individualistic understanding of personhood referred to above, is not accepted by the African delegates. In order to balance the emphasis upon the rights of the child, the Charter places these within a discourse of obligations and duties, making children and their significant others partners in reciprocal relationships that extend beyond the family to the nation, and even to the African continent. Thus, Article 31, entitled 'Responsibility of the Child', states:

> Every child shall have duties towards his family and society, the State and other legally recognised communities and the international community. The child … shall have the duty:
> (a) to work for the cohesion of the family, to respect his parents, superiors and elders at all times and to assist them in case of need;
> (b) to serve the national community by placing his physical and intellectual abilities at its service;
> (c) to preserve and strengthen social and national solidarity;
> (d) to preserve and strengthen their independence and the integrity of his country;
> (e) to contribute to the best of his abilities, at all times, and at all levels, to the promotion and achievement of African Unity.

These provisions are very different indeed from those contained in both the UNDHR and UNCRC. As such, they demonstrate attempts to resist global enforcement of ideas and values concerning family, kinship and personhood.[20] But some go even further in order to assert African originality and creativity. In an essay entitled 'Understanding human rights in Africa', Olusola Ojo claims that, not only was socialism not a European concept, but was one that was native to 'African traditional societies, even if it was not called so' (1990: 118), and further, that the African Charter on Human and People's Rights reflects this in the way that '[t]he main distinguishing features of the charter are the concept of and emphasis on people's rights as opposed to individual rights and the importance attached to "duties" as opposed to "rights"' (ibid.: 119).[21]

Despite my unease about the claim for the reality of *one* African culture, I regard it as highly interesting that fifteen African nations felt sufficiently strongly about some basic assumptions in the UNCRC for them to come together in order to refute them. To my knowledge, no similar action has been taken by any other nation with regard to that convention; but some Southeast Asian countries have attempted in more general terms to circumvent the onslaught of Western values, especially as these were expressed in the UN Declaration of Human Rights, by coining the concept of 'Asian values'.[22] While these have been much criticised (for an overview see e.g. de Bary 1998; Milner 1999), it is also argued that the underlying reasons for the quest for Asian values may be interpreted as a genuine search for identity. In the words of the much-published Singaporean diplomat Kishore Mahbubani: 'It is vital for Western minds to understand that the efforts by Asians to rediscover Asian values are not only or primarily a search for political values. They involve, for instance, a desire to reconnect with their historical past after this connection has been ruptured both by colonial rule and the subsequent domination of the globe by Western *Weltanschauung*' (1998: 35, quoted in Milner 1999).

What has emerged in my study of transnational adoption as a global phenomenon is that the practice gives rise to a number of ambivalent emotional, intellectual and political reactions on the part of many donor countries which can, I argue, be linked to a more general political and ideological discourse that arose in the climate of postcolonialism. I return to this in my next chapter.

The Immorality of Money

From being a charitable act to help an orphaned child, transnational adoption became the means for involuntarily childless couples in Europe and North America to get a child of their own. While adoption from overseas became a source of happiness to many couples, the practice also gave rise to a number of problems – mostly generated by the fact that adoption from overseas was, in many instances, a commercial transaction or, at any rate, appeared so to the Western eye. Spurred into action by the situation in Romania, the initiators of the Hague Convention aimed to regulate transnational adoption so that any semblance of trafficking in children for economic gain could be eradicated and the practice brought under state control.

To exchange children for money is widely regarded as particularly reprehensible. The UNCRC saw it as one of its major challenges to stop it. The theme runs as a thread through the Hague Convention and is a major reason for the continued vigilance accorded to those countries that supply children for transnational adoption. One contested point was, and continues to be, how to define the necessary expenses in donor countries which receiving agencies should be expected to cover; also to what extent gifts may be given to institutions and individuals in donor countries without this becoming corruption,

The *Ethical Rules* of the European organisation of adoption agencies in European countries, EURADOPT, are clear on the issues. Article 2 states, '[t]here must be no promise of direct financial support of the biological parents which could influence their decision to give up their child for adoption'. Furthermore, the rules seek to avoid any personal relationship between the involved parties, and instead reaffirm that expert mediators be engaged: 'If, at a later, stage, the adoptive parents wish to help the biological parents financially, this should not be done by direct contact but through a suitable organization.'

None of these organisations has power to actually interfere in local practices directly. This is not to say that they refrain from exerting influence. A good example is the Hague Convention's effort to control what amounted to the buying and selling of children in Guatemala. Guatemala has not signed the Convention, but was represented at its inception. Reports sent to Headquarters in The Hague indicate that the situation in

Guatemala is far from satisfactory. Corrupt agents and lawyers together with eager prospective adoptive parents result in the transfer of large sums of money in exchange for adoptees. Here, as in most Latin American countries, adoption has to be completed through one or more court hearings leading to a final judgment. Prospective parents must engage a lawyer to act on their behalf. According to the director of one Norwegian adoption agency, this requirement opens the way for corruption. Moreover, lawyers are reputed to run their own adoption agencies. They have agents who travel around the countryside and poor urban areas in search of pregnant women who might feel unable to bring up a child. In addition to medical assistance during pregnancy and birth, the women are paid some money in order to give up their child for adoption. Accusations of false papers also abound. Following the case of a woman who signed herself as the mother of nine babies during a four-year period, some receiving countries now insist on a DNA test of a child offered for adoption and his or her alleged biological mother. A senior Norwegian civil servant told me that what goes on in Guatemala may be described as 'child shopping' and that it has been estimated that as few as 2 per cent of all adoptions out of Guatemala are 'regular', i.e. that they are transacted through accredited agencies. The Hague Convention has asked recipient member countries to put pressure on Guatemalan authorities to improve their ways by refusing to adopt children from the country. The Norwegian government has heeded the appeal and has, as of 2001, imposed a moratorium on adoptions from Guatemala.[23]

While I certainly have no wish to endorse the buying and selling of children, I do wish to reiterate an argument forcefully made by Bloch and Parry in the introduction to the volume *Money and the Morality of Exchange* (1989). They emphasise the not unfamiliar fact of enormous cultural variation in the symbolising of money, and in how this symbolism relates to culturally constructed notions of production, circulation and exchange (Bloch and Parry 1989: 1). Not only is money symbolically represented differently in different countries; it is equally clear that the moral weighting attributed to money and monetary transactions (or transactions that include, inter alia, money), as opposed to other exchanges, also vary. According to Bloch and Parry, one may discern a prominent strand in Western discourse, which can be traced back to Aristotle, that condemns money and trade in favour of household self-sufficiency and production for use (ibid.: 2) The introduction of money can be said to represent a kind of watershed; but rather than arguing with Simmel (1978) that money gives rise to a particular world-view, I agree with Bloch and Parry when they state that 'an existing world view gives rise to particular ways of representing money' (ibid.: 19). Despite the fact that money in Western capitalist economies is usually described as all-purpose money, as opposed to so-called 'primitive money' which is linked to spheres of exchange, the transfer of money is not regarded in Protestant Europe as appropriate in certain types of social transactions. This is particularly so in transactions involving human beings[24] and is reflected in laws and conventions about children and adoption.[25]

Hollinger argues (1992) that US adoption laws and practice are characterised by at least seven principal attributes. One of these, the 'non-contractual nature of adoption', is pertinent in the present context, and she comments on this in the following manner: 'A sixth characteristic of adoptions is that they are unilateral or gratuitous transfers, analogous to testamentary dispositions or the donative deeding over of real property' (1992: 1.02). This implies, she says, that the biological parent 'bestows' the child upon the adoptive parents (ibid.). Although in practice adoptions usually go via some agency, the transfer of money 'or other valuable consideration to be paid in exchange for the child' is forbidden. Prospective adopters may pay for expenses incurred during pregnancy and birth by the biological mother, but 'baby-selling' is banned (ibid.). If we consider this in conjunction with the advertisements in American media for prospective egg donors, surrogate mothers and sperm donors that I quote in Chapter 2, this legal prohibition is curious. While prospective children in the form of eggs to be fertilised (or sperm to fertilise) may freely be bought and sold, or a womb rented from a surrogate mother, a child already born may not be transferred for money.[26]

Notions of gift and exchange are sometimes used in adoption discourses and have been debated by commentators. The ideal of 'gratuitous bestowal', which Hollinger argues is one of the central characteristics of adoption law, is problematic. In open adoption, both parties to the contract (biological and adoptive parents) benefit, according to Modell, from the language of the gift. It is not only a gift of a child, but also a gift to the child, whose best interest it is alleged to serve (1999). In contrast, Yngvesson argues that in a market economy, the pervasiveness of the exchange of goods and services for money makes it difficult (or impossible) to treat some goods as exempt. She further makes the point that in adoption one has to make the distinction between giving and giving up (my emphasis), and that in the latter case, the notion of free gift becomes difficult to maintain (Yngvesson 2002: 227–56). Gifts are alienable, like any other commodity, she argues, but 'relationships constituted through "giving" are interpreted as a function of love'. From this it follows that 'the compelled gift is an oxymoron' (ibid.: 235). While at first sight this appears to be irrefutable, I wish to consider some alternative interpretations based on my Norwegian material. Firstly, it is important to distinguish analytically between the various involved parties' understanding of the event. It is perfectly possible for Norwegian adoptive parents to perceive the arrival of the adopted child as a gift, even though from the biological mother's point of view it might easily be a case of having to give the child up.

We have learned from Marcel Mauss's seminal essay on gift-giving that it is a transaction that involves not just giving, but also receiving and, then, returning the gift in some other form. He characterises this process as a 'total prestation' – this being one manifestation of a 'total social phenomenon.'[27] By this he means that total prestation involves exchanges of much more than property and wealth, but may be in the form of banquets, rituals, women, *children*, dances, festivals and fairs which involve the parties in a moral relationship (Mauss 1969: 5 my emphasis). However, what signifies the return gift, he says, is that it cannot be identical to that received. Furthermore, it need not (ought not) to be returned immediately. Either would be tantamount to negating the exchange, making it in fact a commercial transaction. In other words, we need to think in terms of asymmetry of the gift objects. Exchanges of this kind establish moral relations between the parties, which continue beyond the actual gift-giving/receiving. It is the moral nature of the ensuing relationship that is the crux of the matter. According to Mauss, the giver occupies a superior position to that of the receiver, who may never balance the relationship fully through a counter-gift.

Where does this leave the Norwegian adoptive parents? When I first began my research on transnational adoption in Norway, I was struck by the prevalence of organised transfer of money from adoptive parents to individuals or institutions in the country from which their child had come. One common method is the so-called 'remote adoption' arrangements (*fjernadopsjon*). This is a system by which parents commit themselves to sending regular payment to one specific child in an orphanage who, for whatever reason,[28] is identified as unadoptable. The money is spent on the child's education, medical treatment, clothing and other necessities. The 'adoptive' parents usually receive regular reports on the child's development, and the adults often develop an emotional attachment to the child.

When I accompanied the group of Norwegian families on a motherland tour to Korea, all the families who took part had one such child whom they sponsored. They had photos of the children, and they were all eager to meet them. They had brought presents from Norway. The encounters were emotional, and, on departure, the adults exclaimed that it was heart-rending to leave them to their institutionalised fate. Another method is for groups of adoptive parents to collect money for a specific purpose, such as refurbishing the sanitary arrangements in the orphanage from which they received their child, or purchasing educational material. When asked why they engage in such ventures, I was told again and again that they felt so grateful to the orphanage for giving them their son or daughter that they wanted to give something in return. They would abhor the idea of paying for their child; this would destroy any notion of destiny or of the non-contractual arrangement. They have received the child as gift, just as they would have received a child born to them, and they felt, in true Maussian fashion, the desire and the need to give something in return. So, while they give money, it is not as payment to an institution or individuals, but a means for the institution to improve the services they offer the children in its care, and to enable it to continue sending children to Norway for adoption. The indebtedness that they experience finds an expression which retains the qualities of total prestation because it engages them as total persons.

However, they do not give anything to the person(s) who gave (up?) the child in the first place; the biological mother or parents.[29] The relationship that they establish is with the mediating organisation. Their gift maintains an active relationship with the institution that, in one sense, is their child's place of origin; making it meaningful to activate the relationship at a later stage when they perform a 'pilgrimage' to it as part of their motherland tour. Thus I do not agree with Yngvesson when she concludes, '[w]hat never takes place in these exchange relations [she has in mind the 'gifts' handed over by adoptive parents, via the agencies, at the time of obtaining their child] is a reversal of the flow of children in one direction and of donations in the other' (2002: 246). Rather, the parents and the orphanage establish a meaningful relationship between themselves which is experienced by the parents, at any rate, as non-monetary.

The relationships between the agencies and the orphanages are more mundane. The regular donation by Norwegian agencies to institutions, or, in some cases, the fixed sum paid for each child, may indeed be characterised as an instrumental measure to ensure future allocation of children, resembling a relationship that Sahlins has termed 'balanced reciprocity' (1972). At the same time, it is not a straightforward commercial relationship either, because children are not thought of as commodities – either by the receivers or (in most cases) by the donors.

How the receiving institutions perceive the relationship is an open question. Having talked to employees of orphanages in India, South Korea and Ethiopia that send children to Norway, I learnt that they greatly appreciate the distant adoptive arrangements because these enable them to offer a reasonable quality of life to those children who are left behind. They appreciate the fact that the parents do not just take their child and depart – never to be heard of again, but care about the place and those who live and work there, and that they, through their donations, express a desire to maintain the relationship. These factors provide the orphanage staff with a sense of taking part in something bigger than a number of single transactions. This sense of an ongoing relationship is further enhanced through the return visits that Norwegian families undertake to their children's country of origin. These invariably include a visit to the orphanage. In response to my enquiries, many adoptees expressed the opinion that this visit was the highlight of the trip. This was especially so if they had met someone who remembered them. For the staff, these visits are, by and large, also enjoyable. For the parents, the visit to the orphanage is talked of with profound emotions. Perhaps adoptive parents and orphanage staff share an acceptance of the reality of kinning in adoptive relationships which bureaucrats and law-makers do not.

To Conclude

At a seminar on the trafficking in bodies and body parts held at the University of California, Berkeley in April 2003, Laura Nader said: 'It's great to talk about morality, but what we should be talking about is criminality.' Her statement implied the need for laws and for the means and desire to implement them. Unlike the international trade in organs, transnational adoption is regulated, and the regulations are relatively well implemented. This is due to the number of adoption laws that have been passed both nationally and internationally. The combination of the UNCRC and the Hague Convention means that clear principles and procedures have been established which cover most eventualities. The fact that so many countries have signed and/or ratified the Conventions indicates some degree of willingness to adhere to them. It seems fair to ask why the regulation and control of transnational adoption has been so much more successful than many other attempts at international law. One reason, I suggest, may be attributed to the 'product' itself, namely children. Children have been constructed as a separate category of humanity, one that requires a concerted effort on the part of adults for its members to achieve their full potential; they can no longer be left to themselves to get on with growing up. Children and their well-being have become a major responsibility for the modern state. As a result, the plight of children is high on the agenda for active concern and involvement in the West, and development projects whose purpose is to improve children's quality of life are rarely controversial. Reports and photographs of children as victims of wars, natural and political disasters, invariably provoke strong reactions. Unlike proposals to establish international control of, for example, air pollution, the hunting of seals and whales, or international trade, proposals pertaining to children and their welfare are uncontroversial. Children have come to occupy a special status in the minds of Westerners, and to exercise state control of childhood on a global scale has become a moral imperative.

Notes

1. When the UN Declaration of Human Rights was passed in 1948, the American Anthropological Association issued a response in which they pointed out its lack of understanding of alternative world-views.
2. The most specific discussion of the concept may be found in the White Paper preceding the 1986 Act, where it says, '[t]owards the end of the previous century, and especially during this one, the purpose of adoption has undergone a change. The prime purpose

of adoption should no longer be to ensure the rights of adoptive parents, but to provide a child with a permanent home'. Further, 'Our experience and knowledge today tells us that children's interests and needs are not sufficiently ensured if one only takes account of those laws that regulate the material conditions. It is at least as much a question of psychological, medical and social expertise that is going to ensure the child's needs to obtain adoptive parents who can provide them with care, contact. And security' (NOU 176: 55 in Hognestad and Steenberg 2000: 440). One could hardly wish for a better demonstration of the power of the psycho-technocrats.

3.   Nigel Cantwell was formerly working at the Hague Convention on International Adoption and is currently at the UNICEF Innocenti Research centre in Florence. The paper was presented at a conference in Copenhagen in 2002.

4.   Certainly, as regards transnational adoption, it is not uncommon to hear bureaucrats and local NGO workers in some of the poor donor countries proffer the superior material benefits awaiting the adoptee as the main argument for sending children to new families overseas.

5.   After listing the various rights of the child, such as the right to be brought up in its family, right to a birth certificate and a family name (rights which, one might argue, are also useful for controlling the citizens of a state), she goes on to argue that other rights also need to be safeguarded, such as the right of a birth mother to confidentiality [highly controversial in the drafting of the Hague Convention] and the adoptive parents' right to parenthood (an equally controversial proposal).

6.   Here the concept is further defined as follows: 'Empowerment is the expansion of assets and capabilities of poor people to participate in, negotiate with, influence, control, and hold accountable institutions that affect their lives' (World Bank 2000: vi). The World Bank does not specify the empowerment of children, but the concept has been transferred to those arenas where children are the object of assistance.

7.   The USA – an active participant in all these fora and the self-appointed guardian of worldwide democracy – has refused to sign both the UN Convention on Children's Rights and the Hague Convention on Intercountry Adoption on the grounds that there is no national support in the USA for the involvement of public bodies into issues pertaining to family matters. This may in turn be brought back to the suggestion that US political culture has been framed from the beginning, 'by a language of individual rights that emphasises individual liberty rather than claims to economic and social justice' (*Childhood* 1999: 405).

8.   I regard this point as particularly poignant, especially in light of much current development jargon, which stresses the need for being 'recipient oriented'.

9.   This, apparently, is quite a common phenomenon in the formation of international policy statements concerning controversial topics (Bøås and McNeill 2004).

10.   According to a Norwegian commentator, adoption was included because paragraph 21 dealing with adoption was not phrased as obligatory, but as advisory. In ratifying the Convention, Argentina was the only country to exclude its agreement to the relevant paragraph.

11.   Several commentators have pointed out that it is significant to note that the 'right to privacy' is prioritised above other specified rights of the child. Burman suggests that this may be a reflection of US liberal individualism (Burman 1996: 51). It seems unlikely that privacy is a matter of concern, let alone priority, for the poor people – young or old – of Asia, Africa and Latin America.

12.   The process of drafting the Hague Convention is extremely well documented. Practically all documents and minutes of discussions are published (1994).

13.   Although the proposal coincided with the provisions of the UNCRC, it was made independently of the drafting process (Cantwell 2001a: 1)

14. A precursor to the Convention appeared in 1965, but it was brought out before its time; transnational adoption from the South to the North had only just begun, and only three countries ratified it (Steenberg 1993: 10).

15 Sixty-six countries had ratified the Hague Convention by June 2005. China did so on 16 September 2005. The USA signed it in 1994, but has not ratified it. Attempts have recently been made to achieve this.

16. Indonesia, however, made it difficult for foreign couples to adopt by insisting on a previous three-year residence in the country.

17. According to Sura 33: 4–5, 'God hath not given a man two hearts within him ... nor hath he made your adopted sons to be as your own sons' (Van Loon: 1994).

18. Ethiopia, with a large Muslim population, does not distinguish between the various religious groups but treats all children as equals before the law.

19. This was preceded by the African Charter on Human and People's Rights, which was adopted by African heads of states in 1981 and came into force in 1986.

20. In this connection, it is interesting to note how several senior politicians and policy-makers of African countries perform their own kind of essentialisation of ideas and values when they encompass all of Africa into one African culture. For political and ideological reasons, they cease to be cultural relativists with regard to the huge and socioculturally varied continent of Africa ,while they fight for a cultural relativistic approach on a global scale.

21. While ethnographic studies from African societies demonstrate that the autonomous individual does not represent an overarching value, and hence the meaninglessness of individual rights, it is perhaps too much to claim that 'in African traditional culture [*sic*], there was usually 'no contradiction between personal and communal interest and we accepted that both were dependent upon each other' (Ojo 1990: 120).

22. The promotion of 'Asian values' was developed in the 1980s in Singapore, Malaysia, and other Southeast Asian nation states in direct confrontation with what was perceived by heads of state as the hegemonic effort of former colonial powers.

23. The intervention of the European Union in similar practices in Romania will be discussed in the next chapter.

24. The Christian distinction between that which is God's ('gifts') and that which is Caesar's ('commodities') has influenced Western thinking, and the distinction continues until the present. An abhorrence of monetary transactions in domains characterised as non-economic may be observed. People are not commodities to be bought and sold. Such dichotomous thinking with its heavy moralising overtones underpins much development aid as well as international treaties and conventions that have a human rights intent.

25. An ethnographic example from my own research among the Lio of eastern Indonesia demonstrates some of the moral conflicts that may arise when Westerners encounter alien symbolisation of the meaning of money. Dutch Catholic missionaries strongly disapproved of the Lio bride-wealth system (*belis*) that is practised between wife-receivers and wife-givers. Lio kinship represents a fairly classic example of a matrilateral cross-cousin prescriptive alliance system. Women move in one direction, wealth and services in the opposite. In this the Dutch missionaries saw a system of men buying wives. Despite the fact that the majority of the population today has been converted to Catholicism, people continue to practice *belis*, and money, due to a shortage of gold and buffaloes, is becoming the main part of *belis*. Missionaries fail to understand the wider implication of the system, which gives rise to alliance exchanges of goods and services that stretch far beyond the actual marriage itself and are not thought of as commercial transactions. This example demonstrates how Western thinking constructs money as inherently immoral, and the need to separate it from domains that must be kept morally pure.

26. This clearly tells us something about American notions of personhood. The practice of buying and selling eggs and sperm may further be seen in relationship to debates in American about abortion.

27. According to Mauss, a total social phenomenon is one in which 'all kinds of institutions are given expression at one and the same time – religious, juridical, and moral, which relate to both politics and the family' (1969: 3).

28. The reason for this may be that the child is too old for it to be adopted or that he or she is severely handicapped. These children can expect to spend their whole childhood and adolescence in the institution.

29. This is in sharp contrast to the American practice of open adoption. However, it is in line with Norwegian adoptive parents' focus on the place of their children's origin rather than on the people who gave them life.

Chapter 9

Expert Knowledge: Global and Local Adoption Discourses in India, Ethiopia, China and Romania

Being parents is a challenge ... hence we arrange for continuous inputs on parenting from a panel of experts, child behaviour specialists, child psychologists etc.

> General Secretary, Sudatta Adoption Support Group, India.

Time and again, we cite the most pious international conventions and standards and speak of serving the best interest of the child. Well, what is the best interest of the Ethiopian child?

> Lawyer at the Ethiopian Juvenile Justice Project Office.

Despite all the differences in values concerning children and families, and despite the imbalance in economic and political power between the nation-states, more than 40,000 children are transferred every year – in most cases successfully – from one country to another, from one kinned reality to another. So far in this book I have discussed transnational adoption primarily from the point of view of the receiving countries and the adoptive families. I gave some voice to donating countries in the previous chapter when I discussed the UNCRC and the Hague Convention. I cannot end without looking in more detail at the situation in some countries that adopt children to Western countries. That is the topic of this last chapter, where I focus on India, China, Ethiopia and Romania. The following questions merit consideration: What is the raison d'étre of transnational adoption in donor countries and how is the practice regarded by different sections of society? To what extent do state authorities and orphanage personnel in these countries share, or reject, the values that their powerful partners in Europe and North America present as right and good? To what extent have Western values reshaped local values and practices and to what extent have the psy-discourses affected discursive practices in Asia, Africa and Eastern Europe? From a perspective of indigenous notions of kinship, what value is attributed to the biological tie? What kind of adoptive practices have been engaged in and how have they been regulated? All these questions will be addressed. Thus, I have turned full circle back to the three foci I identified at the outset as the main topics for the book: the anthropology of kinship as a tool in analysis, the growth of psychology and the psychology-based professions which enable the establishment and consolidation of governmentality, and the globalisation of Western morality and rationality. In this chapter the last two foci dominate, but without my theoretical backdrop of kinship (and kinning), my approach would have been very different.

An overall concern in this chapter will be with questions pertaining to the indirect mechanisms of rule, 'those that have enabled, or sought to enable, government at a distance' (Miller and Rose 1990: 83). It is clear that the liberal (wealthy) democratic nations of Europe seek to exercise intellectual domination over those nations that are less favoured, but that, in the case of adoption, have the 'goods' so desired by the Europeans and North Americans. While the goal is to bring children to Western couples, state authorities in receiving countries ensure that they control the transaction – although, as will become clear, donor countries have some means at their disposal to assert themselves. A stated aim by the authorities in the receiving countries, is to ensure that the best interest of the children is achieved, and that the transaction is conducted in a legally and morally acceptable manner – according to the rules that they themselves have made. In order to achieve this, representatives from the Western countries employ a mixture of persuasion and compulsion. They impose conditions before releasing funds or granting legitimacy to local institutions, they monitor practices, they arrange courses and seminars for local staff during which the 'technologies of knowledge' are imparted, they flatter and cajole and invite senior government servants and orphanage personnel to visit (all expenses paid). By and large, those receiving countries that are signatories to the Hague Convention adhere to its principles and rules. They do not bribe, they do not pay illegitimate fees. At least, they claim not to do so; and although the occasional scandal does erupt from time to time, it is fair to say that they do so with decreasing frequency.

The normative edicts and regulations pertaining to the personal and private life of citizens have been on the agenda of the 'advanced liberal democratic state' (Miller and Rose 1990) for quite some time in most recipient countries – with the partial exception of the USA. According to Miller and Rose, governmentality is dependent upon a number of 'technologies of government' that allow for a normalisation of conduct. This not only involves grand concepts like nationhood or the free market, but requires for its success a number of 'apparently humble and mundane mechanisms which appear to make it possible to govern: techniques of notation, computation and calculation; procedures of examinations and assessments, ... surveys, statistics ... professional specialisms ...' (1990: 82). Governmentality, understood loosely as a government's aim to achieve the best life conditions for its citizens, was also, I suggest, the ideology of the former Communist regimes within the Soviet Union and by China. However, here it took a form that was authoritarian, paternalistic and undemocratic and that led to repressive measures. It is from this point of view that I present my discussion of the situation in China and Romania.

There is a further important difference between the governmentality of the liberal democracies of the West and that of the Communist regimes, which has some bearing upon transnational adoption. This concerns the ontological status of the individual. Whereas the autonomous individual occupies pride of place in the West, from which notions of rights, agency and choice have become inseparable from the understanding of personhood, the Communist countries set ontological store by the well-being of the community and the state, and subordinated the needs and rights of the individual to those of the community. Both capitalist and communist ideologies regard kinned relatedness as epiphenomenal; the former to the supremacy of the individual, the latter to that of the community. This is not the case in many countries in Africa, Asia and Latin America from which Western nations adopt children. While claiming democratic aspirations, most do not share in the belief of the supremacy of the autonomous individual, but perceive personhood and community as being constituted through relations. Kinship becomes a determining factor for significant relatedness, but kinship need not necessarily be predicated upon biological connectedness. It is the process of kinning that creates kinship – not biology. I have suggested that abandoned children, whether orphaned or not, fall outside kinship. In the West, this does not matter so much, because personhood is predicated upon the individual. In Asia and Africa, the unconnected, de-kinned, child becomes a non-person. This may account for the neglect shown them by society.

Undoubtedly, all the countries that give up abandoned and orphaned children for adoption overseas do so because they are unable, or unwilling, to provide for the children themselves. The countries that receive children do so because of an increasing demand from their own citizens who are unable to procreate biologically. The networks that are established between public and private bodies in donor and receiving countries are made up of actors whose goals are not necessarily the same – although the rhetoric employed may give that impression – but who nevertheless wish to maintain the relationship. The question remains to what extent the dice are loaded in favour of the recipient countries. They always get what they want (children), although they may not get enough. The donor countries may get part of what they want: help for children unable to help themselves and who the state has not the means to help, and some assistance (financial and professional) to improve existing childcare services – but, in the process, they may get more than they bargained for. They may feel themselves subjected to the humiliation of being regarded as undeveloped (in understanding as well as in means); expected to meekly satisfy the postcolonial demand for what is a scarce resource in Europe and North American.[1]

My discussion of the four donor counties is organised so that, in each case, I start by highlighting 'traditional' values and practices concerning the adoption of children, and then relate these to some effects resulting from the encounter with a normative Western rationality and morality as these are manifested in transnational adoption. My argument will be that all four experience an ambivalence regarding the practice. All are aware of the implicit neocolonial overtones, but the way they choose to deal with this varies from country to country.

Values and Practices in India

Because large sections of the Indian elite are highly ambivalent about their relationship with the West, India is a particularly interesting donor country from the point of view of my study. Indian education has been closely linked to Britain for more than a century. Not only have thousands of Indians attended British universities, the local higher education system is built on the British model. Indian researchers have been actively engaged in international arenas for generations, and it is not surprising that Indian official thinking on children and children's welfare, adoption and transnational adoption, is largely in line with ideas emanating from the West. The 'psy' discourse has been influential, giving rise to the various professions of Indian psycho-technocrats. There is a large body of Indian literature on the psychology of children. As far as I could ascertain, more books on adoption, whether domestic or transnational, have been published in India than in any other donor country. At the same time, there is a noticeable ideological resistance to what is perceived as Western encroachment in Indian intellectual life as well as in social and economic affairs. Of the four countries to be discussed, India expresses the most clearly formulated anti-transnational adoption sentiments. This is manifested in the recent legal provisions which seek to limit, or even reduce, overseas adoption by insisting that no Indian child can be adopted overseas unless another child is adopted by an Indian couple – the so-called 50/50 rule.

The earliest organised transnational adoptions from India occurred in the late 1970s. The children went to Norway, Sweden, Denmark, Switzerland and Holland. Though several children went for adoption to the USA, that does not count as transnational adoption 'since they went to families of Indian origin who had immigrated to the USA' (Damodaran and Mehta

2000: 408). An essentialist, biocentric, approach to personhood and identity may thus be observed in Indian official thinking, a tendency that was confirmed by several Indian speakers and commentators at the Fourth International Conference on Child Adoption which I attended in New Delhi in October 2002.

When we examine figures detailing adoption in India, several startling facts emerge (see Table 9.1).

Table 9.1 Indian adoption figures

Year	Transnational adoption	Domestic adoption
1988	1,661	398
1993	1,134	1,382
1998	1,406	1,746

Source: Damodaran and Mehta 2000: 417

Poverty and illegitimacy are the main causes for abandoning children. Given an estimated number of between half and one million institutionalised children in India, of whom approximately 14 per cent are known to be orphans – i.e. adoptable – (Gudmundsson 2002: 2), the number that are

Figure 9.1 'The Wheel': cot in which to leave a child outside an orphanage in Delhi, India.

found new families is infinitesimal. Recent trends show a stabilisation of transnational adoption, and a slow increase in domestic adoption. Many Indian and foreign adoption workers expressed great frustration with the small number of children placed for foreign adoption, and were critical of the amount of effort invested into processing so few children.

Undoubtedly, transnational adoption is a sensitive issue in India. Sensational media reports appear from time to time that fuel criticism. However, not all are sceptical about the practice. An article in the influential journal *Economic and Political Weekly* argued strongly that the recent drive to encourage domestic adoption must not become a hindrance for transnational adoption just because this is regarded as politically more correct, and that the current imbalance in the procedures required for the two types of adoption cannot be regarded as being in the 'best interest of the child' (Anand and Chandra 2001: 3892). The authors discuss a recent case of corruption in Hyderabad in connection with transnational adoption, as a result of which, several local adoption agencies were closed down, the children seized, and a whole group of high-profile individuals were arrested on charges of child trafficking under the guise of transnational adoption. Allegedly, state administrators and lawyers were also involved in what became a highly publicised case. It was claimed that poor parents, primarily of tribal origin, were tempted by offers of money to sign away their rights in their children. As a result of the revelations, several children who had already been allocated to parents in Europe – who were preparing their journey to pick them up when the scandal broke – were removed from the process altogether and placed in government orphanages. Commenting on the case, Anand and Chandra say: 'the ones who are really being deprived of childhood, homes, families, future and possibly their lives are the children because the adoption process has come to a grinding halt' (ibid.: 3891).

The Indian media are quick to report alleged misdemeanours in connection with transnational adoption reported from other countries. A case involving an American woman in Guatemala in the early 1990s was widely reported in the Indian media and used as an argument against transnational adoption.[2] Such cases give fuel to the opponents of transnational adoption.[3] India ratified the Hague Convention in 2003.

Laws and Regulations

'Endless are the woes of those who have no sons; there is no place for the man who is destitute of male offspring', states the ancient Sanskrit text (Thanikachalam 1998: iv). Adoption of an heir by childless couples in Hindu India has been engaged in for centuries, the purpose being 'the perpetuation of the family name and lineage, protection in old age, performance of death rites and salvation of the adoptive parents' (Damodaran and Mehta 2000: 406). As mentioned in Chapter 3, adoption is subject to a series of complex Hindu regulations. Although kinship systems vary throughout the continent, patrilineal descent and virilocal marriage in some form or other are dominant throughout.[4] Until recently, the adoptee (invariably a boy) was taken from within the circle of family or caste, and the practice did not involve outsiders. To go outside the caste was unheard of. The adoption of an unrelated child began in the 1970s – perhaps as a result of people hearing that children were adopted by European couples – and it is slowly gaining popularity amongst Indian involuntarily childless couples. Social workers, paediatricians and psychologists have taken an active interest, and in the words of two central persons engaged in the development of procedures for controlling adoption, '[t]his professional intervention led to a systematisation of the process so that the best interests of the child, adoptive parents and birth parents could be protected' (ibid.: 407).

Indian authorities were quick to recognise a need to control transnational adoption. The early days of the transaction were often marked by malpractice. Private organisations sent children abroad without any kind of supervision either in India or in the receiving country, and 'there is little doubt that some adoptions to parents overseas were carried out from mercenary motives' (Mehta 2002: 2). The authorities, prompted by concerned psycho-technocrats, wanted to ensure that it was done properly. In 1974 a meeting was arranged in the Mumbai High Court in order to examine the practice. At the meeting there was 'an open confrontation between the lawyers (those involved in sending children abroad and indulging in malpractices) on the one side and the [professionally trained] social workers on the other' (Damania 1988: 7). The presiding judge decided that all inter-country adoptions should be scrutinised and monitored.[5] According to one commentator, the agencies 'were furious at this intervention, but had to perforce follow this procedure' (ibid.).

However, no all-India law of adoption ensued. Two Supreme Court judgments from 1982 and 1984 (the so-called Pandey submissions), following the Hindu Adoption and Maintenance Act 1956, with subsequent petitions in 1986, 1989, 1991, together form the legal basis for the intervention of the state. But these apply only to Hindus, Buddhists and Jains. Muslims, Christians, Jews and Parsees fall outside. They come under the Guardians and Wards Act 1890, which means that they may only engage in a guardian–ward type of relationship (Thanikachalam 1998: vi).

In her review of the Indian adoption programme, Damania states that the Pandey judgments provided 'an excellent opportunity for workers in the field [of adoption] to help shape such an important document'. Pandey had originally called for a ban on sending children abroad due to the many reports of malpractice, but social workers made submissions with the result that, from then on, 'significant steps were taken in promoting adoption as a child welfare service' (1998: 8). Certainly, the judgments and the subsequent Government of India Guidelines from 1995 are perceived by the various experts on children and children's needs as major victories. Their expert knowledge is heeded, and their role as the guardians of 'the best interest of the children' acknowledged and safeguarded. Also, the judgments represent a victory for the authority of the state in-so-far as new state-supervised institutions were established. The Indian state was given new mechanisms for direct involvement in matters pertaining to family and children, and the Guidelines enabled them (at least in theory) to effect strict control over adoption. Privately conducted transnational adoption became banned, and the Co-ordinating Adoption Resource Agency (CARA), a national governmental institution under the Ministry of Welfare, was established by a Supreme Court directive in 1990 as a direct result of the judgments. CARA's functions are to monitor and regulate information about children available for adoption (domestic and transnational), issue licences to placement agencies in India, and supervise their activities – making sure that proper records are kept – issue 'no objection certificates' for children to be adopted overseas and regulate the guidelines (Mehta 2002). There is a general feeling amongst foreign adoption agencies that CARA is negative to transnational adoption. Certainly, CARA actively encourages the growth of domestic adoption. A mixture of motives may account for this bias. A resentment against a perceived Western arrogance which accounts for their interference may be a major reason. Discussing the 1984 judgment, the Director of CARA told me that its provisions preceded the basic principles of the UNCRC and the Hague Convention. 'We encoded the principles and ensuing practices first, and therefore there is no reason not to ratify the Hague Convention', he said.

The Guidelines demonstrate clearly the desire on the part of the state to control matters pertaining to children and family.[6] Again, we find that these regulations are said to be issued in order to ensure 'the best interest of the child' without a clear indication of what this might be. In addition, the regulations now require that 'home-study reports' be provided for domestic as well as foreign adoptions, and the requirements for these mirror those of the Scandinavian and other receiving countries (see below). According to the regulations, the order of priority in allocation should be as follows:

1. Indian families in India;
2. Indian families abroad;
3. one parent of Indian origin abroad;
4. totally foreign.

However, the drafters of the regulations recognised that it might not be easy to find Indian couples willing to adopt totally unknown children – especially if they were older or handicapped – although efforts are engaged in to 'educate' the population in that direction. Consequently, the regulations state, '[h]andicapped children, children over 6 years of age and siblings will be excluded from this calculation' [of dividing adoption on a 50/50 basis between domestic and transnational][7]. What is clear from my own and Roel's researches in India, is that most Indian couples who are willing to consider adopting an unknown child have a strong preference for young babies in perfect health. This means no birth marks, dark skin or other 'disabilities'. People were very open about this. Even individuals who appeared to be hostile towards the adoption of Indian children by Europeans admit that Europeans are useful for taking handicapped, dark-skinned, or older children, as well as 'tribal children that no Indian couple would touch'. The last group is especially difficult to place with Indian couples due also to prejudices concerning their looks and intelligence. And the director of an orphanage in central India told me that tribal people are thought to have very 'hot blood', a quality regarded as inauspicious. Thus, while prospective adoptive parents in Scandinavia (and other European countries) are not permitted to specify what sort of child they are willing to accept, Indians have no such inhibitions. It is hard not to draw the conclusion that a prevailing attitude in some Indian adoption circles is that while they object to Westerners coming to take Indian children, they are nevertheless useful as a dumping ground for the undesirable ones (see also Mehta 2002: 9).

The thinking behind the 50/50 rule on domestic and transnational adoption is problematic. While the hierarchy of preferences correspond to those of Article 21 of the UNCRC, some commentators have linked the formulations of the Indian regulations to anti-West sentiments. Moreover, Anand and Chandra argue that policy decisions regarding transnational adoption have been based on incorrect assumptions. Firstly, the claim that a familiar cultural and social milieu is most appropriate is suspect, they say, because '[h]ow can one, scientifically determine what constitutes a social and cultural milieu?' India has a wide diversity of cultural and social practices. Most children given up for adoption come from a very different caste – and class – from their adoptive parents. It is therefore most unlikely that a child adopted in India would necessarily retain his or her original background. They conclude, '[b]ased on this incorrect assumption, the policy to facilitate in-country adoption has been arrived at. This distinction is not merely one of semantics, but is very real because though the latter is not prohibited it is discouraged at every stage with the aid of the legitimate state machinery' (2001: 3892). They point out that regulations on transnational adoption are much more stringent than those for domestic adoption; at least in most states. This leads to a situation where domestic adoption (the preferential principle) has attained overriding importance, so that 'the welfare of the child has not merely taken a backseat but does not even form a part of the relevant considerations' (ibid.:

3892). The authors conclude by strongly urging that inter-country adoption be encouraged at the same time as efforts are made to promote domestic adoption, and that better procedures for domestic adoption be adhered to in all Indian states.

To judge from this article, the intentions inherent in good government, namely to ensure prosperity for the nation's citizens, have failed dismally in Indian adoption practice. I heard similar sentiments voiced by others. The state's quest for a higher quality of life for its children is hampered by an over-bureaucratisation on the one hand, and an anti-Western ideological stance on the other. In other words, it appears that India has moved from one extreme of no regulations and an attitude of laissez-faire, to another in which over-regulating of procedures becomes detrimental to children in need.

Transnational Flows of Concepts and Values

The involvement of Indian social workers and other professionals in adoption activities, marks the advent of a new approach to thinking about children and family life. The state's role in ensuring appropriate facilities in this previously private sphere has become marked, at the same time as a psy-discourse may be discerned. In his introduction to the *Handbook on Child Adoption in India*, Thanikachalam, the Honorary Joint Secretary to the Indian Council for Child Welfare in Tamil Nadu, states, 'As knowledge in child development grew, it became internationally accepted that no institution can be a match for the care and protection offered by a loving family' (1998: v).

The Fourth International Conference on Child Adoption (organised by the Indian Council for Child Welfare) that took place in Delhi in 2002 was a high-profile occasion and may be regarded as indicative of the contemporary climate of opinion. A couple of hundred people took part from a wide range of organisations, both Indian and foreign. The Indian contingent to the conference was made up of representatives from various State authorities, from orphanages who adopt both domestically and abroad, from voluntary co-ordinating agencies (VCA), and from adoptive parents' associations.

The foreigners were represented by adoption agencies from most of the countries to which India sends children for adoption, as well as, in some cases, representatives of the central state organisation that oversees transnational adoption. The presence of such senior personnel from receiving countries demonstrates that they are eager to show that they are serious and honourable collaborators.[8] Several trends emerged from the Indian side: a strong preference in senior governmental circles for domestic rather than transnational adoption; a sense of frustration from the grass-root-level regarding the bureaucratic procedures that keep the number of children adopted very low; a rising interest in post-adoption services for domestically adopted children; a preoccupation with questions about 'roots' for those adopted abroad; and the recent rise of Indian adoptive parents' associations. From the recipient countries I sensed a concern about an increasing reluctance to send children abroad; a sense of being attributed dishonourable intentions and malpractices; a frustration with the bureaucratic procedures that delay children in joining their new families; an irritation with being made the rubbish dump of unwanted children; and a more positive attitude to the plight of the adoptees who wish to find out about their 'roots'.

Indian attitudes regarding transnational adoption were mixed. While some voiced open hostility to the practice, many actively supported it. The recent case of malpractice in Hyderabad had refuelled negative sentiments and had, according to one speaker, 'impacted the whole Indian adoption programme'. Another stated with passion that 'yes, there are a few bad eggs, but they must not destroy the work of the rest'. The various recipient countries vehemently protested their innocence, though admitting in private that malpractice may sometimes take place. There are rogue agencies, I was told, but only because too many foreign agencies are licensed to adopt from India.[9]

From Adult-centred to Child-centred

All Indian commentators on adoption make the point that until the 1970s, when transnational adoption took off, adoption in India was exclusively thought of as a practice to serve adults in need of an heir for religious and economic reasons. Several speakers at the conference urged for an intensified 'education programme' directed at Indian involuntary infertile couples to consider adopting an unrelated child of unknown caste origin.[10] Following the UNCRC, the attention shifted from 'a child for a family' to 'a family for a child' (ibid.). Posters prepared by CARA to encourage domestic adoption demonstrate the new focus. See next page for examples of two such posters.

Showing an appealingly attractive infant, the text on one poster reads:

I want a Home,

a Father, Mother, Siblings.

Not Donations, Contributions, Cheques.

ADOPT ME

Another poster reads:

Adopt a Child

He has no parents

No home

No hopes....

You can give him

And many others like him

All three

With ideas of children and childhood filtering in from Europe and North America, expressed most clearly in the UNCRC and the Hague Convention, one Indian speaker said that a 'paradigm shift' had begun in India. This is summarized in Table 9.2.

Table 9.2 The 'paradigm' shift in adoption in India

From:	To:
A needs approach	A rights framework
A child for a family	A family for a child
A right to a child	Rights of a child
Custodial care	Holistic development
Minimum standards	Quality standards in child care
Institutional care	Non-institutional family-based alternatives

Source: (Mehta 2002: 10)

In commenting on this proposed shift, Mehta argued that many believed that Western concepts and findings are not relevant to the Indian situation. While this may be the case in some instances, she said, it is not necessarily so. She advocated an attitude of open-mindedness.

A change has been taking place over time. In an early study on adoption in India the author states in her Introduction, 'Adoption *as now understood* is child-oriented and mainly concerned with the welfare of the child', and further, '[t]hese practices are based on the *knowledge derived from the social sciences*, specially the growing science of child development which has emphasised the importance of the parent–child relationship, and the provision of *a proper family for the healthy nurturing of the child* (Billimora 1984: 1, 2, my emphasis). In other words, a transnational flow of concepts has clearly taken place. Mehta was adamant in her acceptance of new (i.e. Western?) ideas when she states,

> a continuous upgrading of knowledge and skills in the adoption field is necessary in order to keep pace with newer development and research. Use of positive adoption language and understanding concepts about the 'Psychology of Adoption like Shared faith, Psychic Homelessness, Primal Wound, Genealogical Bereavement' etc. need to be understood. (2002: 7, 8)

Thus, influential professionals do not reject Western discourses. Mehta's statement bears clear witness to an acceptance of them. I suggest that such Indian attitudes may in part be accounted for by the fact that influential Indian intellectuals regard themselves as equals in the discourse of child psychology; as being contributors to, as well as recipients of, the discourse. To them the 'psy' discourse is global, by and large universally applicable. Politicians and senior civil servants are more dubious about the relevance of some Western precepts.

One consequence of the dissemination of the Western approach is the requirement that a home study of prospective Indian parents be undertaken as part of the process of allocating a child. Applicants must provide personal details as well as information about employment, economic and financial situation, health, and housing – supported by authorised confirmations from doctors, employers etc. On the basis of this, and one or more interviews, a social worker writes an evaluation, taking particular care to 'give an account of the relations between the two applicants, their motive for the adoption, an analysis of the whole environment in which the applicants are living' (Roel in conversation). The profile provided includes the couple's childhood experiences, their relationship with their parents and siblings, their philosophy of life, their interests and hobbies as well as their attitudes to child rearing, in particular to the disciplining of their child, and an evaluation of their relationship as a couple. From this we can see that they are evaluated not just as providers, but also as to whether they are suitable parent material, able to provide psychological care. The criteria and procedures are virtually identical to those in Norway. A major difference is that Indian applicants are allowed to state preferred age, sex, complexion and health status of the child. One report I have read showed the concern felt by the social worker about the couple's desire to keep the adoption secret.[11] Indian adoption workers struggle to persuade Indian prospective adopting parents not to keep the fact of adoption secret. Psychological arguments (e.g. traumatic reaction by the child when s/he finds out by accident), as well as practical ones (others will know or guess), are used in order to discourage secrecy. In her comments, the social worker states: 'Disclosure issues were discussed with them, but the couple, bound by social stigmas, was not open to accept the advice given.' She concludes that although the couple comes across as highly suitable in most regards – being 'psychologically, emotionally and financially well prepared for adoption' – she recommends that before they are accepted, they should be engaged in further talks about disclosure, which will make them realise that the fact of adoption is 'an honour'. This particular social worker had an MA in social work from a highly respected Indian university and was well-read in relevant English and American literature.[12]

Discourses about the Significance of Origins and Roots

In his talk at the conference, the Director of CARA stated with approval that transnational adoption is on the decline, whereas there is an increase in domestic adoption. As regards the fate of the children adopted overseas, he said that once they leave India they ought to be assimilated into their new nationality and culture.[13] He was adamant about the need to protect the biological mother's identity. Indian law insists on the anonymity of biological parents of an abandoned child and he was critical of those receiving countries whose laws on this were different and who maintained that the adoptees had 'a right to know'. 'In India we are sceptical to this', he said.

This view was in stark contrast to that expressed by some of the psychologically trained social workers who organised a session on 'roots' at the conference. One speaker started by saying that 'the question of roots is a very new topic for us'. She explained that she had become interested in it as a direct result of the increasing number of requests she receives from adoptees who wish to find out about their origins. She later told me that she had at first been very surprised by this interest, but was now convinced of its importance, 'having read quite a lot on the subject'. Indeed, in her prepared presentation, she cites the British psychologist Brodzinski who claims that 100 per cent of adoptees[14] desire to make a search. Another Indian speaker stated, '[t]he search for roots has emerged as one of the most challenging areas in adoption. It challenges the secrecy which is the inherent characteristic of adoption' (Maharajasingh 2002: 1).

This session provoked a lot of interest amongst Indian and foreign delegates,[15] many of whom learnt that it is a 'natural desire' to know one's biological origins and that it is positive to search. However, this was not corroborated by another session in which five adult Indian-born adoptees talked about their experiences. They were not preoccupied with roots. Rather, their stories were about life in their adoptive country amongst family and friends. They reported how well received they had been, how integrated they were in their families, and how being brown did not mean discrimination. Noone had felt themselves to be an outsider and they had not had much contact with other transnationally adopted children. To much applause, one Swedish girl said, 'I'm a coconut child. Brown on the outside and white on the inside', and continued that this did not present any problems. They all expressed their pleasure at visiting India and seeing the orphanage where they had spent their first months or years, but none of them had come with any intention to search for relatives. This attitude corresponds well with my findings from Norwegian adoptees' 'return visits'. A couple of the adoptees were very explicit about not making rules about what is right or wrong, and warned against instilling desires and needs.[16] The audience was somewhat ambivalent in its reaction. It seems that although the concept of roots has arrived rather late in India, it finds a resonance with many, but not all, of those involved in transnational adoption. It allows them to maintain that the children are not really abandoned by India, that they continue to be Indian, that adoption abroad does not represent a real rupture, and at the same time, because of this, the practice may be continued.

Associations of Adoptive Families

I noted (Chapter 4) the prevalence of active adoptive parents associations in Norway. I have since discovered that similar associations exist in other receiving countries and I was intrigued to discover that they are being established in India also.[17] It transpired that the Indian initiators were inspired by what they had learnt about such associations in Europe. Taking his cue from European psychological writings, the General Secretary of Sudatta Adoption Support, explained that experts feel that heredity determines the physical characteristics of the child while personality characteristics are a result of nurturing. A support group such as Sudatta is a major component in the nurturing process. The associations have two purposes. Firstly, in the words of one speaker, they wish to be an organ for 'educating the public ... as to the inherent positive possibilities in adopting an unrelated child' and 'to promote the concept of child adoption in a vigorous and sustained manner in schools and various local organisations'. Secondly, they wish to provide a forum in which aspiring parents, as well as adoptive families, may meet and discuss themes of common interest. All present agreed that it is important for adopted children to meet others like themselves. However, one adoptive mother said that her daughter, who was now twelve years old, refused to go to such gatherings, insisting that she had her own friends and did not feel the need to meet other kids just because they were adopted.[18] So, just like the Norwegian associations, the Indian ones stress how their activities are 'good for the children', but upon closer inspection turn out, perhaps, to be good for the parents.

There is a discernible paradox in Indian attitudes about transnational adoption amongst individuals and organisations engaged in the activity. On the one hand, all concerned recognise that India is incapable of looking after its thousands of institutionalised children and that, due to entrenched cultural values, domestic adoption is unlikely to provide a realistic solution for a long time to come. On the other hand, an ideological resentment is apparent in influential circles against what is perceived as a form of neo-colonialism, by which Western countries not only take Indian children away from their homeland, but also dictate the procedures for how to conduct the transaction. The situation is further complicated by the active presence of local experts, the psycho-technocrats whose professional training is to a large extent Western- based, and who are assisting the Indian state in taking control of adoption transactions. Conflicting views amongst Indian adoption personnel arise out of different understandings about family, parenthood and children and out of different attitudes to Western ideas and involvement. The speaker at the conference who argued that adoption in India 'clearly needs a paradigm shift' personifies one voice. The director of CARA, who insists that Indians have little to learn from the West and should be 'pursuing Indian values', personifies another.

I wish to end this discussion about Indian values and practices with a quote from the director of a particularly well-run orphanage. I had asked her about her attitude to the two international conventions and whether she felt that they spoke to the situation in India. She replied, 'the concepts and premises are Western, but they make you think'.

Values and Practices in Ethiopia

I turn next to a consideration of the situation in Ethiopia, another country from which Norway adopts children.[19] Ethiopia is a relatively late comer to the transnational adoption scene, but is rapidly becoming popular. The situation here is very different from that in India. The country is extremely poor. According to the World Bank study, *Voices of the Poor* (2000), the majority of the Ethiopian population is experiencing not only an economic decline , but also a decline in 'well-being' (Rahmato and Kidanu 1999: 12, 13). The postwar period was turbulent, and a coup d'état in 1974 dethroned the Emperor and installed a military Marxist regime. Conflict with Eritrea, decline of the economy and severe droughts, followed by debilitating civil wars, meant that when the Mangiest regime fell in 1991, the country was impoverished economically as well as socially and administratively. The situation is still desperate. Given these facts, the room for manoeuvre by the state is limited. Most commentators, whether local or foreign, agree that Ethiopia would barely survive as a modern nation-state were it not for the aid that the country receives. Accompanying the aid are normative values. In recent years, a large section of foreign aid has been directed at children and the plight of women. Indeed, I was told by one government official that the main reason for producing the recently passed Family Law (which also regulates adoption, see below) was in order to improve the legal position (and hopefully as a result, the actual situation) of women. By all accounts, there is still a long way to go. Low status, enforced girl marriages, and wife beating are all common features of women's lives, regardless of which social group they belong to. In such a cultural setting, where just to survive requires supreme efforts, the notion of children's rights has not been met with much understanding (Berre 2004).[20]

Transnational adoption began in the early 1970s when thousands of children were orphaned or abandoned as a result of drought, famine and severe and prolonged civil wars. The first orphanages were established at this time by the government and by foreign NGOs and missionaries. More recently, the explosive spread of HIV/AIDS in Ethiopia has led to thousands more children being orphaned as a result of one or both parents dying from the disease.[21] According to the Ethiopian delegate to the UN Committee on the Rights of the Child meeting in 2001, an estimated 100,000 children live on the streets in Addis Ababa. Today, there are five state-run orphanages in the country with an overall capacity for 2,000 children. Whereas earlier, local kinship systems would accommodate orphans, the pressures of the past thirty years have, according to several commentators, rendered family and kin incapable of coping with the problem. Ethiopia sends approximately 800 children annually for adoption overseas. This represents only a minute percentage of children that potentially could be adopted. Unlike in India, I could detect no anti-Western sentiments to account for the low number. It seems to be more a question of administrative capacity.

Norway received its first Ethiopian child at the end of 1991, immediately following Ethiopia's ratification of UNCRC. The popularity of the country as a supplier of children to Norwegian couples has been increasing steadily; by the end of 2002, more than 300 children had been adopted from the country. The reason that Ethiopia is a popular country may be found in a combination of circumstances, the most important of which are the relative ease with which one may obtain young infants, and the relatively rapid transaction procedures. These factors seem to override any concerns that might be harboured about colour and race.

Laws and Regulations

All local people I spoke to insisted that biological connectedness – traced patrilineally – is very important in Ethiopian thinking about personhood and relatedness. Adoption is not a traditional practice in most parts of Ethiopia, but there are some well-known exceptions.[22] Until recently, some system of fostering existed, but the children were not regarded by themselves or others as members of the family. As was repeatedly pointed out to me, adoption, in whatever form, was practised exclusively for the benefit of the adults concerned. It was only following the ratification of the UNCRC in December 1991 that children and their needs became a consideration (see also Woldegebreal n.d.: 2).

Adoption as a practice of creating kin-like bonds was covered by the *Civil Code of Ethiopia* (1960). Article 796 (1) runs: 'A bond of filiation may be created artificially by a contract of adoption between the adopter and the adopted child'. In the wake of ratifying UNCRC, the Ethiopian Government amended its Constitution in 1994. Article 36 is devoted to the rights of children and repeats 'almost verbatim the fundamental rights, stated under the UNCRC convention' (Woldegebreal n.d.: 1). At the same time, a Ministry of Labour and Social Affairs (MOLSA) was created as the responsible state organ 'to undertake all acts necessary for the implementation of the convention' (Ibid.: 1, 6). MOLSA, through the Children and Youth Affairs Organisation, produced in 1997 the *National Guidelines on Child Support – Alternative Approaches*, which includes detailed prescriptions for the equipment and running of childcare institutions and 'Directives for the Adoption of Ethiopian Children'. It is an impressive document, striving to make provisions that can ensure the best interest of the child. The aims and underlying values of these reflect the aims of Western organisations involved in development work for children. This is not surprising given that the Preface informs us that the guidelines were produced '[i]n collaboration with governmental institutions, various indigenous and international non-governmental organisations'. International or foreign NGOs are responsible for a very large proportion of child welfare programmes and are, as a result, actively involved in establishing the principles upon which they should be carried out.

Although Ethiopia ratified the UNCRC, they have not signed the Hague Convention. To do so, a lawyer told me, would mean having to change various legal provisions and establish a central government agency to handle all transnational adoption. However, when they had the chance to do this in the Revised Family Code passed in 2000, they ignored the opportunity. They also ignored the Hague Convention's insistence on prohibiting private adoption. Article 192, 1) says; 'Government or private orphanages may give *any child under their custody* to adopters' (emphasis added). This is anathema to European adoption agencies. Adoption workers (Ethiopian and foreign) are somewhat mollified by the requirement that all children given for adoption overseas must be approved by a court of law whose duty it is to look to the best interest of the child, (Article 194). The question remains why the government failed to ban private adoption, especially since two senior lawyers made submissions to the Parliamentary Committee that formulated the Act, strongly urging that private adoption, whether domestic or transnational, should not be allowed. It was suggested to me that one reason might be the financial benefits accruing to the orphanages – and also to some individuals. One local document explicitly criticises private adoption, and states that profit-making agencies inside and outside Ethiopia have 'for some time been promoting the sale of children, making it difficult to distinguish clearly between legitimate adoption and trafficking' (Fadese 1999: 3). Be that as it may, representatives from European adopting agencies expressed concern at this 'loophole' in the law, because they felt that it will make it more difficult for them to follow correct procedures.

A concern with biological relatedness is expressed in Article 183 of the Family Code: 'the adopted child shall retain his bonds with the family of origin'. The reasons for retaining such a provision are stated in a background document prepared for the Parliamentary committee by Seid, the head of legal Services at MOLSA, who argues that this is 'very essential, because [if not] marriage with his relatives, even with his natural sister and mother, is possible' (1999: 11).

According to the Family Code, all citizens are treated as equal regardless of religion. This means that Muslims are subjected to the adoption regulations even though their own traditions do not allow it. Ethiopia thus differs from India where minority populations of Muslims, Christians, Jews and Parsees remain outside the Pandey judgments on adoption. Unlike Indian adoption policy, there is no preference in Ethiopia for domestic adoption over transnational. In fact, virtually no domestic formal adoptions occur. In-so-far as domestic adoption is carried out, it remains a private matter between the adults concerned. Again, in contrast to the situation in India, virtually no attention is paid to transnational adoption in the media; it is not a political or ideological issue.

Transnational Flow of Concepts and Values

In stark contrast to India where 'psy' discourses are well established, there is little Ethiopian professional expertise on child development or childcare. Arguments about basic psychological needs, or the state's role in securing conditions for children to grow up into healthy, well-balanced individuals, are conspicuous by their absence amongst Ethiopians I talked to. All projects aimed at children in need focused on the practical. While everyone expressed concern about the effects of the HIV / AIDS epidemic, their preoccupations were with practical matters of prevention, treatment and care. I heard no Ethiopian mention the possible detrimental effect on children being brought up by other than their families, or suggest that to send them abroad to strangers might have serious emotional effects. Rather, most wished to send many more children for adoption abroad.

The so-called 'community-based child support programme' in which '[f]amily-like environments' are created for destitute children, run by a 'foster-mother', receives a lot of attention from aid agencies. Provisions are based on an understanding of 'the child's uniqueness as an individual and his or her need is recognised;' and further, 'the child's free activity is respected and his creativity will develop'. We see here a manifestation of the preeminence of the autonomous individual, whose individuality must be respected and allowed to develop.[23] While Ethiopian counterparts acquiesce, this does not mean that they are unaware of potential cultural imperialism. One well-known journalist whom I interviewed reacted quite strongly when I asked him what he thought about the UNCRC. He said that, in most regards, it was a good document and that he did not begrudge Western NGOs influence because of the minimal resources available to Ethiopian authorities. However, he objected to the centrality accorded the notion of the individual child. In his opinion, the value of the individual in general, and the individual child in particular, is irrelevant in the Ethiopian context, just as the concept of the nuclear family is irrelevant.

To introduce these values poses a serious challenge to traditional thinking and practice. He referred to his own childhood in the countryside in his father's large compound. All kinds of relatives lived here, and children moved freely between the adults and carried out small tasks for anyone who asked. Poor relatives would bring a child or two to the compound where they would be looked after on a par with the rest. It was the adults who took priority; the children just had to fit in as best they could. No child was abandoned, but any special emotional attachment to them was not on the agenda, he said. Questions of blood connection counted mainly in matters of inheritance. From his point of view, the concept of individual rights is not meaningful in Ethiopia. But, in the words of the journalist, 'what poverty does is to discourage debate about Western values being imposed'. Ethiopia simply cannot provide for the huge numbers of orphans that exist in the country today.

Similar sentiments were expressed by a senior officer at MOLSA who, inter alia, was responsible for transnational adoption. He said that most issues that he had to deal with in his work emanated from Western donor concerns and values. Like the journalist, he said that the Western concern with the value of the individual and the nuclear family in development projects was not very relevant in the Ethiopian context. The fact that both the UNCRC and the Hague Convention base their recommendations upon the centrality of the individual child and the nuclear family makes it difficult for Ethiopians to continue to adhere to traditional values. But, he insisted that the underlying premises of the conventions are shared and that the objectives are good. He added that Western targets for development are very idealistic, especially the stress that is continually placed on the best interest of the child, the meaning of which Ethiopians sometimes find difficult to understand. He was not going to disagree, however, since the resources of the Ethiopian government are very limited and, without the assistance they receive from the West, the situation in the country would be much worse. At the same time, people will continue to practise as they have done for generations, and do whatever is 'suitable to our continent', he concluded.

There is little doubt that the idea of the autonomous individual and his or her rights is a major stumbling block. In a critical article entitled 'On the rights of the child' (2001), Retta, an Ethiopian lawyer who works for the Juvenile Justice Project Office, considers the position of the many street children in Ethiopia and how best they may be helped by the authorities. He poses the question whether the Ethiopians and non-Ethiopians who are engaged in development work in the country share the same understandings when they speak of the rights of children. His answer is that they probably do not, and he insists that the Ethiopians must not allow themselves to be brow-beaten into accepting what, after all, are values and notions more suited to the rich countries in Europe and North America.

'Unlike the child in a rich society who undergoes the "luxury of identity crisis", more often than not, whenever an Ethiopian child in a poor family demonstrates delinquent behaviour … the motive is clear – it is poverty' (2001: 29). He argues for an acceptance of 'indigenous solutions….rather than imitate or import prescription' (ibid.). He even questions the relevance of the basic principles and regulations of the UNCRC and other international conventions. To his own question, ' [a]re the best interests of the Ethiopian and the British and the American child the same?' he replies that institutions and legal provisions that are designed elsewhere are not necessarily suited to Ethiopia. Whereas Retta is outspoken, others may be more cautious, but do not necessarily disagree with his resentment of the rich and powerful nations and organisations which, he says, think that poor nations are 'necessarily backward and inferior [and hence] need to do a lot of "awareness raising" endeavours' (ibid.: 10).

Discourses about Origins, Ethnicity, and Roots

People I spoke to in streets, cafés, and other informal settings were mostly unaware of Ethiopian children being adopted by foreigners. When told about it, most expressed delight at the good luck that came these children's way. It was interesting to observe the staff at the hotel where I stayed together with the Norwegian couples who collected their children. They were used to seeing European couples arriving from the orphanage carrying an Ethiopian baby in their arms and glowing with happiness. During their stay at the hotel, these couples were completely focused on their child and doted on his or her every move. Staff that I spoke to had no misgivings about the practice; if anything they seemed rather envious of the children. Several expressed surprise at the ability of the Norwegian parents to love strangers in such an all-absorbing way. Most seemed to think that they adopted out of the goodness of their heart and praised them for this. When told that their motives primarily were to become parents and to have a child of their own, this was difficult to understand. 'Why come all the way here?' several asked, and added that if they should feel the need for a child they would go to the family for one who 'was of the same blood'. Similar sentiments were expressed by a doctor at the seminar. He admitted to finding it virtually impossible to envisage that couples could bring up an adopted child as if it were their own. Blood relatedness, he said, counts for everything, and he expressed his concern about what would happen to children adopted abroad. He associated the desire to adopt with the desire to help, and wanted to encourage foreign couples to help orphans inside Ethiopia rather than take them out of the country.

Ethiopian authorities, including the orphanage staff, provide very little information on the children that are adopted overseas. In many cases they know nothing, but according to a Norwegian representative of the adoption agency, even when they have background information, they do not see the point of providing this. 'They do not regard it as important for the children as they grow up', she told me. Most adoptive parents find this lack of information very provoking. They are keen to fill in the gaps in the information about their child's background. They interview the workers at the orphanage, read the reports carefully, and ask for elaborations whenever information is unclear or missing. By and large, the staff are not very forthcoming. This difference in attitudes between Norwegians and Ethiopians is the source of some conflict and tension.[25] At the same time, Ethiopian authorities insist on receiving an annual report on the children until they reach maturity – an attempt, perhaps, to assert their independence.

Few Ethiopians I talked to expressed much concern about the adoptees' future identity. Most explained that those adopted overseas are orphans and too young to have developed any sense of being Ethiopian. Although a few come back when they are older (usually with their parents) they do not want to return permanently. An official at MOLSA, however, told me that despite this, transnational adoption should be regarded as a last resort. He was concerned about possible racism in Europe and North America and believed that it is best to grow up in a country where people look like oneself. At the workshop referred to above, several people expressed a strong dislike of transnational adoption. The main reason seemed to be that too many resources were expended to help too few children. Others were concerned about the children losing their Ethiopianness. Unlike the situation in India, where questions about the psychological significance of ethnic identity and roots are becoming a major issue in adoption circles, this is not a matter for concern in Ethiopia.

Because of poverty, AIDS and poor infrastructure, the Ethiopian state does not have much room to manoeuvre. Expert knowledge is represented mainly by foreigners working on specific aid projects, and in so far as one may talk of governmentality in the country, this is primarily exercised by the foreigners. Senior public servants may sometimes be resentful but, realizing their impotence, most are also pragmatic.

Values and Practices in China

I turn next to an examination of China and Romania, countries whose Communist regimes have meant that their relationship with the West was, until recently, highly restricted and marked by mutual suspicion. Only after the fall of the Soviet Union in 1989 did former Soviet bloc countries make it possible for European and North American couples to adopt children. Following the death of Mao Tse Dung in 1976, and the subsequent relaxing of Chinese foreign policy, China also, in the early 1990s, opened its doors to

Western adoption. Romania and China (and also Russia) rapidly emerged during the 1990s as the big new suppliers of children. Both countries had a number of institutions for abandoned children. Once Western observers gained access to these, they were shocked to see the conditions under which many children lived. Reports that were often sensational in character appeared in Western media and served as an incentive to organise adoption to Western couples. Although the political and economic situation in the two countries was, and is, very different, they both had a highly centralised state apparatus that controlled the life of their citizens to a degree that far surpassed that of the welfare state and 'liberal democracies' of Europe and North America. Communist state formation does not conform to a standard understanding of governmentality, but I nevertheless wish to keep this concept in mind in my examination of adoption in China and Romania. Although neither country took much interest in psychology, each developed a highly centralised bureaucracy whose job it was to carry out the state's policies; policies that, ideologically speaking, were supposed to ensure the prosperity and happiness of the population.

With the opening of Chinese society to the West, the new Chairman, Deng, introduced what he called 'Communism with Chinese characteristics'. This entailed an ever-increasing development of the market economy and more active relations with the USA and Europe. The period coincided with a growth in demand by Western couples for children to adopt. Transnational adoption from China began in the early 1990s and has grown rapidly. Today, more than 8,000 children are adopted out every year, and more children are adopted from China than from any other country except Russia. The USA is the major recipient,[26] but most European countries also adopt children from China. For the past four years, it has been the largest supplier of children to Norway: 314 children[27] were adopted in 2002. There are several reasons for the many abandoned children; the most commonly proffered is the introduction of the one-child family policy in 1978 and the strong preference for sons by Chinese families (i.e. the continuation of pre-Revolution cultural values). This has led to a great number of baby girls being abandoned (Johnson et al. 1998).

After the Communist take-over in 1949, one of the main tasks of the new state was to make a clean break with the old social organisation, including kin and family institutions. According to Hsu, this must be understood in the context of 'the overwhelming importance of kinship in the fabric of Chinese society, and the Communist leaders [being] determined to change that society' (1968: 580). No longer was the family to be the focus for sociality; from now on, people's sense of belonging should be with the community, the collectivity and the party.[28] It was therefore no accident that a Marriage Law was passed as early as 1949. It was intended both to protect and liberate women and to enable a clean break with the traditional kinship system which was regarded as oppressive, hierarchical and an obstacle to change and development. The law outlawed concubine and the 'adoption' of future daughters-in law, and insisted on the right to freely choose one's spouse for both parties (Baker 1979: 213). The subsequent family planning policies, which resulted in the law of one-child per family, further confirmed the active role played by the state and the priority accorded the community and the nation above the individual.[29]

China signed the UNCRC in 1990 and ratified it in 1992. Since that time, China has been on the receiving end of much criticism for its alleged failure to follow through the various regulations. After much hesitation, it ratified the Hague Convention in 2005. The conditions in Chinese orphanages, just as those of Romania, have been severely criticised by Western countries. The world was alerted to the poor conditions in Chinese orphanages through a television documentary entitled 'The Dying Room', which led to an investigation by Human Rights Watch in 1996. Inter alia, it was claimed that orphanages were instructed to kill orphans as a measure towards population control. The claim was based on official figures that showed that in the early 1990s 'up to half of the children brought into the orphanages died, usually within the first few months after arrival', and that in poorer orphanages the rate was even higher. Johnson is critical of the report and argues that there were no grounds for claiming a deliberate maltreatment of children in orphanages, nor a state policy of maltreatment. However, the poor economy and the fact that many children arrive at an orphanage in very poor condition contribute to a high mortality rate (Johnson et al. 1998: 469, 505). According to Thune Hammerstrøm, orphanage personnel displayed concern and compassion for the children in their care, but those who were healthy would quickly be adopted out and only the handicapped and sick remained, many of whom could not be saved[30] (Thune Hammerstrøm 2002: 9).

Laws and Regulations on Adoption

Patrilineality, endorsed by Confucianism, is entrenched in Chinese thinking, and for a man and a woman not to have a son is regarded as a misfortune.[31] A son is required not only to look after his parents in old age, but to maintain the continuity of the lineage and perform the ancestral rituals. In the past, concubines might supplement a barren wife, ghost-marriage would ensure the continuity of a dead man without issue, or an abandoned child or a child from a poor family might have been adopted. Although traditional Chinese law prohibited adoption across surname lines, and normative texts argued against the practice, adoption has taken place in China for centuries both within and outside bloodlines, and there is a Confucian acknowledgement of the role of environmental factors in shaping character.[32] (Johnson et al 1998: 483). Abandonment and infanticide were not uncommon and have been reported as far back as the Han dynasty. From the earliest times there has been a strong gender bias; 'all evidence indicates that infanticide and abandonment disproportionately affected females in China' (ibid.: 472). This trend continues with the one-child policy. Johnson estimates that the typical abandoned child today is a healthy, newborn girl who has one or more elder sisters and no brothers. The parents want a son (ibid.: 477).[33] It is difficult to ascertain the number of abandoned children in China. Official estimates range from 100,000 to 160,000, but Johnson suggests that these figures are conservative (ibid.: 471).

Following China's ratification of the UNCRC, the Adoption Law of the Peoples' Republic of China, was passed in 1992 and was the first legislation to regulate the practice. Amendments were made in 1998 and in 2000. The law is intended to regulate both domestic and transnational adoption. Previously, adoption in China had been a private matter for the parties concerned.

In order to implement the laws on transnational adoption, the China Centre of Adoption Affairs (CCAA) was established in 1996. In the words of the Vice-Minister of Civil Affair, on the occasion of the celebration of its fifth anniversary, its purpose was to 'enable the work of foreign-related adoption to embark upon the road of legalization and standardization'. She further pointed out that 'priority should be given to domestic adoption, while allowing appropriate inter-country adoption' (www.china-ccaa.org/ccaa-zdh.hm, 22 November 2001). The CCAA handles only transnational adoption. It examines foreign adoption agencies, scrutinises all individual applications that are sent via the agencies, receives all information about eligible children from the numerous orphanages throughout China, and allocates specific couples to specific children. (As in India, where domestic adoption also is encouraged, Chinese couples who wish to adopt are subjected to a much less stringent and time-consuming bureaucratic procedure than are the foreign couples.)

According to the director of the CCAA, China adopts children to fourteen countries, has arrangements with altogether more than 120 foreign adoption organisations, and has 'placed out tens of thousands of orphans and abandoned children for adoption abroad' (CCAA ibid.) Two main reasons may account for the popularity of China for prospective adoptive parents from North America and Europe. Firstly, the Chinese not only allowed, but stipulated older applicants. They used to insist that both applicants should be thirty-five year or older. This has now been reduced to thirty years. At the same time, they do not operate a strict upper age limit. Secondly, they allow single women to apply, although they must 'submit a statement to show that they are unmarried and not homosexual' (China Centre of Adoption Affairs, internet). However, in 2001 the authorities issued a new regulation that reduced the proportion of children given to single parents. From now on it should not exceed 10 per cent of the total being adopted out each year. They also demanded a thorough investigation of all foreign adoption agencies already licensed to obtain children from China. The purpose was to reduce the total number and, on the basis of this, reconsider the number of children that each agency should be allocated. This provoked panic amongst adoption agencies. No reason was given for the change. However, the measures may be interpreted as a means by which the Chinese authorities assert their independence; a means to counter the explosive growth in demand that has caused some to feel that China was being taken advantage of. The recent encouragement of domestic adoption may be interpreted along similar lines. More recently, Chinese authorities seem to have changed their minds and are allowing more children to be adopted abroad[34] (Ødegård, personal communication).

According to the 1998 amendments to the Adoption Law, Chinese couples may now adopt a second child of the opposite sex to the one biological child that they already have, making adoption an attractive option for many parents. This has led to a sudden increase in domestic adoption. However, Chinese couples, like Indian ones, only want to adopt 'healthy and normal babies' (Wikse 2001: 14). As a result, orphanages throughout China today have a preponderance of handicapped children.

Transnational Flow of Concepts and Values

The closing off of Communist China to the Western world meant that, for a lengthy period, Western values did not reach China. Although the state encouraged the study of science and technology, the social sciences and humanities received very little attention. Psychology and developmental psychology were not paid much attention, and professional expertise based on psychological knowledge did not exist. Confucianism did not encourage the value of the autonomous individual, and neither did the Communist regime. One might therefore not expect to find much appreciation of the basic tenets of the various conventions on human rights. Hammerstrøm and Wikse found that the degree of knowledge that existed about the UNCRC and the Hague Convention amongst orphanage personnel varied between institutions and could be correlated to the degree to which the management interacted with institutions in Europe. Senior staff in one orphanage were highly motivated to implement the regulations. The manageress had regular contact with a Norwegian adoption agency. She had visited Norway and characterised the relationship as 'close and fruitful' and claimed to have learnt a lot. She arranges annual courses for the study of the UNCRC, and staff have to sit exams in order to demonstrate that they have learnt the main provisions. Personnel in the other two orphanages visited were less concerned with the Conventions. They all claimed to know of them,[35] but their actual knowledge was superficial – as became evident when the implications of some specific articles were pursued.

Hammerstrøm and Wikse further noticed that there was minimal discussion about the meaning of the principle, 'best interest of the child'. Treatment of children in care was highly regimented. Virtually no concern was shown about the children's emotional needs, the needs of handicapped children, or of the slow learner. They were struck by the staff's willingness to characterise some children as pretty or intelligent, or dull and stupid, in front of the children themselves; seemingly unaware of any detrimental effects this might have. The main priorities of personnel in all three orphanages studied were: good health, education and training – in that order. Adoption, whether domestic or transnational, was valued because it would provide improved material conditions for the children. Potential emotional benefits were not mentioned. Although they heard no critical comments about the UNCRC, Hammerstrøm and Wikse argue that there were sufficient indications from observed attitudes and practices of the personnel to suggest that the focus on individuality and individual needs and rights so strongly apparent in the UNCRC, carries little meaning in the Chinese context (personal communication).

Western social workers find this Chinese disregard of children's needs particularly provoking. This is illustrated by the experience of an Englishman who was employed to develop a system of fosterage at a new orphanage near Shanghai. This particular orphanage was built in response to Western criticism of the conditions in Chinese institutions for children, and was meant to be a showcase for the good intentions of Chinese authorities. However, to a Western eye the construction and the facilities were far from child-friendly. The Englishman tried to advise on how to achieve a more 'homely atmosphere', but his advice was not heeded. Whether he, and others who bring Western ideas of 'the best interest of the child', were deliberately ignored by the Chinese as a way of resisting an encroachment of Western concepts and values, or whether they just felt that their own notions and practices were better suited for a Chinese reality, is not known. What the example does show, however, is that Chinese authorities are sensitive to Western criticism, that they attempt to take account of it, but that they do so according to their own premises. This may be because they fail to fully understand the Western values. They place their priorities elsewhere. Wikse was told the following by the manager of one orphanage:

> The education and training of a child consists of three parts: school, society and the home. The children at the orphanage lack the last ... That is why we work towards finding ways that can compensate for this, and thereby give the children a chance to manage in society. (Wikse 2001: 16)

In other words, an orphanage should provide conditions deemed necessary for a good learning environment. Possible emotional needs of the children are not relevant. A recent innovation in Chinese policy is the introduction of fosterage. This is only practiced in some of the wealthier parts of the country, and the three orphanages that Hammerstrøm and Wikse visited were all developing some kind of foster arrangement for those children classified as not adoptable.[36] It is an attempt to provide a semblance of a home environment. The focus on education, and not on emotional support, is brought out clearly in an article on the effect of fosterage written by a doctor attached to an orphanage in Shanghai. He studied the development of the children's IQ, and found that the earlier and longer a child lives with a foster family, the better his or her IQ develops. He displays no inhibitions in applying categories such as 'normal', 'abnormal' and 'dubious' in characterizing the intelligence of the children he studied (Wang Jihong 2001, in Wikse 2001: 16).

Discourses about the Significance of Origins and Roots

When asked why they thought foreigners are so keen to adopt Chinese babies, the personnel of the three orphanages suggested that it was because foreigners know that Chinese children are intelligent and hard working, i.e. good students. They further maintained that Chinese children are very beautiful. Regarding the adoptees' identity, the consensus of opinion was that a person born Chinese will in some sense remain Chinese; 'it is in the blood', several stated. But most were of the opinion that if they are brought up in a European country, they would learn to think and behave like the people of that country. At the same time, most thought that they would also remain Chinese in some sense; like the overseas Chinese (*huaqiao*), some suggested, except that, unlike them, they would not speak the language or have relatives here, so they were probably less Chinese than them.[37]

Access to information about the biological identity of adopted persons is not regulated; and in most cases there is none. It is not unusual for a piece of paper to be included in the basket of abandoned babies giving their date of birth, but no other information. The Adoption Act (paragraph 22) states that if the biological parents wish to remain anonymous, it is their right to do so. Files on each child in the orphanages visited by my research assistants contained little beyond dates and some medical information. They found little sympathy for those adoptees who might wish to discover the identity of their biological relatives or the circumstances of their early life. Occasionally, children adopted abroad come back on a visit with their adoptive parents. This was regarded as positive, but not in any way important. No discourse about the significance of roots existed. However, in China as elsewhere, attitudes toward adoption are contradictory. Despite the emphasis upon environmental factors (for example, the myth about the wasp, Note 32), it is common for Chinese couples who adopt to want to keep this secret. In line with a lack of interest in the psychological effects of adoption, no screening is done of prospective parents before they are given a child and no counselling is offered. The general opinion seemed to be that if the child is young enough not to know, it will never be told about the adoption. Nobody to whom Hammerstrøm and Wikse spoke found this objectionable.

Chinese attitudes and practices regarding personhood, family, gender relations, and childhood are noticeably different from those of the contemporary West. The state has maintained a strict control over people's lives, emphasising an ideology of community rather than individual growth. Over the past ten years a softening has been observed in some domains, but the state continues to define the common good and exercises control over its implementation. Although Chinese students increasingly attend universities in Europe and the USA, the majority study the natural sciences, technology and economics. So far, little interest has been shown in the social sciences and the humanities, and the 'psy' effects so noticeable within social services in Europe, and also in India, are not in evidence. However, Chinese authorities appear to be sensitive to criticism from Europe. Changes that are taking place in orphanages in the Jiangsu province indicate an intention to improve the conditions of orphanages and child care. Personnel who have been given the chance to visit European countries that receive Chinese children, return with the desire to implement some of the practices followed there. It remains an open question to what extent they appreciate the philosophical and psychological underpinnings of Western practices.

Values and Practices in Romania

Romania's treatment of abandoned children has been made the acid test for the country's successful application to join the European Union. Because of the appalling conditions in Romanian children's homes and the extent of malpractice in transnational adoption, the EU applied direct and unashamed pressure on the Romanian government to improve the situation. Nowhere has global governmentality been more visible, and nowhere have the expert opinions of foreign psycho-technocrats been voiced more loudly.[38]

After the collapse of the Soviet Union and the fall of President Ceausescu in 1989, Romania became a major supplier of children to adoptive parents in Western Europe and the USA. In less than two years, the number of children adopted out of Romania increased from fewer than thirty recorded instances in 1989 to more than 10,000 in the period from January 1990 to July 1991 (Conley 2000: 77). European media reports, including several heart-rending television documentaries, described the generally terrible conditions in the state orphanages[39] and this led to 'Romania becoming the adoption hotspot of the year' (Kligman 1992: 410).

The political situation in Romania was in many ways similar to that in China. They were both communist dictatorships with a highly centralised administration. The prosperity and well-being of the collectivity were prioritised at the expense of the individual. The state in both cases sought to implement its policies through a centralised bureaucracy, a planned economy and a variety of social engineering programmes – accompanied in many instances by repressive measures. The exercise of direct state involvement in the organisation of family life, indicated not only that the state knows what is best for its citizens, but, more importantly, that the citizens are responsible for the well-being of the state. The notion of individual rights was irrelevant for good government, and little dialogue was engaged in with the population.[40] At the same time, there were important differences between the two countries. The politics of demography in Romania, for example, were dramatically different from those of China. During the regime of Ceausescu, the population was encouraged to produce children. Contraception was not available and abortion was allowed only after a woman had successfully given birth to five children.

These 'pronatalist policies' (Kligman 1992: 405, Serbanescu et al. 1995: 76), led to a large number of illegal abortions, mostly carried out by unqualified persons and often resulting in death.[41] This resulted in many motherless children whose fathers were incapable of looking after them. The law also resulted in a number of abandoned children, as families were financially unable to care adequately for them. 'Many unwanted children were born and abandoned to the care of the paternalistic state that had demanded them' (Kligman 1992: 406). The state acknowledged to some extent its responsibility and operated a number of institutions for children up to eighteen years of age, but these were not given the financial means to provide adequate care. Staff were both unqualified and in short supply and the facilities meagre. Many children were malnourished and showed severe signs of neglect,[42] those deemed too developmentally slow or unhealthy (approximately 20 per cent of the total orphanage population) were placed in institutions for 'the incurable' (Marcovitch and Cesaroni 1995: 995).

Prior to the Communist era, peasant families might give one or two children to be brought up by relatives or childless couples, but this transaction did not involve the judiciary (Conley 2000: 61).[43] During the Communist era there was virtually no legal domestic adoption in Romania.[44] However, it was not uncommon for children to be brought up by people other than their biological parents.[45] With the increased birth rate, many people were unable to cope, and children were given to institutions. The media reports in the wake of the Revolution provoked a number of European and American humanitarian organisations to establish child care services in Romania. The Holt Organisation began by organising domestic, not transnational, adoption. As in India and China, once transnational adoption had become established, domestic adoption emerged locally as the ideologically preferable option.

Laws and Regulations of Adoption

Following the Revolution, the attention of the world was directed at the plight of these children, and at the steady increase in trafficking in children. Not only were many Romanians unscrupulous, but many European and North American adoption agencies and prospective adoptive parents were also unprincipled in their procurement of children to adopt. To deal with foreign criticism and the rapidly growing demand for children, the Romanian government set up the national Adoption Commission in 1990. It was intended to coordinate data about available institutions and children. In spite of this, media reports of 'baby trade' flourished, and the many scandals in the country were a contributing factor to the rapid completion of the Hague Convention.

Upon closer examination, it turned out that most children adopted out of the country did not come from institutions, but through private transactions. To counteract this practice, the first adoption law was passed in 1991. It forbids private adoptions; all orphans must be institutionalised and all adoption take place via them. Not only was this difficult to achieve, but it transpired that far from all the babies and infants that were adopted were orphans. The new law did little to alleviate the situation. It got so bad that, in the words of one Romanian official, 'The child is the object of a traffic in money and goods … in which Romanian citizens as well as foreigners participate … It's as though potatoes are being sold at the market' (Kligman 1992: 411).[46] This went on despite the fact that Romania ratified the UNCRC shortly after its completion, and was the second country to sign and ratify the Hague Convention (1995) – facts which raise some questions about the level of the authorities' understanding of the Conventions' meaning and intentions.

Consistently critical comments kept coming from abroad and led the Romanian government to pass a new adoption law in 1997. A system was established whereby points were granted by each county authority to foreign adoption agencies according to how great a financial contribution they made to humanitarian projects in the county area. On the basis of this, they worked out the number of adoptees to be allocated. The Norwegian adoption agency Children of the World had been adopting from Romania since 1992, but they chose to withdraw in 1998 as a result of this requirement. They did so because they found the *quid pro quo* system highly problematic on moral grounds and because it contravened the Hague Convention (Ulfsnes 2002). The system provoked other receiving countries, demonstrating yet again the gap in basic understanding. When Romania applied for membership to the European Union, the conditions in institutions for children, the treatment of abandoned children, and the existing adoption practices became major issues. The improvement of services for children in need has become a main criterion for membership.

The EU is highly suspicious of the Romanian authorities' intentions and is determined not to be duped. According to a report to the EU Parliament, Romanian authorities regarded transnational adoption 'as an obvious and financially viable solution' (A5-0247/2000). In EU Parliamentary Resolution 05/09/2001, it is claimed that 'the secondary legislation on international adoption of 1996 created a legal framework for child trafficking world-wide, a situation deplored and opposed by the Hague Convention'. A meeting was held between Romanian authorities and representatives of the Hague Convention in the summer of 2001, but the Romanians would not agree that the conditions deserved criticism (ibid). Nevertheless, the newly elected government imposed a moratorium on transnational adoption. It was only following visits by an EU special delegate sent to investigate the quality of care provided for orphans and abandoned children, that the Romanian authorities agreed to reconsider the situation and promised to develop an action plan to reform the child care services. The result of this remains to be seen, and at the time of writing, the moratorium is operative. Meanwhile, the number of children in institutions remains high. According to estimates made by the EU, the number was 147,000 in 2000 while the Romanian National Child Protection Agency claims less than half that.[47]

Transnational Flow of Concepts and Values

The dichotomy between Western and Romanian notions about child welfare is still apparent. According to Kligman, individual rights did not form part of any private or public discourse in Ceausescu's Romania (1998: 6). Not only was it the duty of the state to provide for all the needs of the people (housing, labour, medical provision and education), but matters such as family size and organisation were also its concern. According to the rhetoric, the state 'cared' for them (ibid.). In light of this, it is not surprising that ideas of individual rights, including the idea of children's rights recently introduced by the West, did not find a ready response. The teaching of psychology was stopped in the early 1970s and reintroduced at university level during the 1990s following pressure from abroad. Training in social work with special reference to children in need is slowly being introduced through financial support from abroad.

Romanian national and local authorities have started a publicity campaign in order to encourage adoption and fostering by Romanian couples. They have also initiated a training programme for local personnel in how to think about adoption and the 'best interest of the child'. They do this, however, because of pressure from the EU and UNICEF, and because foreign NGOs organise and pay for it. In its dealing with novel ideas concerning child welfare and transnational adoption, the post-Communist

Romanian state gives a somewhat inflexible impression. It would appear that Romania is not open to new ideas and values about children and childhood emanating from the West. They defend the existing system and only under severe pressure is the state willing to reconsider it. However, as they strongly desire to become a member of the European Union, they are being forced to consider foreign values about the care of children.

Transnational adoption was regarded by many Romanians as a good source of income, and Ulfsnes heard several people express resentment against the moratorium for that reason. Today, the Romanian media devote much attention to the issue of child neglect and malpractice in adoption. However, many Romanians express the (incorrect) opinion that transnational adoption is mostly of children of Gypsy extraction, and therefore none of their concern. Ulfsnes found little sympathy for the women who gave up their children. Despite the apparent disregard for abandoned children and their mothers, popular television programmes show parents (mainly mothers) who search for children they have abandoned, demonstrating that there is some ambivalence regarding the value of biological ties.

There are signs that earlier disregard of 'the best interest of the child' is beginning to change. Ulfsnes found that the UNCRC and the Hague Convention are being read more carefully in some circles. Quoting Western social workers and other experts on children, some Romanian officials within the childcare sector are beginning to voice the opinion that it is best for a child to grow up within a family and a home, and the introduction of fosterage arrangements is rapidly gaining ground. However, just as in China, the fostering facilities available represent only a drop in the ocean of need. It is difficult to ascertain to what extent this new concern with the well-being of children is merely mimicking what they have been told by foreign aid organisations and the EU; the practical acceptance of these Western views carries rewards, and to ignore them entails sanctions. In fact, in response to Western pressure, government policy is now to close institutions established for orphans and abandoned children and actively seek to reunite children with living relatives and arrange for adoption of orphans.

Discourses about the Significance of Origins and Roots

According to Ulfsnes, there was little interest amongst orphanage staff in Romania in the possible significance of roots and biological origin. People reacted with surprise when she suggested that children adopted abroad might desire to return, and meet with biological relatives. As in China and Ethiopia, questions of identity, or troubled identity, were not debated, nor the possible psychological effects on the children of being uprooted and resettled in foreign countries.[48] Romanians interviewed expressed happiness on behalf of the children adopted to families in Western Europe or the USA, stressing the opportunities for improved material conditions that this entailed. They were not surprised by foreigners' desire to adopt Romanian children, because Romanian children 'have much lighter skin colour than that of Asian and Africans'.

Once a legal adoption is effected, the child is issued with a new birth certificate, eradicating his or her biological origins. However, according to Article 34 of the 1997 Adoption Act, the National Authority of Child Protection and Adoption is obliged to keep information of the adoptees' background, including pictures of biological relatives. Article 35 gives an eighteen year old adoptee the right to apply to obtain this information. Such enquiries from transnationally adopted persons must, however, be channelled via other Central Authorities (Article 40 d.I). These provisions indicate continuity in institutional thinking, but also a willingness to accommodate demands from receiving countries.

Compared to China, which has also been the butt of much criticism in its handling of abandoned children, Romania is in a much weaker position and, because it wants to join the EU, has much more to gain from being cooperative. Whereas financial gain by individuals was the main motivation for transnational adoption in Romania and the state did very little to control this, Chinese authorities took charge of the proceedings from the start, and monetary gain has not been a motivation.

To Conclude

The examination in this chapter of values and practices in four very different countries that send children to Europe and North America for adoption, demonstrates the wide variety between them. What they have in common is that, due to a myriad of social, economic and political factors, they all have large numbers of abandoned and orphaned children that they are unable to help. At the same time, transnational adoption represents just a drop in the ocean towards alleviating the condition of these children. The countries arguably expend a disproportionate amount of bureaucratic work and expense on effecting it. This may, in part, be accounted for by the fact that the 'international community' has taken such an interest in the practice and has introduced stringent procedures.

Western media have been more directly critical of these countries' child policies than they have been of many other policies that might be regarded as equally worthy of criticism. I suggest this may be explained by the special moral status attributed to children and childhood in Europe and North America. When children are neglected, this tends to dominate all other human rights issues.

A globalisation – or cultural colonising – of Western ideas and values is discernible within the fields of childcare and adoption in non-Western parts of the world. The mere existence of the UNCRC and the Hague Convention bear ample witness to this. However, against the Western onslaught, the 'weapons of the weak' (Scott 1985) are not without power. An assertion of agency on the part of donor countries is manifest in many ways: local regulations concerning the age and civil status of prospective parents; demands that parents collect their child themselves; specifications as to how long they are required to stay in the donor country and which procedures they have to undergo; and other requirements that the recipient agencies, countries and adoptive parents have to abide by – such as having to provide regular detailed reports on the adoptee's situation.

The reigning discursive practices of adoption spring out of psychological theories of personhood and identity and may be characterised as closed to debate. The most important manifestation of this is the non-negotiable value placed upon the individual and the rights of the individual; expressed in numerous Western European and North American national legislation, and reiterated in the UNCRC and the Hague Convention. To what extent those who seek to implement the conventions are aware of the biased premises on which they are formulated, varies widely. Whereas current thinking about development aid and assistance emphasises participation and 'recipient directed projects' or, in more recent jargon, 'country ownership' (www.worldbank.org/poverty/strategies/overview.htm), such an ideological stance is not reflected in transnational adoption. Of course, transnational adoption is not part of development aid. Direct interventionist action on the part of foreign institutions and authorities may therefore be more acceptable. This is nowhere so stark as in Romania, where the EU has no qualms about wielding power in order to ensure the implementation of its own directives.

The totalitarian Communist regimes developed along very different paths from the liberal democratic West, where democracy and a mixed economy developed side by side. From this perspective, China and Romania display a number of similarities. However, when we look at the practice of transnational adoption, we find that China has more in common with India than it does with Romania, in that both display active resistance to Western attempts to dictate the premises of the transaction. This is due to these two countries' major standing on the world stage, which contributes to their national self-confidence. Chinese and Indian sensitivity to potential humiliation may be more highly developed than that of Romania, and they are more concerned (and economically able) to retain their autonomy vis-à-vis Western organisations. At the same time, India has developed its own corpus of professional psycho-technocrats trained primarily in a Western academic tradition, while Chinese and Romanian authorities and orphanage personnel are, ideologically speaking, far removed from sharing the premises of the Western professionals engaged in childcare. Ethiopia is too poor, and ridden with too many internal problems, to put up any serious resistance to the onslaught of Western interference.

While the influence of Western jurisprudence and cultural values is observable in child and adoption laws in many other countries in the South, it is too simplistic to designate the changes simply as foreign, or Western. Formulations may be Western, but they are subject to local interpretation. They may be incorporated into local thinking and practice in somewhat adapted forms, and be perceived as Indian, Columbian or whatever. The history of ideas in the West, as elsewhere, has amply shown that ideas know no national boundaries, and that discourses change in response to new ideas as well as in response to changing political and economic situations.

Notes

1. How the relationship is perceived varies according to which country and which groups or individuals within each country. Lawyers in Latin America, for example, benefit financially from arranging adoption to couples in the USA and elsewhere.
2. She was observed in a village taking photographs of children and was attacked and beaten to death by villagers because they interpreted her actions as being a preliminary step toward abducting children in order to sell their organs in America.
3. Others believe that transnational adoption is invariably a cover for buying and selling children and that so-called adoptees' vital organs are used in a global trade in body organs. Several Indian NGOs now work actively towards abolishing adoption overseas.
4. For anthropological studies of kinship in India see for example, Dumont (1966); Fuller (1996); Marriot (1990).
5. No such rule was applied to domestic adoption – probably because there was much less demand for it at the time and large sums of money were not involved.
6. India is a continent as much as a country. As a federation of states under federal law and government, it is highly heterogeneous. The degree to which various state governments seek to implement federal laws and regulations varies. What also varies is the level of developed infrastructure established in each state to provide social services generally and adoption services in particular.
7. Infants with very dark skin are not similarly excluded although, from discussions with placement officers, they might as well be so. Having participated in several home visits together with an Indian social worker, Roel reports that these are often conducted with the husband's parents and siblings present. Despite being quite dark-skinned, they often insist on a light-coloured child (Roel personal communication).
8. Countries represented were Norway, Sweden, Denmark, Finland, Iceland, Holland, UK, Ireland, Italy, Australia, USA and Canada.
9. Almost 250 foreign adoption agencies, most of them American, are licensed to adopt (Cantwell 200a: 4) and most people agree that this means that proper supervision is difficult to maintain.
10. 'Blood is important, and blood is passed on through the father' (upper-middle-class Indian male in conversation). Everyone I spoke to told me that involuntary infertile couples who can afford it attempt new reproductive technology. 'Naturally, they want to try this first', I was told again and again.

11. It is not uncommon for a woman who wishes to adopt to go through a mock pregnancy with a pillow on her stomach and to go away in order to 'give birth' and return with an adopted baby. An Indian psychologist talking about the 'psycho-social dimensions of adoption' presented some results of a survey she had conducted among Indian adoptive parents. The findings show that far less than half have told their child that s/he is adopted.

12. She told me she had been very inspired by a presentation at the conference about open adoption in the USA. The idea is appealing, she said, but it will be a long time before we can introduce this in India.

13. If they return to India at some point, this should be as tourists, not as persons seeking an identity by searching for Indian relatives, he said. Of course, the fact of adoption cannot be hidden, he went on, and may give rise to some questions about origins in the adoptee's mind. However, he did not see the need for information about biological origins.

14. His studies are based on domestic adoption in the UK. He has no experience with children adopted from overseas.

15. Pamphlets written by both Indians and Europeans giving case histories of young adoptees who had returned to India in search of their roots and origins were distributed. They all had happy endings.

16. In light of this, it was surprising to hear the next day one Indian delegate say that what she had learnt from the session was that it is important for Indian adoptees to get the support of others like themselves in their new country.

17. Representatives from three different associations presented papers at the Delhi conference: the Indian Federation of Adoptive families (IFAFA), the National Association of Adoptive families (NAAF) and Sudatta (from the Sanskrit, meaning 'good adoption').

18. Another commentator raised the possibility that they might be going too far in endlessly confronting the children with the fact of their situation. 'By all means, inform them about their origins', she said, 'but perhaps we should let the matter rest until such times as our children themselves approach us for a discussion about it.'

19. I visited Ethiopia for two weeks in December 2001 when I accompanied eight Norwegian couples who went to collect their children. I interviewed a number of key Ethiopian personnel in Addis Ababa, visited several orphanages, both state- and privately run, and participated in a conference organised for Ethiopian government officials, lawyers, social workers, and local NGOs by Save the Children and UNICEF, entitled 'Orphans and Vulnerable Children Affected by HIV/AIDS'.

20. For some anthropological studies on Ethiopian social and cultural institutions, see, Levine (1974); Tronvoll (1998).

21. An official at the Ethiopian branch of Norwegian Save the Children told me that there are an estimated one million HIV/AIDS orphans in the country and that about 200,000 children are infected with the virus. They further estimate that approximately 1,300 children under the age of five die every day in Ethiopia from a variety of causes.

22. For example, amongst the Oromo, adoption, called *gudifetcha*, involves a public ceremony supervised by priests and elders in which the adoptive parents swear an oath to treat the adoptee, who may be an adult, 'as if s/she has been born to them' (Fadese 1999: 1). In some highland groups, adopted orphans with some kind of patri-connection to the village may inherit land (Tronvoll 1998: 235).

23. I am not critical of this approach per se, I merely wish to draw attention to the premises upon which it is based. Given the extremely serious conditions facing Ethiopian children, one might ask whether these concerns are the most relevant.

24. It appeared in the new magazine published by the Juvenile Justice Project Office established in 1991 by the Federal Supreme Court.

25. Children earmarked for Norway are provided with a 'birth-book' when they leave the orphanage. This is compiled by the staff, but most parents I talked to found it heart-rendingly incomplete, raising as many questions as it answered.

26. Annual adoption from China to the USA grew from 201 children in 1992 to 5,053 children in 2000 (Rojewski and Rojewski 2001: 3).

27. Only one of these was a boy.

28. The extent to which they succeeded is a moot point. Kinship continues to be very important in present-day China.
29. According to the 'Law Protecting the Right and Interest of Women and Children' passed in 1992, it is a punishable offence to abandon a child. However, despite a noticeable increase in abandoned children in China, few parents have been taken to court for the offence. Of the few cases of prosecution, the basis for sentencing was for breach of the rules concerning family planning, not for breach of the rights of the child or for failing to nurture the child (Johnson et al. 1998: 472).
30. Wikse and Thune Hammerstrøm were graduate students in the Department of Chinese Studies, University of Oslo. With introductions from the Norwegian adoption agency Children of the World, and with some financial support from the research project 'Transnational Flow of Concepts and Substances', they were able to undertake brief field visits under my supervision to three orphanages in Jiangsu Province of China. They were able to 'hang around' and talk to child minders and teachers as well to the managers of the orphanages. In my presentation here I draw heavily on the information and insight that they accumulated. Given the paucity of qualitative knowledge about Chinese attitudes to adoption, I value their reports highly.
31. For discussions of Chinese values and policies regarding family and children, see Croll et al. (1985); Croll (1998); Hsu (1968, 1972).
32. The term 'mulberry insect children' is a common term for adopted children, especially those adopted from outside the patriline. It comes from the belief that wasps take the young of mulberry insects and make them their own. They place the mulberry insects inside the nest and pray 'be like me, be like me'. After a period of time young wasps emerge (Johnson et al. 1998: 484) This is a telling metaphor that indicates an attitude that favours sociality over biogenetics and heredity.
33. The one-child family has been enforced mostly in urban areas. In the countryside it seems that a one son and one daughter family is more acceptable (Johnson et al. 1998).
34. While it is difficult to account for this change, the fact that foreign agencies must pay $1,500 for each child may have something to do with it.
35. The orphanages visited were amongst the best equipped in China. It is likely that staff in more remote orphanages will have very little knowledge of the UNCRC.
36. It is difficult to ascertain with any certainty to what extent this change is due to influences from Europe.
37. In a meeting with a class of high school pupils, the Norwegian researchers discussed the practice of adoption. Most of the young people had not thought about it, but thought it was fine to be able to get another child through adoption – if one could afford it. They had in mind domestic adoption. Opinion was divided about adoption to overseas. Some expressed a strong dislike of 'foreigners meddling in China's problems'.
38. The empirical material from Romania was collected by my research assistant, Kari-Anne Ulfsnes, in June 2002. She has previously conducted anthropological fieldwork in Romania in connection with her M.Phil. thesis (1999). She knows the locality well and speaks Romanian.
39. The situation worsened after the revolution because it led to a collapse of the administrative infrastructure.
40. According to Kideckel (1993), the ideological aim to create the New Man (*Omul Nou*), motivated to action by society's needs, resulted in lonely, self-centred, suspicious and unfeeling people.
41. Kligman reports that between 1966 and 1989, an estimated 9,452 women died from illegal abortions (1992: 406).
42. If the children were deemed healthy at the age of three by a team of health care providers, they were placed in institutions where limited educational and medical care were provided.

43.   For some anthropological studies on Romanian social and cultural life, (in addition to the work by Kligman and Verdrey (1990), see Kideckel (1993) and Livezeanu (1995).

44.   When it did take place it was hampered by bureaucratic complexities and inertia.

45.   Due to a common practice of labour migration within the country, many young couples found it necessary to leave their children with their own parents and to visit only during holidays.

46.   One particularly serious case that received much publicity inside and outside Romania was that of a British couple who paid a baby-dealer £4,000 and obtained a five-months-old girl from her unmarried seventeen year old mother. They sedated the baby, hid her under a rug in their car and tried to bring her over the border illegally. It was discovered and they were sentenced to two years in jail. The baby was sent to an orphanage and was subsequently adopted by a Gypsy couple. Interestingly, many foreigners defended the couple's action. The *Guardian* newspaper presented it as a 'simple case', with needy children on one side and brave, generous Britons with loving homes on the other hand' (Conley 2000: 76).

47.   However, recent reports from Romania indicate that in some regions a sufficient number of children are being fostered or returned to their families for whole institutions to be closed (Ulfsnes, personal communications)

48.   So far, there is little demand for return visits to Romania by adoptees and their families. There could be several reasons for this, one is that the conditions in Romanian orphanages are still so poor that parents may not wish to expose their children to them; another that the children are still relatively young.

Chapter 10

IN CONCLUSION:
TO KIN A FOREIGN CHILD

One thing is the way humans biologically procreate and reproduce, another is how they culturally understand this process, and still a different thing is the social significance that they attribute to the interpersonal links that originate in these processes.

C. Salazar *Kinship and Public Understanding of Genetics*

The purpose of this book has been to locate transnational adoption within a broad context of contemporary Western life, especially values concerning family, children and meaningful relatedness, and to explore the many ambiguities and paradoxes that the practice entails for those concerned. I asked at the outset how it could be possible to move children from one biological, geographical, national, social and cultural reality to another without this leading to major problems. Enormous differences in sociocultural understanding of the meaning of family and kinship, of children and adults, or the role of the state in organising family life, and the sensitive issue of North-South relations in a postcolonial context, all contribute to making the practice fraught with potential tension and difficulties. However, as I hope to have shown, based on substantial empirical material, the transaction is carried out surprisingly smoothly.

The movement of the adopted person from one country to another is a classic case of *rite de passage*. Through rites of separation, liminality and reincorporation, abandoned children are de-kinned from family and country of origin, and kinned into new ones. The child is affected fundamentally and reemerges as one whose personhood is transformed in important ways. But the community into which he or she emerges is also changed by the incorporation. My study demonstrates how children without kinned relations are vulnerable: because they fall outside kinship, in societies where personhood is predicated more upon kinned relatedness than on individuality, they fall outside society also, and, as such, they constitute a highly ambiguous category in their countries of origin. In a certain sense they are not human, and it becomes unclear who is responsible for them, and in what ways. I think this may account, at least in part, for the abysmal conditions in children's homes in many parts of the world.

What kinning does is to transform the autonomous individual into a relational person who becomes fixed in a set of relations expressed in a conventional kinship idiom. But kinning is achieved intersubjectively between all parties involved. Thus, not only are transnationally adopted children affected, so also are their adoptive parents and their kin. Through adoption, men and women are made into mothers and fathers; their siblings are made into uncles and aunts; their parents into grandmothers and grandfathers; just as the abandoned and socially naked child, is made into our child grandchild, niece or nephew.

By and large, Norwegian parents succeed in transubstantiating their adopted children into Norwegians and kinning them into their own family and kin. In doing this they overcome a number of ideological and practical obstacles. The major point I wish to stress is that there is more than one way to create a truly meaningful and lasting relationship expressed in a recognisable kinned idiom. Being biologically connected is the one to which we are accustomed, and it is highly elaborated in Western thinking; but it is not the only way. Adoption is another, and it challenges this biocentrism. Yet, to judge from recent legal changes regarding the right to know one's biological progeny, politicians are not convinced about the plurality of understandings; neither is the population at large. I have been told countless times by adoptive parents with more than one adopted child that complete strangers will ask them if the children are siblings. Upon being answered in the affirmative, the questioner insists, 'but are they *real* siblings?' What is it about this 'reality' that is so important to people? In this book, by exploring the anthropology of kinship, I have sought to provide some answers by demonstrating the heterogeneity of kinship systems across time and space. Minimally, this alerts one to the fact that there is no natural way to organise relationships. Rather, social and cultural predispositions and constraints orchestrate the meaning of sociality and relatedness in every case. Anthropologists know this; but most legislators, bureaucrats and the world at large do not.

There is a universal tendency to assume that the answers that are provided in one's own social world to the existential questions of being are somehow correct and inevitable. They have become embodied knowledge, implicitly shaping most other understandings. To question the unreflected utterance of opinions is therefore, I believe, a worthwhile task. In this book I have developed three main foci to help me in this task: the anthropology of kinship; the growth of psychology and the psychology-based professions which enable the consolidation of governmentality; and the globalisation of morality and rationality. And these three are interlinked. Thus, for example, the link between applied developmental psychology and governmentality in Western Europe is not only close, it is a mutually empowering relationship.

The body of knowledge that has developed within the field of psychology during the twentieth century has had a profound effect upon what we in Europe and North America think about what it means to be a human being, a gendered person, and a child; and what significance we attribute to biogenetic factors ('nature') on the one hand and the social environment ('nurture') on the other. The growth of the expert professions – the psycho-technocrats – has increasingly led to a conformity in state-sponsored activities established to ensure the best interest of the child, whether at home in Europe or abroad in the Third World. The constituting significance of the autonomous individual in Western thinking has meant that national laws and international conventions take such a being as their unquestioned starting point. This, coupled with Western global power and influence in economic and technological fields, has contributed to a globalisation of Western values.

Another aim of this book has been to explore through the lens of adoption the processes and the mechanisms of governmentality, both local and global, that are currently transforming childhood itself. At the same time, it has been equally important to investigate the reactions to these processes in non-Western countries: the manifestations of adaptation, incorporation, resistance and rejection of the Western discourses that can be observed amongst people directly involved in adoption in various donor countries.

Adoption is usually understood as involving three categories of persons: biological parents, adoptive parents and the adoptees; but in recent times, the practice has also increasingly become the concern of the state. Transnational adoption activates one nation-state in a dialogical relationship with other nation-states, at the same time as it has become a global process. The actual transfer of a child is no longer simply a transaction between the individuals concerned. Adoption across national borders has become a matter in which the state in both countries plays an increasingly controlling role. Ultimate power to relinquish a child (a citizen) is held by the nation-state. It transfers these rights to another nation-state, which incorporates the child as its own citizen.

Transnational adoption may thus be analysed as a two-way process between donor and recipient countries; but it is a relationship that is not balanced. While children move in adoption from the South (including Eastern Europe) to the North, posited universal ideas and values concerning personhood, childhood, family life, children and the treatment of children move from the North to the South. At the same time, representatives of Northern adoption agencies approach the donor authorities with circumspection and seek to accommodate their priorities and requests as much as possible, sometimes changing their own procedures in the process. However, the relationship is far from smooth. Authorities and orphanages in donor countries may give the impression that they are accommodating the demands laid down in the international treaties, but they may not actually be doing so. At the request of the 'international community' several donor countries have passed national adoption laws in recent years. By and large, such local laws follow the lead of the Hague Convention, but details may be adjusted so that they fall in line with existing local practices. For example, the recent adoption law in Ethiopia failed to forbid private adoption.

Governmentality, as a mode of thinking that gave birth to liberal benevolent supervision by the democratic state for the best interest of its citizens, is a well-established phenomenon in Western Europe. It is now being extended through international treaties and international bureaucracy to be implemented globally. We may thus discern a globalisation of Western concepts and values that emphasise a discourse of rights of various kinds, a normative ambition that seeks to impose a single moral universe. The slogan of 'the best interest of the child' underpins the two international conventions mentioned above. Although its meaning has received minimal debate, it is nevertheless clear that contemporary Western views of childhood and children's needs predominate, and that minimal account has been taken of the social and cultural diversity of the South. These views are universalistic and allow those concerned to talk in terms of 'the world's children'. Globalisation thus becomes a matter of morally infused intentionality on the part of the Western individuals and institutions, and indeed nations, involved.

My study has shown that a highly charged value in contemporary Western Europe and North America is to 'have a child of one's own'. Those who are unable to achieve this ambition by 'normal' means, for better or worse have to look to the developing world. The process involved in effecting adoption across national, cultural and social boundaries is highly complex, and one might expect it to be doomed at the outset. However, tens of thousands of babies and infants have been 'miraculously' transferred and have adapted well to their new circumstances. Ultimately, I suggest it is the power of kinship, the fact of becoming emotionally and socially related to others, that largely accounts for this success.

POSTSCRIPT: A NOTE ON METHODS

As stated in the Preface, this project has necessarily been both multi-sited and wide-ranging. I argued that social anthropology provides insights which other disciplines cannot provide, but that classic social anthropological methods can be used only to a limited extent when applied to an enterprise such as this. Long-term participant observation was clearly not possible, and the project has therefore been a challenging one. But I suggest that the book may be read as an example of how modified anthropological methods can be effectively combined with a historical approach, supplemented by a wide variety of different written sources, ranging from laws and legal debates to psychological literature and special interest group publications. The need for drawing on such a variety of sources contributed both to the variety of themes addressed, and to the way in which these were presented. I have organised the text according to three main topics: the relationship between biology and sociality, expert knowledge, and the globalisation of Western knowledge. However, it is my firm belief that choosing to interlink these, rather than choose one as being analytically more important than the other two, has resulted in a book which aptly reflects the complexity of the lived world.

In order to grasp and make sense of the cultural issues that are activated in conducting research on transnational adoption, I have involved myself in a multitude of social arenas.[1] In the search for empirical material I cast my net wide: adoptive families; employees of adoption agencies; social workers and others engaged in bringing children from foreign countries into Norwegian families; politicians who passed laws and regulations locally and internationally; and members of the expert professions whose opinions have been influential in establishing the reigning discursive practices. I also visited several donor countries. In the end, rather than suffering from a paucity of material, as I had feared, I found that a major difficulty has been to select from, and render coherent, a large body of disparate material.

I have participated socially with a great number of adoptive families in a great many different contexts and in different parts of the country. The fact that I am the mother of a daughter adopted from Nepal has undoubtedly eased my access into such intimate parts of peoples' lives. At the same time, this has rendered the ethnographic field more personal than I have been accustomed to. To retain a degree of objectivity has, at times, been a challenge, and I have been forced be extra vigilant about my own feelings and reactions.

I have carried out interviews with 120 couples, supplemented by a questionnaire, and participated in many different social gatherings that spring out of the fact of adoption – such as adoptive family summer camps, meetings of local branches of the adoption agencies, and the annual gatherings of associations of families with children from the same country. I have attended meetings and lectures arranged by the adoption agencies and, as my research became known to the adoptive community, I have been invited to speak to such meetings. I have joined courses arranged for prospective adoptive parents in different parts of Norway and courses arranged for adoptive parents whose children are reaching puberty. I spent two days a week, over a period of four months, engaged in participant observation field-work in one of the adoption agencies where I not only chatted to the employees, but was also given routine tasks to perform that gave me an understanding of the procedures for adopting from overseas – as well as some knowledge of adopting couples. I examined the completed application forms by prospective adoptive parents submitted to two adoption agencies over a period of twenty years (Howell and Ulfsnes 2002) and had many conversations with various professionals who facilitate and supervise transnational adoption as well as with some of the civil servants who were engaged in the drafting of the 1986 and 1999 Norwegian Adoption laws. I was also able to interview Norwegians who had participated in the original drafting of the Hague Convention on Inter-Country Adoption. I have had many conversations with psychologists who advise on parental procedures and who counsel adoptees requiring some such assistance.

I have not only studied the various Norwegian legal provisions, White Papers and submissions made in connection with the adoption laws in their historical and social context, but have also kept track of articles, letters and comments related to these in the media. In particular, the magazines published by the three adoption agencies have proved a rich source. By reading all the back-numbers starting from the first in the late1960s, I have been able to track changes in attitudes and practices of bureaucrats, politicians and adoptive parents. I have followed internet discussions by parents and adoptees both in Norway and the USA. Together with the officer of one adoption agency responsible for adoption from India, I conducted an investigation (based on questionnaires), of parents and adopted children who have participated in return visits to India during the past ten years (Howell and Juvet Hermansen 2002).

In order to gain an understanding of attitudes to transnational adoption in donor countries, I visited three countries from which Norway adopts: South Korea, Ethiopia and India. I joined a group of twelve families on a 'motherland tour' to South Korea (see Chapter 6) and a group of eight couples who went to collect their children from Ethiopia (see Footnote 152). I also participated in a large conference in 2002 in New Delhi entitled The Fourth International Conference on Child Adoption. Before attending the conference I spent some time at an orphanage in Old Delhi where my visit coincided with the celebration of their fiftieth anniversary. In all countries I met a number of different people from both government agencies and NGOs (local and international) who are actively involved in both domestic and transnational adoption, and I visited several orphanages in all three countries. Furthermore, I commissioned two graduate students of Chinese at the University of Oslo to undertake a study of Chinese orphanages that sent children abroad for adoption (Thune Hammerstrøm 2001; Wikse 2001; see Footnote 163), and a student of Korean to do the same in Korea. A research assistant whose anthropological fieldwork had been carried out in Romania, spent some weeks back in the country in order to collect information for me on the situation regarding transnational adoption (Ulfsnes 2002, see Footnote 38). I also supervised a student, Audhild Roel, who conducted fieldwork at an orphanage in Delhi with special focus on adoption.

I have interviewed several adolescent and adult adoptees from a number of different countries, read a number of books written by them about their own experiences, and participated in the Second Conference of Adult Korean Adoptees which was held in Oslo in 2001.

What has been striking during my investigations is the similarity of adoptive parents' basic values, hopes, aspirations, frustrations and difficulties encountered – regardless of social class and place of residence. Not only do Norwegian prospective and adoptive parents display many similarities in their concerns and experiences, but these coincide with those in other countries whom I have met. While big differences are observable at the cultural, institutional and political levels in the various receiving countries, at the personal, experiential level, adoptive parents are not very different. The world of adoption is a world full of contradictions and paradoxes. It is also a world filled with emotionality and personal happiness.

Note

1.   I have had to be imaginative in seeking alternative approaches, and serendipity, which, to my mind, lies at the heart of the scientific endeavour, has played a larger role than usual. According to the *Oxford English Dictionary*, serendipity is 'the faculty of making happy and unexpected discoveries by accident'. It is not to be confused with chance, but is the ability to see the potential in chance occurrences.

BIBLIOGRAPHY

Alber, Erdmute. 2003. 'Denying Biological Parenthood: Fosterage in Northern Benin', *Ethnos* 68(4): 487–506.

Altstein, Howard and Rita Simon. 1991. *Intercountry Adoption: A Multinational Perspective*, New York: Praeger.

Anand, S. Arath and Prema Chandra. 2001. 'Adoption Laws: Need for Reform', *Economic and Political Weekly*, 21 September, 3891–93.

Andenæs, Agnes. 2005. 'Natural Claims – Gendered Meanings: Parenthood and Developmental Psychology in a Modern Welfare State', *Feminism & Psychology* 15(2): 211–28.

Anderson, Astrid. 2001. 'Adopsjon og tilhørighet på Wogeo Papua Ny-Guinea', *Norsk antropolgisk tidsskrift* 12(3): 175–88.

Anderson, Benedict. 1983. *Imagined Communities*, London: Verso.

Anderson, Hanne, 2003. 'UKient Opphav', *Magasinet Dagbladit*, June4 2003: 1–9.

Ariés, Philippe. 1962. *Centuries of Childhood*, Harmondsworth: Penguin Books.

Baker, Hugh D.R. 1979. *Chinese Family and Kinship*, London: Macmillan.

Barnard, Alan and Anthony Good. 1984. *Research Practices in the Study of Kinship*, London: Academic Press.

Barnes, John. 1973. 'Genetrix : Genitor :: Nature : Culture?', in J.R. Goody (ed.), *The Character of Kinship*, Cambridge: Cambridge University Press.

Bartholet, Elisabeth. 1992. 'International Adoption: An Overview', in Joan Hollinger (ed.), *Adoption Law and Practice*, New York: M. Bender.

Bary, Wm Theodore de 1998. *Asian Values and Human Rights: A Confucian Communitarian Perspective*, Cambridge: Harvard University Press.

Bauman, Zigmunt. 1998. *Globalization: The Human Consequences*, New York: Columbia University Press.

Beheim Karlsen, Kari. 2002. *Arve – Sonen Min*, Oslo: Gyldendal.

Berre, Kersti. 2004. '"For when the guests come": The Introduction of Child Participation in Northern Ethiopia', University of Oslo. Cand. Polit. Thesis in Social Anthropology.

Billimora, H.M. 1984. *Child Adoption- A Study of Indian Experience*, Bombay: Himalaya Publishing House.

Bledsoe, Caroline and Uche Isingo-Abanike. 1989. 'Strategies in Child-fosterage among Mende Grannies in Sierra Leone', in Jon J. Lesthaeghe (ed.), *Reproduction and Social Organization in Sub-Sahara Africa*, Berkeley: University of California Press.

Bloch, Maurice and Jonathan Perry (eds) 1989. *Money and the Morality of Exchange*, Cambridge: Cambridge University Press.

Bomann-Larsen, Tor. 2004. *Haakon & Maud, vol. 2 Folket*, Oslo: Cappelen.

Boswell, John 1988. *The Kindness of Strangers: The Abandonment of Children in Western Europe from Late Antiquity to the Renaissance*, Harmondsworth: Penguin.

Botvar, Pal Ketil. 1994. *Nysjanse i Norge: Utenlandsadoptertes Levevilkår*, Oslo: Diaforsk.

———. 1999. *Meget er Forskjellig, men det er Utenpå?* Oslo: Diaforsk 2.

Bouquet, Mary. 1993. *Reclaiming English Kinship: Portuguese Refractions on British Kinship Theory*, Manchester: Manchester University Press.

Bowlby, John. 1940. 'The Influence of Early Environment in the Development of Neurosis and Neurotic Character', *International Journal of Psycho-Analysis* 21: 154–78.

———. 1969. '*Attachment*', in *Attachment and Loss*, vol. 1, London: Hogarth Press, New York: Basic Books.

———. 1973. '*Separation: Anxiety & Anger*', in *Attachment and Loss*, vol. 2, London: Hogarth Press, New York: Basic Books.

———. 1980. '*Loss: Sadness & Depression*', in *Attachment and Loss*, vol. 3, London: Hogarth Press, New York: Basic Books.

Bowie, Fiona (ed.) 2004. *Cross-cultural Approaches to Adoption*, London: Routledge.

Boyden, Jo. 1997. 'Childhood and the Policy Makers: a Comparative Perspective on the Globalization of Childhood', in Allison James and Alan Prout (eds), *Constructing and Reconstructing Childhood*, London: Falmer Press.

Brady, Ivan (ed.) 1976. *Transactions in Kinship: Adoption and Fosterage in Oceania*, Honolulu: The University Press of Hawaii.

Brodzinsky, David et al. 1992. *Being Adopted: The Lifelong Search for Self*, New York: Doubleday.

Brooks, C.C. 1976. 'Adoption on Manihi Atoll, Tuamoto Archipelago', in I. Brady (ed.), *Transactions in Kinship*, Honolulu: University Press of Hawaii.

Brottveit, Ånund. 1996. 'Rasisme og de Utenlandsadopterte', *Norsk antropologisk tidsskrift* 7(2): 132–48.

———.1999. *Jeg vil ikke skille meg ut*, Oslo: Diaforsk 4.

Bråten, Stein (ed.) 1998. *Intersubjective Communication and Emotion in Early Ontogeny*, Cambridge: Cambridge University Press.

Burman , E. 1996. 'Local, Global or Globalized? Child Development and International Child Rights Legislation', *Childhood* 3: 45–66.

Bøås, Morten and Desmond McNeill (ed.) 2004. *Global Institutions and Development: Framing the World*, London: Routledge.

Caiani-Praturlon, Graziella. 1991. 'Inter-Country Adoption in European Legislation', in E.D. Hibbs (ed.), *Adoption: International Perspectives*, Madison: International Universities Press.

Cantwell, Nigel. 2002a. 'The International Scenario – the Hague Convention on Intercountry Adoption'. Paper presented to the Indian Council for Child Welfare International Conference on Adoption, New Delhi.

———. 2002b. 'The Best Interest of the Child'. Paper presented at the Conference on Separated Children in Europe, Copenhagen.

Carli, Amalia and Monica Dalen. 1997. *Adopsjonsfamilien: Informasjon og Veiledning til Adoptivforeldre*, Oslo: Pedagogisk forum.

Carp, E. Wayne. 2002. *Adoption in America: Historical Perspectives*, Ann Arbor: University of Michigan Press.

Carsten, Janet. (ed.) 2000. *Cultures of Relatedness: New Approaches to the Study of Kinship*, Cambridge: Cambridge University Press.

———. 2001. 'Substantivism, Antisubstantivism, and Anti-antisubstantivism!' in S. Franklin and S. McKinnon (eds), *Relative Values: Reconfiguring Kinship Studies*, Durham: Duke University Press, pp. 29–53.

Cassels, Manuel. 2000. *The Rise of the Network Society*, Oxford: Blackwell.

Cederblad, Marianne et al. 1994. *Identitet och Anpassning hos Utlandsfødda Adopterada Ungdommar*, Lund: Institutionen for barn- och ungdomspsykiatri.

Cohen, Anthony. 1985. *The Symbolic Construction of Community*, London: Routledge.

Conley, Amy. 2000. *Child Welfare in a Changing Romania 1989–1999*, Boston University Senior thesis.

Couillard, Chantal. 2005. 'Triste terrain de jeu: "Haiti et l'anthropologie"', *Gradhiva* 1: 209–24.

Cowan, Jane K. et al. 2001. *Culture and Rights: Anthropological Perspectives*, Cambridge: Cambridge University Press.

Croll, Elisabeth et al. (eds). 1985. *China's One-child Family Policy*, London: Macmillan.

————. 1998. *Gender and Transition in China and Vietnam*, Stockholm: SIDA.

Cunningham, Hugh. 1995. *Children & Childhood in Western Society since 1500*, Harlow: Longman.

Dalen, Monica and Barbro Sætersdal. 1992. *Utenlandske barn I Norge: Tilpassning – Opplæring – identitetsutvikling*, Oslo: Universitetet i Oslo. Spesiallærerhøgskolen.

————. 1998. 'Utenlandsadoptert Ungdom – en ny Kulturell Kategori?', unpublished manuscript.

Damania, Deenaz. 1998. *Counselling for Adoption: The Setting up of an Indian Adoption Programme*, Delhi: Tata Institute of Social Sciences.

Damodaran, Abdal and Nilima Mehta. 2000. 'Child Adoption in India: an Overview,' in P. Selman (ed.), *Intercountry Adoption: Developments, Trends and Perspectives*, London: British Agencies for Adoption & Fostering, pp. 405-18.

Dumont, Louis. 1966. *Homo Hierarchicus: The Caste System and its Implications*, Chicago: The University of Chicago Press.

————. 1979. 'The Anthropological Community and Ideology', *Social Science Information* (18)6: 785–817.

Duncan, William. 2000. 'The Hague Convention on Protection of Children and Co-operation in Respect of Inter-country Adoption', in P. Selman (ed.), *Intercountry Adoption: Developments, Trends and Perspectives*, London: British Agencies for Adoption & Fostering, pp. 40–52.

Edwards, Jeanette, Sarah Franklin, Eric Hirsch, Francis Pine, and Marilyn Strathern. 1999. *Technologies of Procreation: Kinship in an Age of Assisted Conception*. 2nd edition. London: Routledge.

Elias, Norbert. 1982. *The Civilizing Process*, New York: Panther Books.

Ellingsæter, Anne Lise and Mary-Ann Hedlund. 1998. *Care Resources, Employment and Gender Equality in Norway*, Oslo: Institutt for Samfunnsforskning.

Ennew, Judith. 1995. 'Outside Childhood', in Bob Franklin (ed.), *The Handbook of Children's Rights*, London: Routledge.

Ennew, Judith and Virgina Morrow. 2001. 'Releasing the Energy: Celebrating the Inspiration of Sharon Stephens', *Childhood* 9(1): 5–17.

Erikson, Erik E. 1968. *Identity, Youth and Crisis*, New York: Norton.

Fadese, Fasil. 1999. *Adoption for Commercial Purposes in Ethiopia*, Addis Ababa.

Faubian, James D. (ed.) 2001. *The Ethics of Kinship: Ethnographic Inquiries*, Lanham: Rowman & Littlefield.

Fines, Agnés (ed.) 1998. *Adoptions: Ethnologie des Parentés Choisies*. Paris: Éditions de la Maison des Sciences de l'Homme.

Flydal, Hanna. 2003. 'Retten til bare å være en lykkelig nordmann', *Adopsjonsforum* 28(5): 10–11.

Follevåg, Geir. 2002. *Adoptert Identitet*, Oslo: Spartacus.

————. 2003. Speech given on the occasion of the 50th Anniversary of Verdens Barn. *Verdens Barn* 15(3): 20–22.

Fonseca, Claudia. 2000. 'A Local Practice in a Globalized World: International Adoption as Seen from the Brazilian Favelas', Miami: Paper presented at the Annual Meeting of the Law Society Association.

————. 2004. 'Child Circulation in a Brazilian Favela', in Fiona Bowie (ed.), *Cross-cultural Approaches to Adoption*, London: Routledge.

Foucault, Michel. 1980. *The History of Sexuality: An Introduction*. New York: Vintage.

————. 1991. 'Governmentality', in G. Burchell et al. (eds), *The Foucault Effect: Studies in Governmentality*, Chicago: University of Chicago Press.

Fox, Robin. 1967. *Kinship and Marriage*. Middlesex: Penguin Books.

Franklin, Bob. (ed.) 2002. *The Handbook of Children's Rights: Comparative Policy and Practice*, London: Routledge.

Franklin, Sarah. 1997. *Embodied Progress: A Cultural Account of Assisted Conception*, London: Routledge.

Franklin, Sarah and Susan McKinnon (eds) 2001. *Relative Values: Reconfiguring Kinship Studies*, Durham: Duke University Press.

Franklin, Sarah and Helena Ragoné (eds) 1998. *Reproducing Reproduction: Kinship, Power, and Technology Innovation*, Philadelphia: University of Pennsylvania Press.

Freeman, M. 1996. *Children's Rights*, Vermont: Dartmouth Publishing Company.

Fuchs, Rachel G. 1984. *Abandoned Children: Foundlings and Child Welfare in Nineteenth Century France*, Albany: State University of New York Press.

Fuller, Chris J. (ed.) 1996. *Caste Today*, Delhi: Oxford University Press.

Gailey, Christine Ward. 1999. 'Seeking Baby Rights: Race, Class, and Gender in US International Adoption', in Anne-Lise Ryggvold, Monica Dalen and Barbro Sætersdal (eds), *Mine – Yours – Theirs: Adoption, Changing Kinship and Family Patterns*, Oslo: Department of Special Needs, University of Oslo.

———. 2000. 'Race, Class and Gender in Intercountry Adoption in the USA', in P. Selman (ed.), *Intercountry Adoption: Developments, Trends and Perspectives*, London: British Agencies for Adoption & Fostering, pp. 40–52.

Gell, Alfred. 1999. 'Strathernograms, or the Semiotics of Mixed Metaphors', in Eric Hirsch (ed.), *The Art of Anthropology: Essays and Diagrams*. Alfred Gell, London.

Gillis, John. 1996. *A World of their Own Making: Myths, Ritual and the Quest for Family*, Cambridge, Mass.: Harvard University Press.

Ginsberg, Faye D. and Rayna Rapp (eds) 1995. *Conceiving the New World Order: The Global Politics of Reproduction*, Berkeley: University of California Press.

Goody, Esther. 1982. *Parenthood and Social Reproduction: Fostering and Occupational Roles in West Africa*, Cambridge: University of Cambridge Press.

Goody, Jack. 1969. 'Adoption in Cross-cultural Perspective', *Comparative Studies in Sociology and History* (11)1: 55–78.

Gudmundsson, Ann-Charlotte. 2002. 'From a Receiving Organisation's Point of View', Delhi: Paper presented to the Fourth International Conference on Adoption in India, Delhi.

Gullestad, Marianne. 1997. 'Home, Local Community and Nation', *Focaal* 30(1): 39–60.

———. 2002. 'Invisible Fences: Egalitarianism, Nationalism and Racism', *Journal of the Royal Anthropological Institute* 8(1): 45–64.

Gupta, Akhil. 2001. 'Governing Populations: the Integrated Child Development Services Program in India', in Thomas Blom Hansen and Finn Stepputat (eds), *States of Imagination: Ethnographic Explorations of the Postcolonial State*, Durham: Duke University Press.

Haarklou, J. 1998. 'Adoptivbarn med følelsesmessig skade', *Verdens Barn* 10(2): 4–7.

Handwerker, W. Penn (ed.). 1990. *Births and Power: Social Change and the Politics of Reproduction*, Boulder: Westview Press.

Hjern, Anders et al. 2002. 'Suicide, Psychiatric Illness, and Social Maladjustment in Intercountry Adoptees in Sweden: a Cohort Study', *The Lancet* 360, 10 August: 443–48.

Hognestad, Marianne and Knut R. Steenberg. 2000. *Adopsjonsloven med Kommentarer*, Oslo: Universitetsforlaget.

Hollinger, Joan. 1992. 'Introduction to Adoption Law and Practice. Consent to Adoption', in Joan Hollinger (ed.), *Adoption Law and Practice*, New York: M. Bender.

Howell, Signe. 1999. 'Biologizing and De-biologising Kinship: Some Paradoxes in Norwegian Transnational Adoption', in Anne-Lise Ryggvold, Monica Dalen and Barbro Sætersdal (eds), *Mine – Yours – Theirs: Adoption, Changing Kinship and Family Patterns*. Oslo: Department of Special Needs, University of Oslo.

———. 2001. 'Self-conscious Kinship: Some Contested Values in Norwegian Transnational Adoption'. In S. Franklin and S. McKinnon (eds), *Relative Values: Reconfiguring Kinship Studies*, Durham: Duke University Press, pp. 203-23.

———. 2002. 'Community Beyond Place: Adoptive Families in Norway', in V. Amit (ed.), *Realizing Community: Concepts, Social Relationships and Sentiments*, London: Routledge, pp. 84–104.

———. 2003a. 'The Diffusion of Moral Values in a Global Perspective', in Thomas Hylland Eriksen (ed.), *Globalization: Studies in Anthropology*, London: Pluto Press.

———. 2003b. 'Kinning: Creating Life-trajectories in Adoptive Families', *Journal of the Royal Anthropological Institute* (N.S.) 9(3): 465–84.

———. 2004. 'The Back-packers that Come to Stay: New Challenges to Norwegian Transnational Families', in Fiona Bowie (ed.), *Cross-cultural Approaches to Adoption*, London: Routledge.

———. in press. 'Imagined Kin, Place and Community: Some Paradoxes in the Transnational Movement of Children in Adoption', in Marianne Lien and Marit Melhuus (eds) *Holding Worlds Together*, n.p.

Howell, Signe and Toril Juvet Hermansen. 2001. 'Tilbakereise til India er viktig for både foreldre og barn: Resultater fra en spørreundersøkelse', *Adopsjonsforum* 26(4): 4–8.

Howell, Signe and Marit Melhuus. forthcoming 'Mixed-race Families – Do They Exist?' Some Criteria for Identity and Belonging in Contemporary Norway, in Peter Wade (ed.) *Race, Ethnicity and Nation: Perspectives from Kinship and Genetics*. Oxford and New York: Berghahn Books.

Howell, Signe and Karianne Ulfsnes. 2002. 'Adopsjonsprosessen – hvem er søkerne?' *Verdens Barn* 1: 7–11.

Hsu, Francis. 1968. 'Chinese Kinship and Chinese Behavior', in Ping-ti Ho and Tang Tsou (eds), *China's Heritage and the Communist Political System*, Chicago: University of Chicago Press.

———. 1972. *Americans and Chinese: Reflections on Two Cultures and Their People*, New York: Doubleday.

Hulbert, Ann. 2003. *Raising America: Experts, Parents and a Century of Advice About Children*, New York: Knopf.

Ingvaldsen, Siri. 1996. *Rette Foreldre og Virkelige Barn: Norsk Adopsjonslovgivning 1917–1986*, Universitetet i Bergen: Hovedfagsoppgave i historie.

Irhammar, Malin. 1997. *At urforska sitt ursprung*. Lund: unpublished manuscript.

Itéanu, André. Cultural Identity as a Theory of Conflict. Unpublished manuscript.

James, Allison and Alan Prout (eds) 1997. *Constructing and Reconstructing Childhood: Contemporary Issues in the Sociological Study of Childhood*, London: Falmer Press.

James Wendy et al. (eds). 2002. *Remapping Ethiopia. Socialism and After*, Oxford: James Currey.

Johnson, D. Gale. 1994. 'Effects of Institutions and Policies on Rural Population Growth with Application to China', *Population and Development Review* (20)3: 503–31.

Johnson, Kay et. al. 1998. 'Infant Abandonment and Adoption in China', *Population and Development Review* (24)3: 469–510.

Kalve, Trygve. 1998. 'Utenlandske barn sjelden I barnevernet', *Samfunnsspeilet* 6: 1–6.

Katz, Madeleine. 1990. *Adoptivbarn Vuxser Upp*, Stockholm: Bonnier Alba.

Kertzer, David I. 2000. 'The Lives of Foundlings in Nineteenth Century Italy', in Catherine Panther-Brick and Malcolm T. Smith (eds), *Abandoned Children*, Cambridge: Cambridge University Press.

Kideckel, David A. 1993. *The Solitudes of Collectivism: Romanian Villagers to the Revolution and Beyond*, Ithaca: Cornell University Press.

Kirk, H. 1964. *Shared Fate: A Theory of Adoption*, New York: The Free Press.

Kim, Wun Jung. 2002. 'Benefits and Risks of Intercountry Adoption', *The Lancet* 360, 10 August: 423–24.

Kligman, Gail. 1998. *The Politics of Duplicity: Controlling Reproduction in Ceausescu's Romania*, Berkeley: University of California Press.

————. 1992. 'Abortion and International Adoption in Post-Ceausescu Romania', *Feminist Studies* (18)2: 405–19.

Kramer, Julian. 1984. 'Norsk Identitet – et Produkt av Underutvikling og Stammetilhørighet', in Arne Martine Klausen (ed.), *Den Norske Væremåten*, Oslo: Cappelen.

Lappegård, Trude. 2002. 'Flere føder flere', *Samfunnsspeilet*: 6.

Larsen, Tord. 1984. 'Bønder i Byen – På Jakt etter den Norske Konfirgurasjonen', in A.M. Klausen (ed.), *Den Norske Væremåte*. Oslo: Cappelen.

Latour, Bruno. 1993. We Have Never Been Modern, New York: Harvester Wheatsheaf.

Leira, Anlaug. 1996. *Parents, Children and the State: Family Obligations in Norway*, Oslo: Institute for Social Research.

Levine, Donald. 1974. *Greater Ethiopia. The Evolution of a Multiethnic Society*, Chicago: Chicago University Press.

Lévi-Strauss, Claude. 1969 [1948]. *The Elementary Structures of Kinship*, Boston: Beacon Press.

Lifton, Betty Jean. 1994. *Journey of the Adopted Self: A Quest for Wholeness*, New York: Basic Books.

Livezeanu, Irina. 1995. *Cultural Politics in Greater Romania: Regionalism, Nation Building and Ethnic Struggle*. 1918–1930, Ithaca: Cornell University Press.

Locke, John 1953 [1690]. *An Essay Concerning Human Understanding*, New York: Dover.

Lowie, Robert. 1930. 'Adoption, Primitive', *Encyclopaedia of the Social Sciences*, Volume 1: 459–60.

Maharajasingh, Dipika. 2002. *Destiny's Child: The Adopted Child's Search for Completion*. Paper presented to the Fourth International Conference on Adoption, Delhi.

Mahbubani, Kishore. 1998. 'Can Asians Think?', *The National Interest* 52(Summer).

Maine, Sir Henry. 1917 [1861]. *Ancient Law*, London: Dent.

Mayne, J.D. 1892 [1878]. *A Treatise on Hindu Law and Usage*, London.

Marcia, J. 1966. 'Development and Validation of Ego', *Journal of Personality and Social Psychology* 3: 551–58.

————. 1980. 'Identity in Adolescence', in J. Adelson (ed.), *Handbook of Adolescent Psychology*, New York: Wiley.

Marcovitch, Sharon and Laura Cesaroni. 1995. 'Romanian Adoption: Parents' Dreams, Nightmares, and Realities', *Child Welfare* 74(5): 993–1118.

Marre, Diana and Joan Bestard. 2003. 'Governance, Globalisation and Associations: Collaboration/Conflict between Public Administration and Association with Regard to International Adoption', Unpublished paper.

Marriot, McKim. (ed.). 1990. *India through Hindu Categories*, New Delhi: Sage.

Marshall, M. 1976. 'Solidarity or Sterility? Adoption and Fosterage on Namoluk Atoll', in I. Brady (ed.), *Transactions in Kinship*, Honolulu: University of Hawaii Press.

Mauss, Marcel 1969 (1924). *The Gift: The Form and Reason for Exchange in Archaic Society*. London: Routledge & Kegan Paul.

Meigs, A. 1986. 'Blood, Kin and Food', in P. Spradley and D.W. McCurdy (ed.), *Conformity and Conflict: Readings in Cultural Anthropology*, Boston: Little Brown Higher Education.

Meir, J. 1929. 'Adoption among the Gunantuna', *Catholic Anthropological Conference* (1)1: 1–98.

Melhuus, Marit. 2001. 'Kan skinnet bedra? Noen meninger om assistert befruktning', in Signe Howell and Marit Melhuus (ed.) *Blod – tykkere enn vann?*, Bergen: Fagbokforlaget.

————. 2003. 'Exchange Matters: Issues of Law and the Flow of Human Substances', in Thomas Hylland Eriksen (ed.), *Globalisation: Studies in Anthropology*, London: Pluto Press.

————. 2005. '"Better Safe than Sorry": Legislating Assisted Conception in Norway', in Christian Krohn-Hansen and Knut Nustad (eds), *State Formation, Anthropological Formations: Anthropological Perspectives*, London: Pluto Press.

Melhuus, Marit and Signe Howell. Forthcoming 'Adoption and Assisted Conception: One Universe of Unnatural Procreation'. Jeanette Edwards and Carles Salazar (eds), *Kinship Matters*. Oxford and New York: Berghahn Books.

Melosh, Barbara. 2002. Strangers and Kin: *The American Way of Adoption,* Cambridge, MA: Harvard University Press.

Mehta, Nilima. 1992. *Ours by Choice: Parenting Through Adoption*, Bombay. Privately published with support by UNICEF.

———. 2002. 'An Overview of Child Adoption in India: Background, Current Scenario and Future Challenges', Paper presented to the Fourth International Conference on Adoption, Delhi.

Miller, Peter and Nicolas Rose. 1990. 'Governing Economic Life', in G. Burchell, C. Gordon and P. Miller (eds), *The Foucault Effect: Studies in Governmentality*, London: Harvester Wheatsheaf.

Milner, Anthony. 1999. 'What Happened to Asian Values?', in David S.G. Goodman and Gerald Segal (ed.), *Towards Recovery in Pacific Asia*, London: Routledge.

Modell, Judith. S. 1988. 'Meaning of Love: Adoption Literature and Dr. Spock, 1946–1985', in Carol Z. Stern (ed.), *Emotion and Social Change: Towards a Psychohistory*, New York: Holmes and Meier.

———. 1994. *Kinship with Strangers: Adoption and Interpretations of Kinship in American Culture*, Berkeley: University of California Press.

———. 1999. 'Freely Given: Open Adoption and the Rhetoric of the Gift', in Linda L. Layne, *Transformative Motherhood: On Giving and Getting in a Consumer Culture*, New York: New York University Press.

———. 2002. *A Sealed and Secret Kinship: The Culture and Practices in American Adoption*, New York: Berghahn Books.

Morgan, L.H. 1871. *Systems of Consanguinity and Affinity of the Human Family*, Washington D.C.: Smithsonian Institution.

Morton, K.L. 1976. 'Tongan Adoption', in I. Brady (ed.), *Transactions in Kinship*, Honolulu: University Press of Hawaii.

Needham, Rodney. 1971. 'Remarks on the Analysis of Kinship and Marriage', in Rodney Needham (ed.), *Rethinking Kinship and Marriage*, London: Tavistock Press.

Nieuwenhuys, Olga. 1999. 'The Paradox of the Competent Child and the Global Childhood Agenda', in R. Fardon, W. van Bins Bergen and R. van Disk (eds), *Modernity on a Shoestring: Dimensions of Globalisation, Consumption and Development in Africa and Beyond*, Leiden: EIDOS: African Studies Centre Leiden and the Centre of African Studies London.

O'Collins, Maeve. 1984. 'Influences of Western Adoption Laws in the Third World', in Philip Bean (ed.), *Adoption: Essays in Social Policy, Law, and Sociology*, London: Tavistock.

Ojo, Olusola 1990. 'Understanding Human Rights in Africa', in Jan Berting et al. (eds), *Human Rights in a Pluralistic World: Individuals and Collectivities*, London: Meckler Westport.

Ortner, Sherry. 1996. *Making Gender: The Politics and Erotics of Culture*, Boston: Beacon.

Panther-Brick, Catherine. 2000. 'Nobody's Children? A Reconsideration of Child Abandonment', in Catherine Panther-Brick and Malcolm T. Smith (eds), *Abandoned Children*, Cambridge: Cambridge University Press.

Panther-Brick, Catherine and Malcolm T. Smith (eds). *Abandoned Children*, Cambridge: Cambridge University Press.

Parra-Aranguren, G. 1994. *Explanatory Report on the 1993 Hague Intercountry Adoption Convention*, The Hague: Proceedings of the Seventeenth Session (1993) tome II, Adoption.

Penn, Helen. 2002. 'The World Bank's View of Early Childhood', *Childhood* (9)1: 118–32.

Prout, Alan and Allison James. 1997. 'A New Paradigm for the Sociology of Childhood? Provenance, Promise and Problems', in Allison James and Alan Prout (eds), *Constructing and Reconstructing Childhood: Contemporary Issues in the Sociological Study of Childhood*, London: Falmer Press.

Queseth, Harald. 1985. 'Det tomme barneværelset'. In *Adopsjon av Utenlandske Barn*. Oslo: Univesitetsforlaget.

Qvorup, Jens. 1997. 'A Voice for Children in Statistical and Social Accounting: A Plea for Children's Rights to be Heard', in Allison James and Alan Prout (eds), *Constructing and*

Reconstructing Childhood: Contemporary Issues in the Sociological Study of Childhood, London: Falmer Press.

Radcliffe-Brown, A.R. 1952. *Structure and Function in Primitive Society*, London: Routledge & Kegan Paul.

Rahmato, Dessalegn and Aklilu Kidanu. 1999. *Consultations with the Poor: A Study to Inform The World Development Report on Poverty and Development* (National report Ethiopia). Addis Ababa.

Rasmussen, Marianne. 2000. 'Når eplet faller langt fra stamen: En studie av voksne utenlandsadopterte I Norge'. Thesis submitted for the Degree of Cand. Polit. University of Oslo.

Retta, Markos. 2001. 'On the Rights of the Child'. Addis Ababa: The Federal Supreme Court Juvenile Justice Programme (1): 1: 9–10, 28–31.

Roalkvam, Sidsel. 2001. 'Det Står Skrevet i Sten'. In S. Howell and M. Melhuus (eds), *Blod – Tykkere enn Vann?*, Bergen: Fagbokforlaget.

Roche, J. 1999. 'Children's Rights, Participation and Citizenship', *Childhood* 6(4): 475–94.

Rojewski, Jay W. and Jacy L. Rojewski. 2001. *Intercountry Adoption from China: Examining Cultural Heritage and other Post adoption Issues*, Westport, Conn.: Bergin & Garvey.

Roll-Hansen, Nils and Gunnar Broberg (eds). 1996. *Eugenics and the Welfare State: Sterilization Policy in Denmark, Sweden, Norway and Finland*, East Lancing: Michigan University Press.

Rose, Nikolas. 1999. *Governing the Soul: the Shaping of the Private Self*, London: Free Association Books.

Rousseau, Jean-Jacques. 1963 [1762]. *Émile*, London: Dent.

Russell, Audrey T. 1995. 'Transracial Adoptions Should be Forbidden', in David Bedner and Bruno Leone (eds), *Adoption: Opposing Viewpoints*, San Diego: Greenhaven Press.

Sá, Isabel dos Guimaraws. 2000. 'Circulation of Children in Eighteenth-century Portugal', in Catherine Panther-Brick and Malcolm T. Smith (eds), *Abandoned Children*, Cambridge: Cambridge University Press.

Sahlins, Marshall. 1972. *Stone Age Economics*, London: Tavistock.

Salazar, Carles. 2002. 'Kinship and Public Understanding of Genetics', Manchester. Unpublished paper.

Salisbury, R.F. 1970. *Vunamami*, Melbourne: Melbourne University Press.

Scheper-Hughes, Nancy and Carolyn Sargent (eds). 1998. *Small Wars: The Cultural Politics of Childhood*, Berkeley: University of California Press.

Schneider, D.M. 1968 (1980). *American Kinship: a Cultural Account*, Chicago: University of Chicago Press.

———. 1984. *A Critique of the Study of Kinship*, Ann Arbor: University of Michigan Press.

Scott, James C. 1985. *Weapons of the Weak: Everyday Forms of Peasant Resistance*, New Haven: Yale University Press.

Seid, Hussein. 1999. *Adoption Under the Ethiopian Laws*, Addis Ababa: MOLSA.

Selman, Peter (ed.). 2000. *Intercountry Adoption: Developments, Trends and Perspectives*, London: British Agencies for Adoption & Fostering.

———. 2005. *Trends in Intercountry Adoption 1998–2003*, School of Geography, Politics and Sociology: University of Newcastle.

Seltzer, M.R. 1976. 'Rasisme, Marginalitet og det Adopterte Utenlandske Barn i Norge', NOU 1975: 55.

Serbanescu, Florina et al. 1995. 'The Impact of Recent Policy Changes on Fertility, Abortion, and Contraceptive Use in Romania', *Studies in Family Planning* 26(2): 76–87.

Simmel, Georg. 1978. *The Philosophy of Money*. London: Routledge and Kegan Paul.

Simon, Rita J. 2000. *Adoption across Borders: Serving the Children in Transracial and Intercountry Adoptions*, Lanham: Rowman & Littlefield.

Steenberg, Knut R. 1993. 'Haagkonferansen for international privatrett', *Juristkontakt* 8/93: 2–11.

Stephens, Sharon. 1995. 'Introduction', in Sharon Stephens (ed.), *Children and the Politics of Culture*, Princeton: Princeton University Press.

Sterett, Susan M. 2002. 'Introductory Essay', *Law & Society* Review 36(2): 209-26.

Strathern, Marilyn. 1988. The Gender of the Gift, Berkeley: University of California Press.

———. 1992. *After Nature: English Kinship in the Late Twentieth Century*, Cambridge: Cambridge University Press.

Strong, Pauline Turner. 2001. 'To Forget Their Tongue, Their Name, and Their Whole Relation: Captivity, Extra-tribal Adoption and the Indian Child Welfare', in Sarah Franklin and Susan McKinnon (eds), *Relative Values: Reconfiguring Kinship Studies*, Durham: Duke University Press.

Sundby, J. and B. Schei. 1996. 'Infertility in a Sample of Women Aged 40–42', *Acta Obstet. Gynecologica Scandinavia* 1996: 832–37.

Svendssen, Lais. 2004, *Kineseven fra Königsberg – Immanuel Kant (1724–1804)*, Oslo: Transit Forlag.'

Sætersdal, Barbro and Monica Dalen. 1999. *'Hvem er jeg?' Adopsjon, Identitet, Etnisitet*, Oslo: Akribe.

Talsethagen, Gro Fivesdal. 2004. 'Adoptivforeldre – plageånder eller medspillere?' *Adopsjonsforum* (29)1: 12–16.

Telfer, Jon. 1999. 'In-dividual but In-complete: Adoption, Identity and the Quest for Wholeness', in Anne-Lise Ryggvold, Monica Dalen and Barbro Sætersdal (eds), *Mine – Yours – Theirs: Adoption, Changing Kinship and Family Patterns*, Oslo: Department of Special Needs, University of Oslo, pp. 247–65.

Thanikachalam, Chandra. 1998. 'Introduction', *Handbook on Child Adoption in India: Laws, Procedures, Guidelines and International Convention*, Chennai, Tamil Nadu: Indian Council for Child Welfare, Tamil Nadu.

Tonkinson. R. 1976. 'Adoption and Sister Exchange in a New Hebridean Community', in I. Brady (ed.), *Transactions in Kinship*, Honolulu: University Press of Hawaii.

Triseliotis, John. 1973. *In Search of Origins: The Experiences of Adopted People*, London: Routledge & Kegan Paul.

Tronvoll, Kjetil. 1998. *Mai Weenie: a Highland Village in Eritrea: a Study of the People, Their Livelihood and Land Tenure during Times of Turbulence*, Lawrenceville, N.J. : Red Sea Press.

Thune Hammerstrøm, Sissel. 2001. *Implementerig av FNs konvensjon om barns rettigheter i kinesiske barnehjem – Hva anses som barns behov i Kina?* Universitet et i Oslo. Storfag i kinesisk.

Ulfsnes, Karianne. 2002. 'Notions of Transnational Adoption and its Relation to Family- and Kinship Values in Romania', Oslo: Report on fieldtrip.

Van Loon, J.H.A. 1994. 'Report on Intercountry Adoption'. The Hague Convention of Intercounty Adoption.

Van der Waal, Koo. 1994. 'Collective Human Rights: A Western View', in Jan Berting et al. (eds), *Human Rights in a Pluralistic World: Individuals and Collectivities*, London: Meckler Westport.

Verdrey, Kathrine. 1990. 'The Production and Defence of the "Romanian Nation" 1900 to World War II', in R.G. Fox (ed.), *National Ideologies and the Production of National Cultures*, American Ethnological Association Society Monograph series.

Vike, Halvard. 2002. 'Culminations of Complexity: Cultural Dynamics in Norwegian Local Government', *Anthropological Theory* 21(1): 57–75.

Volkman, Toby and Cindy Katz (eds). 2003. *Transnational Adoption*. Special issue *Social Text* 21(1).

Weigl, Kerstin. 1997. *Längtansbarnet: Adoptivforeldre beratter*, Stockholm: Norsteds.

Weinstein, C.A. 1968. 'Adoption'. *International Encyclopaedia of Social Sciences*, New York: Macmillan.

Weismantel, M. 1995. 'Making Kin: Kinship Theory and Zumbagua Adoptions', *American Ethnologist* 22(4): 685–709.

Wikse, Tone Helene. 2001. *Barnehjemsinstitusjonen i Kina – med spesiell focus på perioden etter innføringen av familieplanleggingspolitkken*. Universitet et i Oslo. Storfag i kinesisk.

Witoszek, Nina. 1998. *Norske naturmytologier: Fra Edda til økofilosofi*, Oslo: Pax.

Woldegebreal, Yohannes. n.d. *Legislative Measures on the Implementation of Inter-country Adoption in Ethiopia*, Addis Ababa.

World Bank. 2000. *Voices of the Poor*, Washington.

———. 2002. *Empowerment ad Poverty Reduction: A Sourcebook*, Washington.

Yngvesson, Barbara. 2002. 'Placing the "Gift Child" in Transnational Adoption', *Law & Society Review* (36)2: 227–56.

——— 2004. 'National Bodies and the Body of the Child: "Completing" Families through International Adoption', in Fiona Bowie (ed.), *Cross-Cultural Approaches to Adoption*, London: Routledge.

Youngblood, D. 2001. 'Rainbow Family, Rainbow Nation: Reflections on Relatives and Relational Dynamics in Trinidad', in J. Faubion (ed.), *The Ethics of Kinship*, Lanham: Rowman & Littlefield.

Øhren, Andreas. 1995. *Consuelo: en adopsjonshistorie*, Oslo: Gyldendal.

INDEX

Related Titles of Interest

A SEALED AND SECRET KINSHIP
The Culture of Politics and Practices in American Adoption
Judith S. Modell

"Accessible and interesting, the book is suitable for all academic and public libraries." **–Choice**

"This book offers a thought-provoking exposition of the ironies of adoption, and by extension, the inconsistencies of our social attitudes toward parenting in general." –Journal of Sociology and Social Welfare

Adoption has long been a controversial subject in the United States as well as in other western countries, but never more so than in the past three decades. Why that is and how public attention affects the decisions made by those who arrange, legalize, and experience adoptive kinship constitutes the subject of this book. Adoption, the author argues, touches on major preoccupations we all have: who we are; why we are what we are; the balance of "nature" and "culture" in self-definition; the conflict between individual rights and social order. The problematic nature of adoption in western societies is effectively contrasted by the author with cultures in many other parts of the world in which children are exchanged frequently, openly, and happily. Adoption thus reveals itself as one of the keys to western ideas about human nature, the person, rights, privacy, and family relationships.

Judith S. Modell is Professor of Anthropology, History and Art at Carnegie Mellon University. She is currently the director of the Center for the Arts in Society at the school.

2002. 232 pages, bibliog., index
ISBN 1-57181-324-1 Pb $19.95/£13.50
ISBN 1-57181-077-3 Hb $49.95/£35.00
Volume 3, Public Issues in Anthropological Perspective

MEDIA AND NATION BUILDING
How the Iban became Malaysian
John Postill

"... very well written, lively, incisive and clear. Students will learn a lot about anthropology and media from this book... it should be recommended or essential reading for students."
–Andrew Beatty, Brunel University

From Eastern Europe to East Timor, Afghanistan and recently Iraq, the United States and its allies have often been accused of shirking their nation-building responsibilities as their attention – and that of the media -- turned to yet another regional crisis. While much has been written about the growing influence of television and the Internet on modern warfare, little is known about the relationship between media and nation building.

This book explores, for the first time, this relationship by means of a paradigmatic case of successful nation building: Malaysia. Based on extended fieldwork and historical research, the author follows the diffusion, adoption, and social uses of media among the Iban of Sarawak, in Malaysian Borneo and demonstrates the wide-ranging process of nation building that has accompanied the Iban adoption of radio, clocks, print media, and television.

John Postill is a Research Fellow at the University of Bremen. He is currently studying e-government and ethnicity in Malaysia. Trained as an anthropologist at University College London, he has published a range of articles on the anthropology of media, with special reference to Malaysian Borneo.

Spring 2006. 256 pages, 28 ils, bibliog, index
ISBN 1-84545-132-5 Hb $80.00/£50.00
Volume 1, Asia Pacific Studies: Past and Present

Berghahn Books, Inc. 150 Broadway, Suite 812, New York, NY 10038, USA

Berghahn Books, Ltd. 3 Newtec Place, Magdalen Rd. Oxford OX4 1RE, UK

orders@berghahnbooks.com ~ www.berghahnbooks.com

Related Titles of Interest

MANAGING REPRODUCTIVE LIFE
Cross-Cultural Themes in Fertility and Sexuality
Edited by Soraya Tremayne

"[This] ... excellent overview ... should be valuable in medical anthropology, gender and demography studies. It demonstrates the value of anthropology in exploring the varied cultural and economic contexts for reproductive decisions and sexual power relations."
—Social Anthropology

"... the authors provide innovative ethnographic data and analysis ... This edited volume is notable for its coherence and the consistent attention to the themes of the three sections." **—American Ethnologist**

In this book a group of anthropologists set out to throw new light on the dynamics of human reproduction in the world today, looking at the intricate ways that people manage their reproductive life across different cultures, and highlighting the wider meaning of human reproduction and its impact on social organization. The importance of human agency, ethnic boundaries, the regulation of gender relations, issues of fertility and infertility, the significance of children and motherhood and the problems of two large vulnerable social groups, youth and refugees, are all considered in their broader social contexts.

Soraya Tremayne is Co-ordinating Director of the Fertility and Reproduction Studies Group and a Research Associate at the Institute of Social and Cultural Anthropology, University of Oxford.

2001. 300 pages, bibliog., index
ISBN 1-57181-317-9 Pb $25.00/£17.00
ISBN 1-57181-500-7 Hb $69.95/£50.00
Volume 1, Fertility, Reproduction and Sexuality

CULTURE, CREATION, AND PROCREATION
Concepts of Kinship in South Asian Practice
Edited by Monika Böck and Aparna Rao

"I would advise everybody who is interested in new directions in anthropological theory on kinship to read this volume." **—L'Homme**

"[This volume] offers a nuanced exploration of the complexities of the ideology and practice of kinship in this diverse region." **—Folklore Bulletin**

As reproduction is seen as central to kinship and the biological link as the primary bond between parents and their offspring, Western perceptions of kin relations are primarily determined by ideas about "consanguinity," "genealogical relations," and "genetic connections." Advocates of cultural constructivism have taken issue with a concept that puts so much stress on heredity as being severely biased by western ideas of kinship. Ethnosociologists in particular developed alternative systems using indigenous categories. This symbolic approach has, however, been rejected by some scholars as plagued by the problems of the analytical separation of ideology from practice, of largely overlooking relations of domination, and of ignoring the questions of shared knowledge and choice. This volume offers a corrective by discussing the constitution of kinship among different communities in South Asia and addressing the relationship between ideology and practice, cultural models, and individiual strategies.

Monika Böck is Lecturer at the Institut für Völkerkunde, University of Cologne, and Aparna Rao[†] was Research Associate, Department of Anthropology, Cologne University, Germany.

2000. 336 pages, 1 map, 13 figs, 6 tables, bibliog, index
ISBN 1-57181-912-6 Pb $25.00/£17.50
ISBN 1-57181-911-8 Hb $69.95/£47.00

Berghahn Books, Inc. 150 Broadway, Suite 812, New York, NY 10038, USA

Berghahn Books, Ltd. 3 Newtec Place, Magdalen Rd. Oxford OX4 1RE, UK

orders@berghahnbooks.com   www.berghahnbooks.com